# 'FOR WOMEN, FOR WALES AND FOR LIBERALISM'

**Gender Studies in Wales**
**Astudiaethau Rhywedd yng Nghymru**

**Series Editors**
Jane Aaron, University of Glamorgan
Brec'hed Piette, University of Bangor
Sian Rhiannon Williams, University of Wales Institute Cardiff

**Series Advisory Board**
Deirdre Beddoe, Emeritus Professor
Mihangel Morgan, Aberystwyth University
Teresa Rees, Cardiff University

The aim of this series is to fill a current gap in knowledge. As a number of historians, sociologists and literary critics have for some time been pointing out, there is a dearth of published research on the characteristics and effects of gender difference in Wales, both as it affected lives in the past and as it continues to shape present-day experience. Socially constructed concepts of masculine and feminine difference influence every aspect of individuals' lives; experiences in employment, in education, in culture and politics, as well as in personal relationships, are all shaped by them. Ethnic identities are also gendered; a country's history affects its concepts of gender difference so that what is seen as appropriately 'masculine' or 'feminine' varies within different cultures. What is needed in the Welsh context is more detailed research on the ways in which gender difference has operated and continues to operate within Welsh societies. Accordingly, this interdisciplinary and bilingual series of volumes on Gender Studies in Wales, authored by academics who are leaders in their particular fields of study, is designed to explore the diverse aspects of male and female identities in Wales, past and present. The series is bilingual, in the sense that some of its intended volumes will be in Welsh and some in English.

# 'FOR WOMEN, FOR WALES AND FOR LIBERALISM'

## WOMEN IN LIBERAL POLITICS IN WALES, 1880–1914

Ursula Masson

CARDIFF
UNIVERSITY OF WALES PRESS
2010

*www.uwp.co.uk*

*British Library Cataloguing-in-Publication Data*
A catalogue record for this book is available from the British Library.

ISBN 978-0-7083-2253-6
e-ISBN 978-0-7083-2254-3

Printed in Wales by Dinefwr Press, Llandybïe

Ursula Masson (1945–2008), Lecturer and subsequently Senior Lecturer in History at the University of Glamorgan from 1994 to 2008, was the author of a number of journal articles and book chapters on Welsh women's history. Her editorial work included co-editing *Llafur*, the Welsh people's history journal, *Women's Rights and 'Womanly Duties': the Aberdare Women's Liberal Association, 1891–1910* (2005) and for Honno Press, Elizabeth Andrews's *A Woman's Work is Never Done* (2006) and *The Very Salt of Life: Welsh Women's Political Writings from Chartism to Suffrage* (2007). She was involved in setting up and chairing Archif Menywod Cymru/Women's Archive of Wales and initiated its highly successful series of roadshows. In recent years she also chaired the west of England and south Wales Women's History Network. In all these activities she proved a lasting inspiration to those who worked with her or were taught by her. This current volume, based on her successful Ph.D. thesis, was at the point of going to press when she died; the editors of the Gender Studies in Wales series would like to thank Professor June Hannam of the University of the West of England for her help in preparing the final draft.

# *Acknowledgements*

I want to thank June Hannam and Deirdre Beddoe for their expert help and guidance and, above all, patience and friendship during the course of my studies. Many thanks too to all those archivists and librarians of the collections listed in my bibliography for their assistance in locating and accessing the materials which form the basis for this work. To colleagues at the University of Glamorgan, to friends and students too numerous to name, thanks for invaluable discussions about sources and interpretations. And to my family, especially, all my thanks for support through the rough and the smooth, without which I could not have completed this book.

Earlier drafts of chapters in this book have been published elsewhere and I am grateful to the publishers for permission to reproduce versions of them here. For a more extensive account of the history of the Aberdare Women's Liberal Association given in chapter 5, see the introduction to my edited volume *'Women's Rights and Womanly Duties': The Aberdare Women's Liberal Association, 1891–1910* (Cardiff, 2005). Some of the material in chapter 6 was published as Ursula Masson, 'Women *versus* "the People": language, nation and citizenship, 1906–11', in T. Robin Chapman (ed.), *The Idiom of Dissent: Protest and Propaganda in Wales* (Llandysul, 2006).

# Contents

## Contents

# Abbreviations

| | |
|---|---|
| *AL* | *Aberdare Leader* |
| APEGW | Association for Promoting the Education of Girls in Wales |
| *AT* | *Aberdare Times* |
| BC | Aberdare Reference Library Biographical Collection |
| BWTA | British Women's Temperance Association |
| CCL | Cardiff Central Library Local Studies Collections |
| C&DWSS | Cardiff and District Women's Suffrage Society |
| CLA | Cardiff Liberal Association |
| *CN* | *Cambrian News* |
| CNSWS | Central National Society for Women's Suffrage |
| COS | Charity Organisation Society |
| CPLWU | Cardiff Progressive Liberal Women's Union |
| BUL | Bristol University Library Special Collections |
| *DLB* | *Dictionary of Labour Biography* |
| EFF | Election Fighting Fund |
| GRO | Glamorgan Record Office |
| ILP | Independent Labour Party |
| LNA | Ladies National Association for the Repeal of the Contagious Diseases Acts |
| *ME* | *Merthyr Express* |
| NLF | National Liberal Federation |
| NLW | National Library of Wales |
| NUWSS | National Union of Women's Suffrage Societies |
| NVA | National Vigilance Association |
| NWLF | North Wales Liberal Federation |
| *ODNB* | *Oxford Dictionary of National Biography* |
| SDF | Social Democratic Federation |
| *SWA* | *South Wales Argus* |

| | |
|---|---|
| *SWDN* | *South Wales Daily News* |
| *SWDP* | *South Wales Daily Post* |
| SWLF | South Wales Liberal Federation |
| SWMFWSS | South Wales and Monmouthshire Federation of Women's Suffrage Societies |
| *SWR* | *South Wales Radical* |
| *SWWA* | *South Wales Weekly Argus* |
| UDMD | Undeb Dirwestol Merched y De |
| UDMGC | Undeb Dirwestol Merched Gogledd Cymru |
| WCG | Women's Co-operative Guild |
| WFL | Women's Freedom League |
| WGS | Women's Guardians Society |
| *WHR* | *Welsh History Review* |
| WLA | Women's Liberal Association |
| WLF | Women's Liberal Federation |
| WLGS | Women's Local Government Association |
| WLL | Women's Labour League |
| WLUA | Women's Liberal Unionist Association |
| WNLA | Women's National Liberal Association |
| WNLC | Welsh National Liberal Council |
| WNLF | Welsh National Liberal Federation |
| WSPU | Women's Social and Political Union |
| WTUL | Women's Trade Union League |
| WUWLA | Welsh Union of Women's Liberal Associations |
| *WM* | *Western Mail* |
| *WR* | *Welsh Review* |
| WWP | W. W. Price Collections, Aberdare Reference Library |
| WWP BI | W.W. Price Biographical Index, Aberdare Reference Library |
| *YW* | *Young Wales* |

# Introduction

This book examines the relationship of women to feminism, to political parties and to national identity, through a history of women's Liberal organization in Wales from the 1880s to the outbreak of the First World War. The introduction outlines the subject matter and structure of the book and the survival and interpretation of sources; it provides a brief discussion of historiographical issues relating to the three themes of party, feminism and nation; and, finally, considers the theme of 'place' and the value of the local studies which form a large part of the volume.

## Argument, aims, structure

The book demonstrates that the intersection of party, feminism and nation in Wales from the 1880s to 1914 made for a distinctive politics: women's liberalism in Wales was different from men's liberalism because it was women centred, shared the ethos and values of British women's liberalism and needed to accommodate feminism. The material supports recent historiography which suggests that women were instrumental in a reinterpretation of liberalism, developing a distinctive view of the meaning of citizenship, and that Liberal women in Wales shared that world-view and sense of their place in the political public sphere with their British sisters. However, Welsh women's liberalism was distinct from the liberal feminism dominant in the Women's Liberal Federation (WLF) because it had to reach an accommodation with 'Welsh' questions and conditions. National identity, which the Welsh Liberal party had made its own in this period, was always a question for Liberal women, whether through close identification with Welshness and Welsh interests in the 1890s, or in the necessity, embraced by some, consciously to reject that identity in favour of a feminist and suffragist position from 1910. The three strands – party, feminism and nationalism – were, therefore, in constant tension, as activists attempted to construct from them a meaningful women's liberalism.

The volume constructs a narrative through which these themes can be explored. While the use of the term 'narrative' is not intended to suggest that this is an unproblematic concept in history-writing, the creation of a narrative tracing continuity and change is in itself a useful contribution in a notably neglected area of Welsh women's history. It is structured by the three dimensions in which women's politics was enacted: the 'British', embodied in the WLF;[1] the Welsh, in the Welsh Union of Women's Liberal Associations (WUWLA) and its relationship to the Welsh party; and the local, in the Women's Liberal Associations (WLAs). In part I, the focus is on the Wales-wide creation of WLAs; on the WUWLA and its relationship to British liberal feminism; and on its relationship to the Liberal party and Liberal nationalism in Wales. These chapters begin the examination of the characteristics of women's liberalism, and the interplay of its elements, continued in greater depth in part II through the examination of two local associations, Cardiff and Aberdare. My concluding chapter will suggest ways in which the narrative might be expanded or revised by further research.

I have taken a broad conception of the political, to encompass the moral, religious and social aims which provided the drive in women's public life, while focusing on one party political strand. The Liberal party exercised political hegemony in Wales from the 1880s until the 1920s, and for most of that time successfully projected itself as embodying Welsh political, religious and cultural identity; the issue of women's representation within such a hegemony (as in that of the Labour party, which replaced it) is of vital interest. Thus, I am concerned with the 'formal structures of radicalism . . . the press, the public demonstration, and organised societies', a focus on which, it has been suggested, 'inevitably' marginalizes or denies women's political agency in the pre-enfranchisement era.[2] However, as well as events, and cause and effect, the book is concerned with women's political language. It is my contention that, in the 1890s, women placed themselves at 'the spoken centre' of the Welsh nation. The phrase is Patrick Joyce's: he suggests that Gladstonian discourse brought women to 'the spoken centre' of British liberalism in the

1880s.[3] The religious and moral appeal of Gladstone's 1879 Midlothian campaign, and his direct call on women to involve themselves in Liberal politics as a peculiarly womanly and moral duty, had been remembered as a watershed moment by Liberal activists,[4] and the terms and tenor of his address were often to be echoed in the speech of Nonconformist Liberal women in Wales. Joyce has represented this as a development in which women exercised no agency, and from which they derived no power; they were included in a discourse of nation and 'the people', but had no role in shaping meanings.[5] I suggest that in the Welsh context of the 1890s, discussed in part I, women were active in shaping political and populist language. This case, for women's agency in the construction of national identity, will be supported by analysis of those formal structures, press representations and organizations; but also by close reading of the texts and speech of Liberal women themselves, in the context of, and sometimes in contention with, the wider discourses of party and nation (see chapter 3). In the long run, however, women did not gain a secure hold on influence in Welsh liberalism, or secure ownership of meanings of the 'nation'. This was to be strongly demonstrated in the Edwardian period of deteriorating relations between women and Liberalism (see chapter 7).

## Sources and approaches

Nora Philipps, later Lady St Davids, first president of the WUWLA, is a key figure in the history outlined here. When she died in 1915, she bequeathed to her eldest son and, after him, his brother, 'all her MSS, letters, papers, notebooks, copybooks, memorandum and family papers ... "to be preserved for future generations in the hope that they may become of interest to posterity"'.[6] That despite Philipps's historicizing instincts the collection cannot be located seems like a simple demonstration of the marginalization of women's political history, but it also at least partly reflects the dislocations of the period: her eldest son was killed in France between his mother's funeral and the publication of her will; by the end of the following year, his brother too had died in France. Lord St Davids remarried, and the present family contains no descendants of Philipps; inheritance and heritage thus become confused and discontinuous. Much of the obituary material at Philipps's death focused on her cultural and charitable activities and dramatic and rhetorical skills; the combative feminist politician of the 1890s became lost in the conventional portrayal of a good, if artistic, upper-class woman. However, it is possible to construct a political biography of Nora Philipps (though maybe not the one she herself constructed in the lost personal archive)[7] because, thanks to her social class and networks and undoubted platform and meeting-room skills, she was able to play a prominent part in women's Liberal and suffrage activities of the 1890s; her name appears in their records, she published lengthy articles and pamphlets, she gave speeches which were fully reported and she was commented upon by others.

As the example vividly shows, the survival of any historical material, and the emergence of individuals into the historical public sphere, owes much to circumstance, to the social position of the subject and, crucially, to value-laden choices and decisions about recording and conservation. The gendered practices of archiving and the organization of memory have long been problematized by feminist scholars.[8] In late nineteenth-century Wales, the creation of local libraries and a national library, connected to local and national pride and the construction of historical nationhood, encouraged the deposit of material, but, as suggested, not equally for all sections of society. The perception that women have been peripheral to Wales's political traditions means there has been no comprehensive archiving of their records. However, historical comprehensiveness is probably an illusion,[9] and records have survived. As the bibliography demonstrates, the sources for this book, despite their focus on women, have been the conventional ones of the political and social historian: newspapers and journals; minutes, reports and leaflets, printed and manuscript; autobiography; the census and local directories. All such sources, much as they can tell us, have their limitations and problems of interpretation, which are discussed more fully at appropriate points in the text. This section will briefly suggest some of the ways in which I have pressed them into service.

The newspaper and periodical press is an essential source for the period. Historians have explored the growth of the press in Wales, its 'significance as a social agency' and its close relationship with the Liberal party,[10] making it 'a vital aid in understanding the structure and essence of the Liberal movement';[11] but it must be handled with care. It can legitimately be used as a quarry of information, tempered by an understanding of the processes of selection and mediation which produced not reflections but representations of the world. In the late nineteenth century, women increasingly presented themselves and their organizations on the public platform, to speak directly to at least a part of their intended audience. But these attempts at self-representation were and are mediated by the press which reported on them; it is difficult to judge what the organizers wished their public to take away from the meeting, and what they did take, as opposed to what the newspaper editors presented as significant. Some meetings were reported very fully, their importance or novelty signified; some women were signalled as worth listening to and were reported at great length, audience reaction indicated ('Hear, hear' 'Applause') and the flattering remarks of other speakers recorded;[12] others were not equally valued. Our understanding of how Liberal women understood their politics, their relationship to ideas and issues, therefore, relies in part on the representation in the press of relatively few individuals. For lesser-known women, there are a number of ways the historian can attempt to establish their social and political identities. One is through their connection with better-known men: 'Mrs (Rev.) Rees Jenkin Jones, Broniestyn' of the newspaper reports is intended to be identified as 'the wife of . . .'. Drawing conclusions about political, or even religious, identity from this information involves assumptions about shared beliefs and practices within marriages and families, assumptions which the press readily made in the case of wives, but of which the historian must be wary. Census data and local directories can be used alongside the press reports, but interpretation of these rather intractable sources may also involve assumptions about the connection of political identity to household, community status and position within families. All of these methods have been used to some extent in this book; I hope I have not pressed them further than they can bear. The issue of the naming of women in the past, and in our histories of them – identifying a woman's 'real' name – has been integral to feminist history, especially as it concerns itself with concepts of experience, autonomy and agency.[13] But recent understandings of 'identities', emphasizing multiplicity and fluidity, problematize the assumption that there is a 'real' name. Does the revelation of 'Mrs G. George (Beehive)' of the newspaper report, as Winifred, then Winnie George, in her signature to the minutes of her WLA, represent a more authentic identity than that of her marriage and her commercial activity in the locality? Did the introduction of 'Mrs John Wynford Philipps' to a public meeting in terms of her husband's name and politics rob Nora Philipps of autonomy, or provide her with a useful platform in a context in which she was relatively unknown?[14] Representations of women, in the press, in art and literature and in prescriptive texts, have provided fertile ground for feminist historians for many years; increasingly, though, it has been felt that such sources have given rise to an overemphasis on lack of agency of women in the nineteenth century in particular.[15] Material generated by women themselves appears to tell another story.

This book has been able to make use of unexpectedly rich, though patchy, records produced by women's organizations which, I suggest, contain material which allows us to speak about the self-representation of political women, amongst themselves and, through their resolutions, letters, appeals and memoranda, to the public political world. Such a record is the minute book of the Aberdare Women's Liberal Association, apparently unique as a handwritten record of a WLA in Wales, spanning the 1890s, a particularly lively period for women's political activity. Printed material from the period has survived better: some annual reports of WLAs, including Cardiff and Aberystwyth, have survived, in the case of Cardiff including subscription lists which enable some analysis of the social characteristics of the membership; agendas, annual reports and printed discussion papers of the WUWLA in its period of greatest activity, 1892–6, are also available. This material, women's reporting of their own activities, can be read as examples of group 'self-writing', reflecting collective aspirations and self-perceptions, emanating mainly from a class of women well below those upper-class and aristocratic women who usually produced autobiography for this period. They are a rich source for the morally informed political ethos of the Welsh middle class: like most of the sources used, they tell us nothing of working-class women's politics.[16]

As at the beginning of this section, I have used the device of exemplary biography at a number of points in the book and in the appendices. Biography has been used in recent feminist histories to show women's lives as embodying the complexity of the times and the places they inhabit. In exploring the history of groups and organizations, a number of biographies brought together may vividly illustrate the background and ethos in which the politics was developed, and the device humanizes discussion which might otherwise remain rather abstract. Their use inevitably raises the issue of the role of individuals in history. The role of a number of key women in shaping women's

Liberal politics in the 1890s, locally and nationally, cannot be ignored. They were able to take that role because other conditions were in place, so that what they had to say made sense to many others. Like many historians, therefore, I have presented these individual subjects as a point of convergence of historical forces, or as indicative of the intersection of local and other identities, or as embodying change and new potential.[17] These are the kinds of narrative techniques which historians share with writers of fiction (which is not to say that history-writing is the same as creating fiction). These fictive elements are also easily recognized in the autobiographical materials I have used, notably the autobiography of Margaret, Lady Rhondda.[18] Unique in its reflection on the pre-1914 movements of women and the creation of political identities in the Welsh context, it is also representative of the spate of autobiographical writings by women, particularly former suffragists and upper-class women, of the late 1920s and 1930s.[19] Rhondda's narrative is, among other things, a vivid example of the tensions between 'paternal and maternal narratives, these fictions of male and female selfhood' which, it has been suggested, provide a characteristic dynamic in women's autobiography.[20] This had implications for the way Rhondda represented her mother Sybil, who is more important for this book than Rhondda herself, as well as her own relationship to Liberal politics. While only briefly explored, these considerations necessarily affect the reading of the autobiography as evidence.

The discussion above indicates the extent to which approaches arising from the turn to language, textuality and the discourses of gender are a part of the analytical toolbox for this book. As a contribution to the creation of a political history of women in Wales, this is an exercise in feminist women's history,[21] a piece of 'recovery' history, attempting to make women visible. I hope that the account will shed some light on the gendered political culture of the country, and so strengthen change in the present and future. To some these will appear as outdated aims and practices, but for many feminist historians, perhaps especially in 'small nations', the concept of 'women's history' remains useful in its ability still to transform the historical narratives.[22] However, 'we need all the tools we have at our disposal'.[23] Shifting the focus towards gender and utilizing textual analysis and the concepts of representation, self-representation and identity suggest more fruitful ways to recast some old questions. For example, how should historians interpret the rhetoric of a sometimes very conservative Celticism used by feminist women, some not themselves Welsh in origin or upbringing? Did such women, who otherwise dedicated their lives to the getting of the vote, to party politics and to education and work opportunities for women, really believe in the 'platitudes [of] romanticise[d] and exaggerate[d] notions of Welsh freedom and justice'?[24] It is possible, and in some contexts plausible, to explain their language as a disingenuous tactic to flatter the Welsh Liberal establishment into giving ground to women's demands. However, it is more interesting to take seriously the attempt by progressive women to engage with the discourse of nationalism, to take a part in the imagining of Wales, past and future, and to write into it a role for women's citizenship which took account of their fullest hopes and desires. My discussion of Liberal nationalist meetings and writings engages with this gendered language of nation. The focus on gender also offers a way out of the cul de sac of 'contribution' history; it allows us, for example, to do more than merely note the absence of women from the political organizations, events and literature. To explore the way that such institutions were gendered, with masculinity built into their culture, enriches our understanding of the past, and may enable a greater understanding of the persistence of these exclusions long after material conditions have changed.

*Party*

Party political activity of women accelerated in the 1880s with the formation of the mixed-sex Conservative Primrose League and the WLF. The appeal of Gladstonian liberalism for women has been noted but, more pragmatically, the franchise and electoral reforms of the 1880s enlarged and transformed electorates, creating the need for more sustained party machinery and many voluntary workers. The creation of the WLF has been understood as a response to the effectiveness of the Primrose League as an electoral machine; there is evidence for this in the south Wales coalfield.[25] Rather than party and electoral factors only, this book explores other reasons for its formation, on the one hand, in the context of specifically Welsh conditions and, on the other, in a women's and feminist agenda. Nevertheless, the pattern of local, regional and national structures developed by the male parties provided a model for women's organization.[26] At the British level, after 1887, associations in England, Wales and Scotland were affiliated to the WLF; from early 1892, there was a separate Scottish federation. In Wales, from March 1892, the majority of local Women's Liberal Associations were also affiliated to the Women's Union of Welsh Liberal Associations. Two further bodies were formed as a result of splits in the WLF. The Women's Liberal Unionist Association (WLUA) was formed in 1888, mirroring the party split over Irish Home Rule. In 1892, when the WLF enshrined women's suffrage amongst its objectives, those opposed formed the Women's National Liberal Association (WNLA). Associations in the larger towns and cities developed into federations of ward-based associations, as in Cardiff, Swansea and Newport, while there were also county federations, as in Pembrokeshire. Local delegates met at the annual meetings, or councils, where they made policy, framed objectives and passed resolutions. At their peak, while not approaching the strength of the Primrose League, these were impressive bodies. In 1896, the membership of the WLF was about 82,000 in 476 associations; despite a period of decline, by 1912 the 837 associations represented a membership of over 133,000.[27] In the mid-1890s, the Women's Union of Welsh Liberal Associations (WUWLA) represented fifty-seven associations and 9,000 members.[28] However, the period of strength in Wales was short lived; an arc of rise and decline shapes the narrative. Chapters 1, 5 and 6 of this book examine that rise and decline in relation to local associations, while chapters 2 and 3 consider the issue in relation to the WUWLA.

The history of the Liberal party in Wales has been almost entirely blind to any involvement of women.[29] For the most part, the history of British Liberal women's politics has been analysed for the extent to which it helped or hindered the suffrage struggle. Writing in the 1920s, Ray Strachey acknowledged the importance of party organizations in breaking down the notion that the world of electoral politics was not for women; for the WLF, her interest was mainly in the strains and schisms over the suffrage issue.[30] Writing in the late 1960s, at the very beginning of the 'second wave' examination of Victorian and Edwardian feminism, Constance Rover concluded that Liberal women were, on the whole, 'markedly suffragist', briefly examining Liberal women's dilemma of party loyalty versus suffragism. Her discussion effectively ended with 1908.[31] David Morgan's 1975 volume placed women's suffrage in the context of the wider politics of the day, of reform of the House of Lords and Irish Home Rule, a crucial context for these years. However, the WLF was reduced to a background to ministerial speeches on the subject, ultimately represented as loyal to, if not happy with, the male leadership and their party in government.[32] Martin Pugh's 'revisionist' study of the women's movement treats Liberal women's dilemma with deeper and more lasting significance, both for women and the party. Describing liberalism as 'the unexpected enemy', he explores the party's difficulties with the suffrage issue; Liberal women and their organizations mainly feature as they intersect with this story.[33]

Feminist political histories in the 1980s and after have produced more fruitful conceptual frameworks. Jane Rendall emphasized the necessity for historians to free themselves from nineteenth-century conceptions of public and private spheres, in order to move beyond the focus on the suffrage struggle and to 'recover the language which women used, and the meaning of their politics . . . to grasp the range of women's political activity . . . [and to] expand our definition of what is properly political'.[34]

These concerns were reflected in Linda Walker's comparative study of Liberal women and the Primrose League.[35] Walker examined the political culture of party women, analysing their self-representation in using, but also sometimes stretching and subverting, the notion of separate spheres, and emphasized the close connection for Liberal women between religion and their politics.[36] This is a theme that has been more fully developed in recent years, as a way of exploring the meanings of women's involvement in the public sphere and their reinterpretation of liberalism. In this book I make an argument for the distinctive nature of Welsh Liberal women's politics, but it is important to remember that its intensely moral and religiose tone was shared more widely with the evangelically inspired feminist tradition identified by Olive Banks.[37] This is not to detach it from the sense of national identity; but the identification of morality and religion as the qualities which women, par excellence, brought into politics meant that at times gender trumped nation as a core identity, and at others women were seen as a safeguard for the aspirations of the nation.[38]

Walker's suggestion that the WLF leadership was likely to be more suffragist than the WLAs, demonstrating 'a conviction that women should shape their own political destiny', has been subject to some revision, to some extent arising from different chronological focus: like Rover, Walker does not provide a detailed examination of the years 1906–14.[39] The extremely destructive strains within the WLF arising in the period of Liberal government, explored in depth by

Claire Hirshfield, form a more convincing context for the picture of the decline of the organization described in this book, and the bitterness and schism in Cardiff 1910–11.[40] Hirshfield describes a WLF in which the executive resisted suffragist pressure from the localities.[41] Welsh records too suggest that local associations sometimes wished to go further in a radically suffragist direction than the WLF and WUWLA leadership, but in moments of political crisis differences between women were highlighted at all levels. Walker's characterization of Liberal women has also been challenged from the perspective of attempts by Catherine Marshall of the National Union of Women's Suffrage Societies (NUWSS) to encourage WLA pressure on the government. Walker had ignored, argues Jo Vellacott, WLF 'failure to show effective commitment to women's suffrage in the crucial period of 1910–1914'.[42] Vellacott emphasized both lack of leadership from the WLF and 'the tendency both locally and nationally' to defer to the male party leadership.[43] However, from the perspective of the WLAs themselves, the picture is rather more complex. In Wales, WLF leadership, or lack of it, must be judged to have been an issue in this period, but so was an inability of Liberal women in Wales to unite for action, following the failure of their own national organization, and the difficulty of abandoning articles of faith which had for so long been part of a Welsh Liberal identity. Local conditions, the specific context in which Liberal women made their politics, were crucial, as the studies of Cardiff and Aberdare will show. Overwhelmingly, events demonstrated the destructiveness of the male liberalism's disregard of the suffragists in the party, rather than supine loyalty of Liberal women.

Sandra Holton's work has influentially placed the consideration of 'democratic suffragists', and the NUWSS Election Fighting Fund (EFF) policy at the centre of historiographical debates.[44] Liberal women enter the story as the majority group within the NUWSS, and as disillusioned party women. In both Vellacott's and Holton's work, the south Wales opposition to the EFF is examined in some detail, and I have contributed to that debate, which this book revisits.[45] Cardiff WLA presents a vivid example of such disillusionment among Liberal women; nevertheless, they were not 'democratic suffragists' eager to embrace the labour movement. On the contrary, as I show in chapter 6, it was their distrust of the Labour party and miners' MPs in south Wales which was at the bottom of their resistance to the EFF, and not blind Liberal loyalty.

Krista Cowman's work departs from the work reviewed above to approach political organization directly, in a broad survey of women's activities in Liverpool from 1890 to 1920.[46] As would be expected, Liverpool's Liberal women display many similarities to those in south Wales, and bear comparison with Cardiff WLA, located as they both were in important regional commercial and port cities. The similarities highlight the issues and characteristics which united Liberal women around Britain: as in Cardiff, women's candidacy for local government, the gendered discourses which accompanied the elections and divisions over the suffrage issue were all evident. The differences probably reflect the importance of local and regional conditions. In Liverpool, unlike Cardiff, there was no cross-party alliance between women on local government candidacies, and only belated and grudging support from men, in marked contrast to Cardiff, and Wales generally, where the candidacy of women was linked to national, humanitarian and civic progress. In the militant era, Liverpool women succeeded in maintaining their party organization and were not compelled, like Cardiff women, to reject long-held Liberal beliefs. Cowman's approach usefully sets Liberal organization in a broad context of women's political activity in one locality. However, the constraints of a broad survey mean that the examination of the ethos and ideology lacks depth. Cowman proposes three ideological models for political women: separate spheres, socialism and a 'sex–class' analysis; and depicts Liberal women wedded to the separate spheres model, reinterpreted to claim a place in the world of politics based on 'the notion of female superiority'.[47] In Wales, too, the model of 'female excellence' was used, by women and men. But it was perhaps especially from men, and especially from Nonconformist ministers supporting women's political claims, that this discourse was to be heard in Wales. Women's language was differently inflected, centrally utilizing the language of 'duty' in relation to citizenship. Rereadings of liberalism as an evolving ideology, discussed below, take us beyond the 'equal or different' dichotomy.

Both the suffrage movement and women's Liberal politics have been approached by Megan Smitley through the lens of Scottish women's temperance campaigns.[48] Despite this oblique approach to Liberal women's politics, Smitley's work explores themes which occur in this book: the importance of temperance, the creation of an urban feminine public sphere and the suggestion, already discussed, that in British women's history religion should be added to the intersections of class, gender and race in explorations of 'Englishness, Britishness and "Otherness"' (and, of course, Welshness).[49] Smitley's exploration of the Scottish women's temperance union draws comparisons with other parts of Britain, contrasting the 'overwhelmingly suffragist' Scottish temperance advocates with Welsh and English campaigners.[50] This argument for regional diversity is partly based on a study of the Welsh-language Undeb Dirwestol Merched Gogledd Cymru (North Wales Women's Temperance Union, UDMGC) who kept their temperance campaigning independent of official support for the suffrage struggle.[51] I suggest that the women's temperance movement in Wales, in its broad entirety, is in need of further research which would link it more firmly to suffragism, at least partly through the WUWLA and the WLAs. Like the Scottish Women's Liberal Federation, the WUWLA declared its suffragism from the beginning, but the intersection with issues of Welsh politics and national identity made for a tense relationship. This does not appear to have been the case in Scotland, despite the decision to maintain separate organization on grounds of national distinctiveness. Smitley sees their feminism and their Scottish consciousness as sitting comfortably within their British and imperial 'concentric identities'.[52] Welsh political women also displayed 'concentric identities', but the fit between Welshness and feminism was not comfortable when nationalist Wales felt insecure (see chapter 3).

In Welsh women's political history, a brief exploration of Liberal women's politics has been set in the context of the suffrage movement.[53] Decline of organization is linked to the defeat of Cymru Fydd, while a suffragist heritage within the party is outlined, though it is suggested that for the suffrage movement 'the stimulus came from elsewhere'.[54] This book develops and explores these themes.

## Feminism

So far, I have used the term 'feminism' without defining it, or asking what kind of feminism, if any, Welsh Liberal women espoused. Welsh Liberal women were, on the whole, suffragists. Some were not, taking an anti-suffragist position, or putting other issues, such as disestablishment, first; but the evidence suggests that suffragism was the majority position in the WUWLA as in the WLF. Suffragism was not, on its own, a sufficient condition of feminism; however, the writings and speeches of Welsh Liberal women make it clear that their suffragism was part of a wider politics. A 'feminist consciousness' has been defined as viewing 'women's collective situation in the culture as unjust, [attributing] it to social and political institutions established by men, and [believing] it could be changed by protest and political action'.[55] On such terms, the position expressed by much of the membership of Welsh WLAs can be described as feminist, and many of them saw their distinct and autonomous organizations, and the political culture developed in them, as an expression and vehicle of that world-view.

Historians of the nineteenth century have further identified different kinds of feminism.[56] Perhaps most influential in British feminist history has been the division into 'equality' and 'difference' feminisms, based on understandings of male and female nature and culture, and making claims for emancipation based on those understandings.[57] Increasingly, it has been recognized that many women used both sets of arguments, and that the 'difference' arguments, apparently grounded in an acceptance of 'separate spheres' ideology, were frequently used to stretch and undermine the boundaries between 'public' and 'private'. 'Women's sphere' became very elastic indeed, both discursively and in fact, as women reconstructed in turn the realms of philanthropy, local government and national and imperial politics as the business of women. However, to understand late nineteenth-century feminism, it is necessary to add to this synthesis their understanding of what citizenship was for, and the importance of the *duties* of citizenship, in addition to, and perhaps over and above, *rights*.

Liberal suffragists believed the enfranchisement of women, along with the other reforms they sought, was an essentially Liberal measure, which would one day be delivered by a Liberal government. So if liberalism seemed 'the best available vehicle'[58] for women's social and political goals, what sort of liberalism was it? At a public meeting in Aberdare in 1892, a visiting speaker referred scornfully to 'what the men call Liberalism'; her audience laughed, suggesting that they thought they knew what she meant and shared her sentiment.[59] What was it that women called liberalism? A growing historical literature examines the relationship of women to liberalism as a British ideology, and feminism's critique and transformation of that ideology. While party and ideology were not identical, Liberal women, claiming their emancipation and their broader social goals as essentially Liberal, insisted on making the party the vehicle for that ideology, and judging it accordingly.

14

Liberal feminism has been equated with equal-rights feminism, drawing on the individualist creed of the right of individuals to the fullest development of their potential, avoiding a universal suffrage position by emphasizing the constitutionality of the demand, based on the independent tax-paying or householder woman.[60] The problems of women's relationship to this version of the liberal subject have been influentially analysed from the perspective of political science by Carole Pateman.[61] Other strands in the history of liberal ideas have also been very fruitful, in particular the emphasis on the conception of 'altruism' from the mid-nineteenth century and the extension of that to women's conception of liberalism.[62] Historians have analysed the impact of this re-visioning of liberalism for the first generation of British feminists, in the 1860s and 1870s. Additional influences have been identified as Giuseppe Mazzini's *Duties of Man*, newly translated in these decades, providing a European framework for ideas about women's relationship to society and humanity; and Josephine Butler's leadership of the anti-Contagious Diseases Acts campaigns, injecting religious fervour and the conception of citizenship as a sacred trust.[63] It has been argued that the repeal campaigns represented an important moment in the redefinition of liberalism, when arguments for extensions of the franchise in terms of individual taxpayers' and householders' rights gave way to a rhetoric which constructed the vote as a trust, for the use of which men would have to answer to 'the GOD of purity'.[64] This 'new liberal subjectivity' provided women with 'a view of citizenship which transcended sharp boundaries between domestic, social and political responsibilities'.[65]

This has provided a useful framework for Welsh Liberal feminism, enabling an interpretation which goes beyond a narrow identification with Welsh Nonconformist evangelicalism, placing Welsh Liberal women in a wider framework of British and European ideas. Such ideas found a receptive public in Wales. There, in the 1890s, as the following chapters show, the concept of duty, of engaged and effective citizenship, driven by moral and religious precepts (and timely new translations of Mazzini which were clearly influential in Wales), enabled a second generation of feminists to see their version of liberalism, not 'what the men called Liberalism', as the standard. The speech and writings of many women who feature in this book can be understood within this framework. The echoes of Butlerian language were strong. Butler's world-view was a touchstone for Welsh Liberal suffragists in the 1890s and in the Edwardian period.[66] They used the language of 'separate spheres' because they spoke from their own experience of the world. A representative figure in this regard is Nora Philipps. For those women who did not wish to claim rights for themselves – recognizing the difficulty for women of making claims not based on altruism – she reminded them of the needs of other women, of 'that great mass of workwomen who were downtrodden, overworked and underpaid'.[67] Her affirmation of women's familial role was always a preamble to an equally trenchant 'but . . .', as she launched into what she and many others saw as a moral imperative, women's necessary engagement with the world. The construction in the Liberal national movement of a moral 'mission to the world' (itself a Mazzini-esque idea) for Wales within the British empire facilitated the rapprochement between feminism and the party. However, as confidence in that vision of the nation dissolved, many women thought their feminism was best served outside the party.

Did the stimulus come from elsewhere?[68] To a degree; but to the extent that there was support for women's suffrage, the conditions in its favour brought together the 'outside' stimulus with elements usually considered as impeccably 'national', the forces of Welsh Nonconformity. Two sets of circumstances appear to have come together in Wales in the 1870s to create support for women's suffrage. One was undoubtedly a succession of touring suffrage speakers and the links set up between south Wales and the west of England through the Bristol and West of England Society for Women's Suffrage.[69] But the visiting speakers and the presence of a small number of unusually active women, like Rose Mary Crawshay and Gertrude Jenner, whose connections and social position enabled them to ignore pious conventions, does not in itself explain even the little that is known about early manifestations. The second set of circumstances was provided by Nonconformity which, while distinctively Welsh in language, national feeling and political ambitions, was nevertheless not sealed off from British networks of dissenters bent on social and moral reform, connected through temperance societies and with a history of political activism going back to the anti-slavery campaigns. In the 1870s these networks were animated by the campaign to repeal the Contagious Diseases Acts, providing support for changes in the political position of women (see chapter 4).

By the 1890s, therefore, there was fertile ground for the feminist message. Social changes and women's campaigns had expanded educational and professional opportunities and increased participation in the public sphere, especially for middle-class and lower-middle-class women. The contradictions in the position of such women, of opportunity hedged about by continuing constraints of gender, created the conditions for feminism in Wales as in England. For the Liberal nationalist supporters of feminist demands, the improved position of women would be one of the marks of the unique and progressive culture of Wales.[70] So an examination of the nationalist period and women's nationalism and feminism, pre-dating the later, better-known period of suffrage struggle, can demonstrate a history of support for feminism.

## *Nation*

Two key periods have been identified in the shaping of national identities in nineteenth-century Wales. The first, beginning in the middle of the century, followed the events dubbed 'the Treason of the Blue Books', when a parliamentary commissioners' report on the state of education in Wales, published in 1847, saw the Welsh reflected in the unsympathetic gaze of the British establishment, their lack of enlightenment blamed on the very marks of their distinctive nationality, religion and language. The national trauma produced by these characterizations was followed by religious, moral and cultural efforts to reconstruct Wales, identified as a historic moment in the growth into national self-consciousness of a Welsh Nonconformist people. This cultural effort had implications for constructions of gender.[71] While this period and these events fall outside the subject matter of this book, relevant aspects will be discussed in the context of gendered representations of nation (see chapter 3).

The second period of nation building came in the period from 1886 to 1896, when the Cymru Fydd movement saw the possibility of using political means to bring about Welsh religious, social and cultural objectives, including a measure of self-government, following extensions of the franchise in 1867 and 1884.[72] If liberalism in the late nineteenth century could be identified with militant Nonconformity,[73] Wales was its stronghold. Welsh political demands arose from issues which had salience for Liberals all over Britain: 'Education, temperance, land reform and disestablishment . . . were essential food for every Liberal's digestion.'[74] What made them 'Welsh' issues, as they were increasingly acknowledged to be at Westminster, was the dominance in Wales, numerically and culturally, of Nonconformity. Cymru Fydd was an attempt to make the Liberal party in Wales a vehicle for this version of the nation.

Historians who have analysed the gendering of nations and nationalisms have been interested in the way this impacted on women's citizenship, or lack of it.[75] They have analysed women's place in nationalist struggles and the representations of women and gender in nationalist discourses and discursive practices – in 'national symbolism and national citizenship'.[76] European nationalist movements, and the ideas which fuelled them, were influential in Wales, but Wales also shared many of the characteristics of nationalism, and manifestations of it, more globally.[77] Nationalisms, while insisting on distinctiveness and separation, were at the same time sharing in a global phenomenon while, in their own struggles for inclusion in the nation, women were also participating in local manifestations of an international and worldwide spirit. These convergences exemplify the 'coeval rise' of nationalisms and women's claims for citizenship, in which nationalisms became 'narratives[s] of progress', marked by the progress of women.[78] Welsh Liberal nationalism in the 1890s displayed these characteristics very strongly. Recent interdisciplinary work on Wales's relationship to 'the other', both within its borders and in the empire, particularly through missionary work, has enriched the understanding of the way national identity has been shaped.[79] There is, however, still room for historical work on gender and nation in the context of political developments in the period covered by this book. As a political movement, looking towards Parliament for the realization of its aims, Cymru Fydd has not, until recently, been examined by historians of women or gender.[80] While the theme of women's representations within national identities runs through this book, chapter 3 focuses on these questions for the end of the nineteenth century, while chapter 6 develops them for the Edwardian period.

### Place, politics, gender and class

This book contributes to developments in women's political history which have moved attention away from the metropolitan 'centre' and into the so-called 'periphery' and 'Celtic fringe'. While no attempt has been made to draw thorough-going comparisons with Scotland or

Ireland, recent work on both those areas, and work on women's political activity in English regional centres, has been useful and where appropriate, as in this introduction, comparisons have been drawn. By examining the neglected history of Welsh Liberal women, I aim to 'reconfigure a familiar historical landscape',[81] for both British women's political history and Welsh political history. As a study structured around the 'local' and the 'national', this book is also concerned with the *real* landscapes, places and locations which were the context within which women lived, worked and pursued politics.

Wales in the late nineteenth century was a politicized landscape: the word 'heartland' was both a geographical expression and a term which contributed to the 'imagined' nation of values and culture. Wales was also a place in which the landscape, and the difficulties of communication within it, obstructed attempts at united action. Nora Philipps, the first president of the WUWLA, appears to have understood these things very well. She represented women's organization as making a new political map of the country, through the will to unity.[82] Philipps had recognized that the language of Welsh political geography was often divisive, that identity in Wales at the end of the nineteenth century had in it an assertion of difference expressed as location. A pamphlet on disestablishment circulated to WLAs in Wales and England in 1894 was signed by its author 'Un o'r Gogledd' ('One from the North', or 'Northerner').[83] As a statement of personal and political identity, this would have been fairly opaque to English readers, but would have invoked a bundle of meanings for Welsh Liberals. Attachment to the land and to rural life as the source of national values were key elements in nationalist writings and rhetoric, but were strongly located in the north, or the 'heartland'. The 'south' – really the industrial and cosmopolitan south-east – was frequently identified with 'de-nationalizing' forces and values. These divisive conceptualizations emerged in women's Liberal politics; challenging them required political, rhetorical and literary efforts to construct Wales and its people as one. For some women, the identity contained in the feminist notion of 'womanhood' offered a solution, for others it threatened to undermine the nation and its goals (see chapters 2 and 3).

The identification, from 1867, between the Liberal party and Welshness, the party and its leading figures being understood to embody the history and destiny of Wales, exemplifies the concept of a 'politics of place', in which 'myths of community and myths of party intertwined'.[84] This presented a site of ideological contest for women, on both nationalist and feminist grounds. Chapter 3 looks at some of the ways in which party women attempted to rewrite the myths of the nation and its history to include women. While there was always the possibility that such representations were exclusive, they also offered a sense of place in which the party itself, as the embodiment of values, rather than 'blood and soil' nationalism, provided the sense of belonging.[85] At the national level, Nora Philipps, and at the local, Mary Lloyd of Aberdare, could connect to 'place' and be identified with it by others, not just through marriage, but by their dedication to values and institutions, their contribution to the construction and representation of community.

Developments in the second half of the twentieth century rescued the local study from the realm of the antiquarian. The first was the rise of social history, in particular of histories of working-class struggles and 'history from below'. The feminist practice of women's history, in which the validation of women's experience and knowledge was a key object and in which hierarchical notions of leadership and centralization were challenged, led to a flowering of locally focused research. The growth of cultural history and the postmodern turn to identities and diversity also make the study of local organizations and individual actors central to the history of women's politics. Such approaches are especially appropriate for the period covered by this book, since in the Victorian understanding of the political sphere, the local, bounded and specific were the areas of feminine activity par excellence, while the national, imperial and general were masculine.[86] These understandings were expressed, for example, in the famous 'Appeal Against Female Suffrage' of 1889, and again in the Edwardian high imperial era, when the essential masculinity of imperial government and the state was emphasized to refute the demand for women's suffrage.[87] Women's emancipation, as its opponents recognized, was a fundamental challenge to this gendering of the geographical and conceptual spaces of politics, as of work, education, culture and leisure. As the studies of the Liberal women of Aberdare and Cardiff will show (in chapters 4 to 6), that challenge was made most effectively at the local level, perhaps especially through the disruption of the boundaries of the local by women's political networks; the demonstration that 'the local', far from being the bounded and static space especially suited to women, was permeated by other spatial and social dimensions, from family and home to the national, imperial and international. However, women's claim to the public and political spaces of a locality was not secure, and could be challenged by assertive and even violent masculinity (see chapter 6).

The notion of the permeability of local boundaries should not dissolve away the local altogether. Aberdare and Cardiff do not just stand for local Women's Liberal Associations everywhere; if that were the case, it would be enough to study one of them. The emphasis on 'Welsh conditions' is not intended to suggest an essential and uniform experience for the women's associations throughout Wales. The contrasting orientations of the early Denbigh and Newport (Mon.) associations are telling while, in the Edwardian period of overall decline in women's organization, the experience of the industrial south was different from that of the north of the country and, amongst the largest urban associations, the histories of Cardiff and Swansea WLAs developed very differently in the same period. The depth possible in local studies enables exploration of class and social identities and the extent to which they did or did not contribute to political identity, and this book examines the available sources to attempt some conclusions. If subordinate groups are identified by their lack of cultural and social as well as economic capital,[88] most of the women who took leading roles in Liberal politics cannot be described as 'subordinate'. Women without wealth and unknown beyond their localities nevertheless had enormous social capital, in the shape of their religion, families and networks, to be invested in their activities. The consciousness of these cultural resources, of being in a more 'fortunate' position than others, drove a sense of duty; it also imbued such women with a very strong sense of their own fitness for active citizenship and its duties: their reflections on their roles as poor law guardians strongly display that consciousness (see chapter 4). However, the women without such resources are not, for the most part, made visible or audible in the sources for this book; social duty appears not to have been their prerogative. Is this simply because of the class composition of the WLAs? There are some clear differences between Aberdare and Cardiff WLAs on this ground. In Aberdare it has not been possible to identify many working-class women amongst the WLA activists. While not wishing to make inflated claims for the class composition of the Cardiff activists, working-class women made up a good proportion of subscribers, and there was some involvement of women who could be identified as coming from working-class backgrounds and the Lib–Lab positions in local politics. There were some differences on other grounds too. The politics of place, the intertwining of myths of party and community, operated more strongly in Aberdare than in Cardiff. The part played in such a politics by religion, temperance and moral-reform ideologies, while inclusive of women like the migrant Scot Mary Lloyd, were exclusive of others, such as Roman Catholics and, while encompassing 'progressive' ideas about women's role, might rule out more libertarian and New Liberal approaches to social action. In Cardiff, the diversity of the larger and more cosmopolitan society, a coalition of disparate elements, made more room for difference and therefore, perhaps, a looser attachment to the older forms of politics, and hence the possibility for women to repudiate them, as they did in 1910–11.

Such local diversity Welsh associations had in common with their English counterparts, making for debate, controversy and divisions in the WLF throughout its history. Bringing together the histories of two associations supports and suggests some general understandings of women's politics, but also points to the rich diversity of beliefs, practices, characteristics and contexts still to be studied elsewhere, all of which found a place in the rich mixture of women's liberalism. For the majority of women, their local association was their main, and often only, sphere of political activity. The study of women's activity at the local level, therefore, 'is crucial for understanding the process by which women become politicised, and the meaning of political activity in their lives'.[89] The study of local organisation contributes to the national picture, and reveals the relationship between 'centre' and 'periphery'. But it also reveals the particular circumstances in which women, organized and as individuals, have forged their political identities and made their histories.

PART I

THE THREE DIMENSIONS OF WOMEN'S LIBERAL
POLITICS IN WALES, 1880–1914

# 1

## *'A groove to work in': Women's Liberal Organization in Wales, 1880–1914*

### Introduction

This chapter will explore the circumstances of formation of Welsh Women's Liberal Associations (WLAs), their activities and characteristics, and the conditions of their decline in the period, roughly, 1880–1914. The aim is to construct a broad narrative of women's political organization and activity, and an examination of the ethos of their politics. As I have argued, the provision of such a narrative has value in itself for Welsh women's political history, but it also provides a context for the more closely focused chapters which follow. While the British context of the development of political parties and their parallel or auxiliary women's organizations (as set out in the introduction) is a vital part of the background, the chapter explores specifically 'Welsh' conditions, the ways in which the organization of women was linked to those conditions, and their intersection with more feminist aims, especially women's suffrage.

The first association in Wales seems to have been formed in 1883, in Denbigh. During the rest of the 1880s, development of women's organization was extremely slow, but by the middle of the next decade, fifty-seven associations representing about nine thousand members were organized in the Welsh Union of Women's Liberal Associations (WUWLA). In a period when Liberal party organization in Welsh constituencies was notoriously poor, commentators were impressed not just by numbers, but by the effectiveness of organizations which in many cases put the male associations to shame, with a high degree of zeal for aspects of the Liberal programme and for Welsh Nonconformist 'national' aims, such as disestablishment.

However, the period of strength was short lived. The decline of associations will be broadly explored, with a number of aspects, such as the relationship to nationalism and the impact of the suffrage movement, being more fully discussed in subsequent chapters.

It has been common to understand women's increasing presence in the 'public' world of local government and party politics in terms of a journey from the private world of the home, through an intermediate 'social' or 'civic' sphere of philanthropic activity motivated by religious faith.[1] More recently, however, historians emphasize the necessity of dismantling the distinction between women's political lives and their domestic, religious and philanthropic activities, in order to enter into 'the meaning of their politics'.[2] The forms taken by Welsh Liberal women's activities, and the language in which they represented those activities, support the contention that it is essential to expand definitions of the political.[3] The local associations were contributing to an ethos which was reflected and nurtured at the national level in the WUWLA, to be more fully discussed in the next chapter.

## The rise and decline of Women's Liberal Associations, 1883–1914

The annual reports of the WUWLA (1893–6) and of the WLF (1888–1920s) provide records of 168 WLAs in Wales. The information in the reports was supplied by the associations themselves: some disappeared from the records after a year or two, some reaffiliated after a break; so, while not an exact reflection of the number of societies in existence at any one time, over the longer term the figures supply a pattern of Liberal activism among women in Wales. The pattern of rise and decline of associations appears to have been different for Welsh and English WLAs, and also for WLAs and male Liberal Associations in Wales. Clear explanations for these differences are not easy to find in the available sources, and to some extent remain speculative. The graph (figure 1) shows the pattern of affiliations of Welsh WLAs to the Women's Liberal Federation: the available sources for affiliations to the WUWLA do not provide figures over a comparable length of time; the union seems to have effectively ceased operating shortly after the turn of the century.

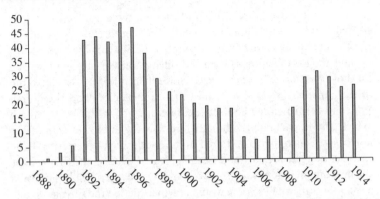

**Figure 1.** Women's Liberal Associations of Wales affiliated to the Women's Liberal Federation, 1888–1914
Source: WLF Annual Reports 1888–1914

### *The first phase, 1883–1891: foundations and structures*

When the Denbigh WLA was formed, it was amongst the earliest in Britain. By the 1891 annual conference of the WLF, five Welsh societies had affiliated. Four were in south Wales, in the large centres of urban liberalism, Cardiff, Swansea, Newport and Pontypridd. One was in the north Wales seat of the recently elected David Lloyd George, Caernarfon Boroughs. The earliest north Wales associations – Denbigh (1883), Bala (1887) and Bangor (1890) – had not affiliated to the WLF by 1891. However, all of these associations, along with others numbering in all around thirty, were represented at the inaugural meeting of the WUWLA at Aberystwyth on 30 March 1892.[4] By the publication of the WLF annual report for May 1892, the number of affiliated Welsh associations had shot up to forty-three. The 1895 figure of fifty-seven associations represented the peak of WLA affiliations to WUWLA, reflected in the high point of WLF affiliations in Figure 1.[5]

The earliest organizations occurred in key areas for the national resurgence. This can be seen most clearly in a quartet of WLAs created in counties bordering each other in north Wales, Denbigh, Bala, Caernarfon and Bangor, the last two both in Caernarfon Boroughs constituency. The formation of Denbigh WLA occurred during preparations for an election, in 1885, in which the Liberals brought an end to more than one hundred and sixty years of representation by a powerful land-owning dynasty. Denbighshire gained its place in the history of late nineteenth-century Nonconformist liberalism as the arena of political activity of the Gee family, notably the Revd Thomas Gee, Methodist publisher of the influential journal *Baner ac Amserau Cymru*.[6] Since the tripling of the electorate in the constituency in 1867, the Liberation Society and the North Wales Reform League had set the agenda and, in the 1880s, north Wales, and in particular Denbighshire, saw the intensification of the land issue, which then also flared in the south-west. When Anti-Tithe Leagues merged with a Land League created by Gee, the first rule of the new organization was that 'women as well as men will be admitted as members thereof'.[7] Some women farmers defied the tithe laws: one of the iconic figures of anti-tithe campaigners in the late 1880s was Peggy Lewis, an elderly farmer, who briefly came to embody all the oppressions to which Wales was subject when she was prosecuted and imprisoned. Rosemary Jones's work on community and collective action shows women active in the tithe wars utilizing traditional 'rough music' styles of social protest and resistance;[8] the language used in celebration of Peggy Lewis situated her too in the rural and 'traditional' which embodied Welshness in nationalist discourses.[9] But, with the enfranchisement of the affected social groups and classes, opportunities had now also been created for women to involve themselves in the public political sphere in the newer, more respectable, and successfully urban, forms of party auxiliaries. The women of the Gee family took a leading role: Susannah Gee (Miss Gee) and her sister, Mrs Sarah Matthews, were amongst the leaders of the temperance movement, instrumental in the creation in 1892 of Undeb Dirwestol Merched Gogledd Cymru (UDMGC, the North Wales Women's Temperance Union).[10] The family also took the lead in the Denbigh WLA in 1892. The association was absent from WLF records from 1898/9, not reappearing until 1927. In the 1890s, records suggest, the association orientated its work almost exclusively towards Welsh Nonconformist liberalism rather than the political claims of women. As a member of the executive of the WUWLA, Miss Gee provided the link between it and the Welsh Disestablishment Campaign Committee, getting the committee's financial support for propaganda on disestablishment amongst English Liberal women, some of which she wrote herself.[11] It becomes clear (see especially chapter 3) that Miss Gee put her nationalism before the WUWLA's agenda for women, and that she and her association represented a distinct and important strand in Welsh women's liberalism; the formation of the Denbigh WLA had more to do with Welsh national aims of the 1880s than with goals which can be ascribed to Liberal feminism. However, the political power of women was increasingly being seen by Welsh Nonconformist Liberals as essential in the battle, as a cleric put it at a suffrage meeting in 1881, 'on the side of right and justice'.[12] Up to a point, the movements progressed side by side, sometimes hand in hand, exemplifying 'the legitimating power of the sentimental concept of "woman's mission"',[13] but also reflecting the real commonalities between the agendas of women's organizations and reforming dissent.

The Bala WLA, in neighbouring Merionethshire, was formed three years after Denbigh. In Merioneth, the martyrology of Welsh Nonconformist liberalism had been created with the politically motivated evictions of tenant-farmer voters following the 1859 election. The county 'was the *exemplar* of the new political awakening ... providing the inspiration and drive in the Welsh parliamentary party'.[14] In 1886, Merioneth elected Thomas Edward Ellis as its MP in a campaign fought first on the issue of Irish Home Rule and then on disestablishment and land reform in Wales. Ellis's own family history, and the source of his political faith, was also traceable to the political evictions of 1859, and he compared the disregard of Welsh claims to the case of Ireland. The campaign 'marked a new era in the history of Welsh politics', with Ellis including the aim of Welsh self-government in his election address.[15] When Ellis envisaged the future for Wales, his vision included women on terms of equality with men, active in the political institutions of the nation; two years after his election, he was to be one of the sponsors in the House of Commons of the Women's Disabilities Removal Bill on behalf of the Women's Franchise League.[16] The Bala WLA had been formed in the optimism of his 1886 campaign. Its president in the 1890s was Mrs Hugh Williams, wife of a professor of church history at the Bala Theological College; the theological colleges were active in local reform campaigns from the 1850s onwards.[17]

Two more north Wales associations, Caernarfon and Bangor, were to be formed before the creation of the WUWLA. Both were in the constituency of Caernarfon Boroughs, both were formed in 1889/90, in time to work for the election of David Lloyd George, who took the seat from the Conservatives, though with a tiny majority, attributed to his premature support for Welsh home rule.[18] The by-election that

29

returned Lloyd George took place in April 1890, and Caernarfon WLA had affiliated to the WLF at least in time for the printing of the annual report in the spring; Bangor affiliated in 1891/2.[19] Denbigh and Bala had been formed when there was no WLF, and local women, members of Nonconformist leadership families, appear successfully to have taken the initiative. In the case of Caernarfon Boroughs, it was one of a number mentioned in the WLF annual report for 1890 as demonstrating some of the problems of organizing WLAs where no active association existed before the election, where there was 'an absence of any women in the locality with experience of political work',[20] requiring WLF election workers to be sent in. The result was the creation of a WLA or, as the report put it, 'it was only the spark needed to kindle the abundance of energy and interest in public affairs, latent amongst the women of the district'.[21] The first president of both Caernarfon and Bangor WLAs was Mrs Arthur Acland, wife of the MP for Rotherham, a supporter of Welsh causes with a home in Caernarfonshire. The two associations shared a secretary, although Bangor also had a local president. After 1892, the presidencies passed to local women.

These associations fit the pattern of creation of WLAs in response to the new electoral conditions. Like many associations, they were created by the 'sudden need for practical help during a time of hard work and excitement'.[22] They also reflect the observation that early associations were most often not found in 'notoriously Liberal' constituencies. According to WLF secretary Miss Macdonell, 'most have been formed amidst great difficulties and much discouragement, and in places where there is a hard task set before all the active adherents of the Liberal cause'.[23] Denbigh, Caernarfon Boroughs and Bangor were such constituencies. As we have seen, their WLAs were also created in conditions which were premonitory of women's relationship with the burgeoning national movement, to be discussed in the following chapters.

The first Welsh association to affiliate to the WLF was Newport and Monmouth Boroughs, in 1888. Its first president was the Honourable Evelyn Pelham, a vice-president of the WLF, and wife of the vice-president of the South Monmouthshire Liberal association. Despite its president's residence in Monmouth, the association seems to have been effectively a Newport society. The town was an important coal, steel and tinplate port, with an expanding working-class population in which, particularly in town and dockland areas like the

Central ward, employer interests, trade unionism, Irish politics and religious interests made a rich mix at election times; women added themselves to this mix in local elections after 1894.[24] Monmouth Boroughs (Newport, Monmouth and Usk) and South Monmouthshire were both marginal seats so there was everything to fight for. To the extent that it answered the need for improved electoral machinery, the association resembled the early north Wales associations and, like the north Wales women, Newport women were also prominent in the temperance activity of which the town was a centre,[25] with leading members in the Women's Christian Temperance Union and the British Women's Temperance Association (BWTA), which were well established before the creation in 1902 of the Welsh-language Undeb Dirwestol Merched y De (UDMD, South Wales Women's Temperance Union). However, the early support by Newport women for the women's suffrage progressive faction within the WLF[26] prefigured the second phase of organization of Women's Liberal associations in Wales, linked to British Liberal suffragism, a link to be explored in the following chapter.

A group of important south and south-west Wales associations was formed in 1890 and 1891, providing a basis for the intensive organization of 1891–2 and the creation of the WUWLA. Cardiff WLA was formed in 1890,[27] and the following year Carmarthen, Pembroke Dock, Pontypridd, Swansea, Aberdare and Tenby followed suit. Cardiff and Swansea were to become large associations, the latter having an unbroken record of WLF affiliation to the mid-1920s. Carmarthen disappeared from the records after a few years, while Pembroke Dock, Pontypridd and Tenby had broken histories, with reaffiliation part of the pattern. In the absence of good local records, it is difficult to know whether this represented the demise and revival of associations, or simply periods of relative inactivity.

Case studies of Cardiff and Aberdare WLAs appear in part II of this book. Swansea WLA represented two constituencies created in the redistribution of 1885, Swansea Town and the widespread Swansea District, which embraced the towns of Morriston, Aberafan, Neath, Kenfig and Loughor as well as parts of Swansea itself. Swansea Town was Liberal from 1885 to 1895, and again from 1900 until the 1920s. Swansea District was so safely Liberal that a contested election was the exception rather than the rule until redistribution in 1918. The WLA was organized on a ward basis, but affiliated to the WUWLA and WLF as a single association.[28] Some of its far-flung districts had their own associations for a while, including the tinplate-producing town of Morriston (1893–6) with a membership reaching about two hundred and fifty, Cadoxton (1892) and Neath (1893).[29] Swansea WLA drew its president and other officers from amongst local women from the beginning. Like Cardiff, the town had a history of activity in the early suffrage movement, and the anti-Contagious Diseases Acts campaign, a history discussed more fully in the context of the Cardiff study. The town provided one of only three women on local government bodies in Wales before the 1890s.[30] The association continued to be strongly suffragist throughout its history.

In the group of 1891 associations, it is also worth looking briefly at Pembroke Dock and Tenby, in the Pembroke Boroughs (Pembroke and Haverfordwest) constituency. Pembroke Dockyards provided a relatively strong Conservative enclave, and the constituency was captured by the Unionists in the Home Rule election of 1886.[31] The creation of the WLAs in these two towns, and another in Haverford-west the following year, shows all the signs of electoral machinery being put in place for the fight back in 1892, and credit for the role of the WLAs in regaining the seat was duly given.[32] The secretary of the Tenby association in its first year was Mrs C. F. Egerton Allen, wife of the successful Liberal candidate, though he was to lose to the Unionists in 1895. More significantly, the president of both associations was Nora Philipps, who was to become the first president of the WUWLA. The following year, she was also president of the newly formed Pembroke association. Her presidency of these associations gave her a first official foothold in Welsh Liberal politics in her own right, and in the longer term will have helped her husband regain the county seat for the party with a very much increased majority in 1898, giving him a more secure place in Welsh politics.[33] The role in this election of the Liberal women of the county, and of Nora Philipps, were seen to have been crucial: 'the ladies are a power in the Pembrokeshire constituency'.[34]

The typical structure of associations emerged in this period. Local associations had a president, a number of vice-presidents and an executive committee, all elected by the general body of members at the annual meeting. Some, like Aberdare, also had a general committee. The secretary was usually honorary, though Cardiff was to have a number of paid secretary-organizers, adding to the growing body in this period of professional female political organizers. If an association was in need of help, for recruitment, revival, or special events and campaigns, an organizer might be seconded by the WLF.[35] Cardiff, Newport and Swansea were later to reorganize their associations on a ward basis, each with its local officers, and with a central committee drawn from them. This was WLF policy for large associations, and in each case a WLF organizer spent some time in the towns facilitating the reorganization.

Despite its early formation, membership of the Newport WLA had remained rather static in the early 1890s, and low compared with the other important port and commercial centres. Like Cardiff WLA, in the mid-1890s Newport felt it should aim at a membership of about one thousand; instead, it bumped along under three hundred. As a result, reorganization into ward associations took place in November and December 1894, when Mrs Louisa Martindale, from Brighton WLA,[36] advised the Newport women to work 'on the same lines as the men' – that is, with five ward-based organizations and a central committee. The association relaunched itself with a new statement of rules and objects which were said to be 'in strong contrast to the more modest and hesitating propositions adopted in January 1888', including a clear statement on women's suffrage.[37] The reorganization came, as Evelyn Pelham pointed out, at 'a critical moment for our association'. There was the 'possibility of much power', she said, in local and parliamentary elections; the association was working for the election of women to Boards of Guardians and Parish Councils, following the 1894 reforms in the local government franchise, with women voters being urged to use their votes in the temperance cause. Pelham was herself elected to the new parish council of Penallt in Monmouthshire.[38]

The role played by the presidents of the associations probably varied according to locality and individuals. Perhaps an important attribute for a president was the confidence which came from class and status, as well as experience. Relatively inexperienced local women, dealing with the press and with local male organizations, as well as with national organizations of women, may have felt they needed the extra political heft provided by higher social class and political connections. Despite Evelyn Pelham's suggestion that Newport WLA needed a president who lived closer to the town and could be more actively involved, she retained the position until 1902, though the association, on her advice, appointed a 'local' president.[39] As we saw, the early associations like Denbigh and Bala, less concerned with the national stage, consisted of active local women, with a president from a local leadership family. As the WLF increasingly intervened in election campaigns, as in

Caernarfon, someone like Acland, a woman with leadership connections and experience, even though with rather tenuous local connections, was seen to be necessary. In Cardiff, from 1894, the position of Eva McLaren as president was clearly an acknowledgement of the admiration in which she was held in the town, while the 'working' presidents from 1894 were local women. McLaren's presidency of Barmouth WLA (1891–6) indicates a role in setting up the association, but also perhaps weak local organization, since it disappeared from the records for fourteen years after 1896. As already proposed, Nora Philipps's presidency of west Wales associations is suggestive of the ground being prepared for a longer-term strategy, involving both her feminist aims and the career of her husband. Where a constituency had a Liberal MP, it was usual for his wife to take the presidency; Lady Reed (1889–91) and later the Hon. Mrs Ivor Guest (1907–8) in Cardiff, Sybil Thomas in Aberdare and Mrs Arthur Williams in Bridgend are just some examples. Some must have been more willing than others to take the role: Margaret Lloyd George, for example, despite being described as 'the member *in* Caernarvon District, while he was the Member *for* it',[40] became president of several north Wales WLAs in her husband's constituency only when he was Chancellor of the Exchequer after 1908, and then in at least one case with a local president also in place.[41] The position and role of the president, and of political wives and daughters, will be more fully discussed in the context of studies of Aberdare and Cardiff WLAs. The vigour, effectiveness and longevity of an association depended on its committee, and on an active core amongst the committee members. The class and social composition of an association will also have depended on the success of the committee in getting beyond what a speaker in Cardiff called 'villadom' in its organizing efforts. These issues are explored in some depth in the context of the studies of Cardiff and Aberdare associations (see part II).

## The second phase, 1890–1895: growth and characteristics

In 1891, there were just six Welsh WLAs listed in the annual report of the WLF. In 1892, over forty associations, all with voting rights at the annual council meeting, were now affiliated to the federation. The great effort which saw so many new WLAs created was not confined to Wales: in that year, the number of associations in England and

Wales more than doubled, from 177 to 367. The proportionate increase in Wales, however, was much greater, almost 700 per cent, from a very low base.[42] While some of these newly affiliated associations had been in existence for some time, the vast majority had been created in a burst of organizing activity in the autumn and winter of 1891–2.[43] Some were very short lived, and perhaps inherently weak, but served their immediate purpose, for it will be argued in chapter 2 that the organizational effort of those months was intended to boost the progressive faction in the WLF, helping them to ensure that women's enfranchisement became one of the objects of the federation, as it did in the council meetings of May 1892. However, the auxiliary role of the associations, and the local electoral needs of the Liberal party, were not forgotten: the annual report of 1891 pointed out that the party was 'placing its general organisation in a state of efficiency' for the coming general election (of July 1892), and that constituency demands for the help of women organizers and workers were high. The delegates at the council meeting agreed on the need for 'lady lecturers' to organize new WLAs and ginger-up existing ones. The report of May 1892 issued a high-minded reminder that Liberal workers should employ 'only such methods of electioneering as are worthy of the great cause whose triumph they are striving to achieve'.[44] In the creation of a number of associations in Wales, the activities of the women of the Primrose League were cited as creating the need for organization by Liberal women, calling good women out to do their duty in the noble cause, 'to counteract the insidious influence of the dames'.[45]

While these were the wider and 'top down' conditions in which WLAs were formed, there was also the possibility for the construction of local collective identities. This process could be seen at work in the various rules, aims and objects adopted by WLAs. The WUWLA had produced a six-point model:

> The aim of the Welsh Union is to teach what women need, what the world wants, and what Wales wishes for. Its immediate objects are as follows:
>
> 1. To organize new Associations, and to strengthen those which already exist; and to publish special Liberal literature in both the English and Welsh languages.
> 2. To win the victory for Mr Gladstone's policy of Home Rule for Ireland.
> 3. To teach the great principle of religious equality, and ardently to

support a measure for the Disestablishment and Disendowment of the Church of England in Wales.

4. To press forward very zealously in the country all Liberal principles and especially to promote measures of reform for Wales.
5. To strenuously support all measures of just legislation for women, including their parliamentary enfranchisement, and to work for the incorporation of this important measure of reform into the programme of the Liberal Party.
6. To protect the interests of children.

The model had been modified and adopted by many associations by 1893;[46] the variations from the model indicated that it was debated by the local groups, and altered to fit, rather than simply taken off the shelf. The common elements were support for Liberal principles and Liberal party aims (disestablishment and Irish Home Rule might be specified), and usually a statement on maintaining the 'purity' of conduct of elections, reflecting the WLF admonitions noted above, and Liberal women's sense of their ethos in contrast to that of Unionist women. These propositions were combined with a variety of aims which showed that associations considered themselves to be working for women rather than party, with statements aimed at their political rights, including the vote, and at their educational, social and economic needs. The protection of children was usually included. The pattern provided a general statement of the field of women's Liberal politics in this period: while statements of aims by male Liberal associations appear to have confined themselves to Liberal electoral objectives, the women's organizations were more likely to emphasize Liberal principles and to address themselves to a constituency of women.[47] There were differences of emphasis between WLAs which are suggestive. Both Newport and Aberystwyth used the WUWLA model as the basis for their rules. Aberystwyth WLA, which included members of the radical Women's Franchise League amongst its leadership, and which liked to think of itself as 'sound on suffrage', included the objective of 'the cause of women's suffrage', and added a seventh object: 'To insist on the perfect equality of the sexes before the law.'[48] Newport WLA produced a new set of aims in 1894, which was also largely based on the WUWLA model, but used the phrase 'the claims of women to the Parliamentary franchise'; strengthened the aim of 'equal justice and political rights for all' by naming 'rich and poor, men and women'; and inserted a statement on 'the unsatisfactory economic position of women' and their need for technical training and trade unionism ('trade combinations'). These differences of emphasis may indicate some social and political diversity of membership in different communities, and a spectrum of political possibilities, probably tempered by an understanding of what might attract or repel local support. In addition to sensitivity to local cultures and conditions, women had also to be mindful of the broader context of prescriptive discourses about women's role and women's nature; their self-representations, therefore, should be read as 'dialectical – that is very sensitive and responsive' to these prescriptions.[49] The detailed examination of the founding of Cardiff and Aberdare WLAs in part II bears this out.

The brief period from 1893 to 1896 when WLAs were sending accounts of their activities for publication in the annual reports of the WUWLA coincides with the period of greatest optimism in women's political organization, and it is safe to suggest that changes in the reports reflected what was happening to organization. From 1893–5, the associations sent in information on membership, speakers and activities and reflected on their progress. From 1894, the names of the presidents and secretaries were listed. In 1896, the reports included those details and membership figures for fewer than half the associations, but no information on activities. During that time, memberships ranged from a group of thirty in Mid-Rhondda to 900 in Cardiff; after Cardiff, the largest were a group of associations with membership around the five hundred mark – Aberdare, Llanelli, Pembroke Dock – and Swansea with just over four hundred. The returns covered brief statements of work done for the 1892 general election – canvassing, literature distribution and transporting voters. Rhosllannerchrugog said they had 'urg[ed] women to get their husbands to vote for disestablishment', while Merthyr and Milford Haven associations had questioned candidates about their views on women's suffrage. The same kinds of work were undertaken for local elections, when some associations recorded that they had canvassed women local voters in particular, and a few reported that the value of their work during elections had been acknowledged by candidates and agents. Speakers to associations during these years included some familiar names from the federation, such as Countess Alice Kearney, a much admired speaker in Wales, Mrs Stanbury, Mrs Morgan-Browne, Miss Morant and Miss Conybeare; WUWLA and local speakers and MPs were regulars.[50]

Associations used meetings to help women develop their skills of public speaking and presentation, with local women reading papers which were often the means by which positions on women's suffrage, and the status of women more generally, were developed. In 1893 and 1894, associations held meetings in support of petitions for the Special Appeal on women's suffrage, and reported large numbers signing at enthusiastic meetings.[51] The importance of women's suffrage, though sometimes as a means to an end, was frequently mentioned by associations: Newtown in 1893 stated that it was '*particularly* anxious to help forward Women's Suffrage, Disestablishment and Temperance Reform'; in the Vale of Towy 'enthusiasm for the woman's movement was great; the Petition in favour of Women's Suffrage was eagerly signed by men and women in large numbers'. There is no sign here of any problems with the 1892/3 suffrage controversy in the WLF, though some associations, such as those headed by the anti-suffragist Lady Osborne Morgan, emphasized disestablishment and temperance, and omitted any mention of women's suffrage. In some of the early reports, associations represent themselves as the instrument of growing political consciousness amongst members. Rhyl WLA, with 229 members in 1893, while more complimentary than others, expressed the optimistic sense of progress:

> The meetings are well attended by thoughtful women who are gradually feeling their way towards taking a more active part, and who are steadily increasing in numbers and becoming more and more convinced that the suffrage for women is an absolute necessity in face of the great reforms which the Association is pledged to vote for.[52]

The association's account of its year's activities – 'Vigorous help in the C.C. election', 'One tea and social evening', 'Monthly [meetings] with papers' – gives few clues to the discussions, arguments and speeches which must have contributed to the political awakening described. However, the reports from the WLAs, while brief, allow some reflection not just on activities but on the ethos of women's liberalism at a local level. The entry for Merthyr and District WLA in 1894 suggests some of the energy of the time, as well as the breadth of focus:

> Good work has been done for the Welsh Union. Petitioned the members to support amendments in favour of Female Franchise under Parish Councils Bill; also memorialised Parliament urging the abolition of the State Regulation of Vice in India and throughout the British Dominions. Collected 890 signatures for Special Appeal in favour of Women's Suffrage. Sent petition to Parliament in favour of Peace and Arbitration.[53]

From the other end of the country, on the north Wales coast, the Rhyl WLA described its work in the same year:

> The four public meetings were arranged for specific purposes, *viz.*, Opium Traffic in India and China; Zenana Work; and a Temperance Demonstration; all these were large and enthusiastic – evidence of the vitality of the Association; while the numerous petitions sent up to Members of Parliament are a further proof of its industry.[54]

The list of subjects suggests some of the characteristics of Welsh women's liberalism: an overriding concern with moral and social reform issues, including the international and imperial dimension, allied to an equal interest in gaining political power locally and nationally. The use of the term 'Zenana work' is interesting in this context. A form of missionary activity developed by Nonconformist women in India, which reached into the zenana, or segregated quarters of Hindu women's households, the term signals the taken-for-granted connection between politics and religious faith in Wales – as well as, of course, the enthusiastic participation in empire of evangelical Christians. While the 'zenana' – women's work amongst women in women's quarters – might be read as constructing Liberal women's work in terms of the innermost circle of the domestic sphere, and of a distinct and separate women's culture, nevertheless, the knowledge gained there led straight to the critique of imperial governance understood by many to be beyond the limits of what was politically permissible or legitimate for women. An example was to be found in the wide support in Wales for Josephine Butler's extension of the anti-Contagious Diseases Acts campaign to India.[55] The entry does not tell us whether the Liberal 'missionary' work in Rhyl was party political or attempted to reach women primarily through moral and social issues. These workers for liberalism would have found the distinction irrelevant. In Swansea too, while not describing its work in the same terms, the association branched out into active social work, setting up a Provident Club and a Girls' Club with a membership of ninety, meeting three evenings a week and collecting funds for miners' families during a coal lock-out.

Enthusiasm and high ideals did not necessarily result in effective organization: in 1894, Caernarfon WLA noted ruefully that the style of their meetings had not 'been the means of reaching the masses', and decided, in some unspecified way, to change tack. In 1895, the returns reported the satisfactory results of WLA efforts to get women elected to parish and district councils and boards of guardians. In that year, large associations reported rising membership figures, while others held their own. Some struggled, though optimistically, with scattered rural populations, severe weather and consequent social distress, all of which affected their work and attendance at meetings. Generally, there was little in the reports to suggest that organization was on the point of collapse. However, if not giving up work altogether, associations were to draw in their horns in the next few years, many dropping their WLF affiliation.[56] Some surviving reports of the Aberystwyth WLA provide more detail of the decline of one association, which may have reflected the experience of others.

Despite very buoyant returns of its activities and progress in the WUWLA annual reports, Aberystwyth had never been one of the largest associations, with 152 members at its peak in 1893. The secretary, Elizabeth James, and a member of its committee, *Cambrian News* editor John Gibson, had been members of the inaugural council of the Women's Franchise League in 1889, and Aberystwyth hosted a conference of the league in 1895;[57] the association was therefore strongly suffragist, supporting the use of a 'test question' to Liberal candidates. In 1895, Aberystwyth reported that it was 'in a flourishing condition and a great many of the members are very active workers'.[58] However, the association's own annual report of 1897 painted a rather different picture, in retrospect as well as on future prospects. Not only had 'little progress' been made in the past year, but the committee felt 'that as a political society the Association had failed in attaining its first aims and expressed objects'. It revealed that no public meeting had been organized by the association since 1893, when Countess Alice Kearney had visited, and that its membership and committee meetings were 'sparsely attended'. In 1897, meetings had been held with papers on women's suffrage, women's work, boards of guardians and 'Our Duty to the Labouring Classes' (a title highly suggestive of the social composition of the society); resolutions on Armenia and the use of the Contagious Diseases Acts in India had been passed, the queen had been memorialized on her sixtieth anniversary and the NLF on women's suffrage. 'Your Committee venture to think that this association is sound on suffrage', Mrs James wrote, but membership was now down to eighty and, though the association kept going, and kept up its affiliation to the WLF until 1903–4, membership continued to fall. The year 1896–7 was clearly a turning point for associations in Wales. After this time, they found it increasingly difficult to combine for an annual council of the WUWLA.[59]

## Decline, 1895–1914

From 1895 to 1914, there was an absolute decline in the number of WLAs in Wales affiliated to the WLF. The graph (figure 1) shows an important period of decline: 1895–1909. Broadly speaking, the decline of 1895–1906 can be connected to a number of factors affecting liberalism in Wales and in Britain. From 1906, the relationship of women to their party deteriorated and, in England and Wales, associations disaffiliated from the WLF, and individual women chose to work with suffrage societies instead of in their WLAs, as liberalism became 'the unexpected enemy' of women's suffrage.[60] While the graph shows an uneven revival of affiliated WLAs in Wales from 1909 to 1914, it appears to have been almost entirely confined to the northern constituencies, under the impetus, possibly, of the 'Lloyd George factor', and, certainly, of a push for reorganization under the WLF's 'Area Scheme'. This section will attempt to examine some of these factors in some detail.

Allowing for likely incompleteness and inaccuracy of national, regional and local records, affiliations to the WLF may well be a distorting mirror for the state of Liberal organization in Wales. For example, in the mid-1890s eight associations in the WUWLA were not affiliated to the WLF, although some of them had been. This was despite the fact that affiliation to the union required a membership of fifty (though there is evidence of flexibility on this), while after 1893, the WLF required a membership of only twenty-five.[61] So some societies were choosing to affiliate only to the WUWLA. Without knowing exactly why that was, it is difficult to know how it may be reflected in the pattern of affiliations to the WLF over the years; when compared with the majority which did affiliate, it is difficult to draw firm conclusions from either location or size. While it may have been the case that some of the northern associations preferred to conduct their business in Welsh, it would not be safe to assume that 'nationalist' feeling made north Wales women pursue a separatist line in relation to English organization; they used the British stage to promote arguments for disestablishment with some success from 1892, when key northern associations like Denbigh affiliated to the WLF. The language map of Wales for the 1890s provides no clear lead: while in north and north-west Wales a substantial proportion of the population were monoglot Welsh speakers, and Welsh had become 'a major language of politics' in the late nineteenth century,[62] the five north Wales associations not affiliated to the WLF in 1895 were located in towns which were either bilingual or English speaking, though mostly surrounded by Welsh-language zones.[63] It may be that before the creation of the WUWLA, which brought the possibility of exerting influence for Welsh causes such as disestablishment within the WLF, the earliest associations saw little to be gained from union with the English associations.

Another explanation for non-affiliation or intermittent affiliation to the federal bodies may be the costs involved. These could be a problem even for apparently large and healthy associations: in 1901–2, Cardiff WLA found there was a gap of almost two hundred and fifty between its nominal and its paid-up membership.[64] Affiliation to the WLF cost associations one guinea per annum, and each year associations were also asked to contribute to the costs of hospitality for the meetings of the WLF Council in London, along with other occasional calls on their support.[65] Delegates' expenses were another drain on resources, and could not always be met. Aberdare WLA was probably not the only association whose affiliation and other costs were being subsidized by its president and other better-off individuals.[66] Affiliation to the WUWLA cost just 2s. 6d. but, from the beginning of 1896, associations also paid one guinea a year towards the wages of an organizing secretary and, as membership fell, these costs had to be cut back, inevitably affecting the union's work.[67] In 1904 the WLF made affiliation cheaper, but in the period 1910–12, an 'Area Scheme' to provide regional organizers for the WLF constituted a major call on extra donations.[68] As the study of Aberdare WLA will show, the more active an association was, the more money it was likely to spend; but, at times when the level of general political interest was low, or support for liberalism slackening, the returns were likely to diminish.

Early in the new century, the novelist Gwyneth Vaughan, a delegate for Flintshire St Asaph WLA, but also speaking as WUWLA secretary, told the WLF Council that 'there were many small and struggling Welsh Women's Liberal Associations who know absolutely nothing about the Federation'.[69] By the beginning of 1903, only five counties, and only nine constituencies in those counties, contained associations affiliated to the WLF. Only one of those, Flint, was a northern constituency, with two associations, both of which disappeared over the next couple of years. The rest were in south and west Wales, where, however, by 1905 only Glamorgan and Monmouthshire were represented.

## Women and the party, 1895–1905

What do these patterns of rise and decline tell us about women's Liberal organization in the period covered, about its relationship to the fortunes of liberalism in the country more generally, and about its relationship to the party in and out of power? The graph (figure 1) can be read as reflecting the fortunes of liberalism on the national level. The rise from the late 1880s to the mid-1890s reflects the Liberal recovery after the splits over Home Rule – splits which affected women's organization, and may well have hindered the formation of more associations in Wales in this period. Welsh Liberals, their voting power massively increased after the 1884 franchise reforms, became loyal supporters on Home Rule, and were especially enthusiastic for the government's programme in the mid-1890s, which included Welsh Church disestablishment. The growth of women's organization in this period, as the following chapters will show, was connected to both British feminism and Welsh Liberal nationalism. The falling away of membership and organization coincides with the long period of absence from power from 1895, the fall of the government having been connected with the 1895 Welsh Church Disestablishment Bill and fissures in the Welsh parliamentary party.[70] Writing her annual report for 1901–2, Mary Ellis, secretary of Cardiff WLA, wrote of the fall in membership the large association had experienced. She identified a number of local, organizational and non-political factors (further discussed in the Cardiff context), but 'above all' loss of faith, divisions and powerlessness.[71] Ellis wrote in terms very similar to WLF Executive Committee reports, which spoke of a time 'of depression as regarded Liberal work', of the death of the queen, the general election defeat of 1900 and 'a year of considerable stress and anxiety in the Liberal Party ... a period of discouragement and depression arising largely from the continued tension caused by the war'.[72] The South African War of 1899–1902 was a troubling and divisive experience for Liberals. As K. O. Morgan has shown, neither Wales nor its Liberals were as united in opposition to the war, or in support of the Boers, as has been supposed, and the mood of jingo seems to have been as lively in parts of south Wales as anywhere else, infecting the general election campaign of 1900, the 'khaki election'. According to Morgan, the party split along urban and rural lines; in industrial and urban south Wales, a majority of Liberal party activists appear to have supported the war.[73] If such was the case, women were out of step with the party. The WLF was 'to the fore of a vociferous anti-war movement'[74] and it is clear that some WLAs in south Wales shared the federation's position. This was clearly the case in Aberdare and in other south Wales WLAs: in Bridgend, the association was 'much dismayed by the threat of a khaki election' but determined not to be diverted 'by any false cry of Imperialism'.[75] It would seem that the Liberal women of urban and industrial south Wales were closer to the position on the war of male party activists in the rural areas than to those in their own communities. Such divisions will have weakened the party; the language used by Mary Ellis in Cardiff and in the WLF report suggests a psychological impact of disillusion and hopelessness.

From 1895, liberalism in Wales presented 'a consistent picture of disintegration of organization and morale', and was characterized by 'stagnation'.[76] The pattern of activism of women in Wales was related to these issues of Welsh liberalism, in the constituencies and in Parliament. The question is: how closely related, and how was that reflected in the figures for affiliations to the WLF? Delegates from Wales were most active within the WLF in the mid-1890s, when the Welsh party had its greatest impact in national and parliamentary politics. To this extent, they formed a parallel presence to the Welsh Liberal party in British politics, eager to use the WLF to push the aims of Welsh liberalism, as they succeeded in doing, putting disestablishment at the centre of debates in the WLF.[77] It is conceivable that Welsh WLA affiliations fell off from the mid to late 1890s because Welsh associations felt that the WLF, dominated by a weaker English liberalism, had less to offer. From 1896, the support of the WLF for Welsh disestablishment was reaffirmed annually in a composite 'Declaration of Reaffirmation', along with Irish Home Rule and reform of the House of Lords.[78] There was, therefore, no debate on the question, though there were rousing speeches, and nothing new to be said except when bills were going through the House of Commons. Some of the excitement of the early part of the decade, when women from Wales felt they were proselytizing and creating a broad base of support for the national cause, must have been lost.

It has been assumed that there was a decline in women's Liberal organization in Wales which was tied to the collapse of Cymru Fydd.[79] The relationship between the women's organization and the national movement will be examined in chapter 3 but, as already suggested, the slump in women's Liberal activity in the late 1890s and the first years of the twentieth century was not confined to Wales, though the patterns of decline and recovery were not exactly the same as in England. The WLF lost in all some sixty associations between 1897 and 1903. The reports comment on the missing societies but, from 1902, the WLF reported signs of increased activity, and in 1904 its report 'rejoiced' at new associations being created 'at a remarkable rate' in expectation of the coming general election.[80] The experiences of Wales and England diverge strongly at this time.

## Women and the party, 1906–1914

In Cardiff, Mary Ellis too believed that the worst had passed, and that revived Liberal energies were beginning to show themselves amongst women,[81] but the graph had some way to fall yet, and the pattern of response seen at the Liberal victory in the mid-1890s cannot be discerned around the landslide of 1906. The pattern of Welsh affiliations to the WLF differs from that of English associations most markedly in this period leading up to and immediately after the general election of 1906. While there may have been a 'hidden' recovery before that, not yet reflected in affiliations, not until the 1908 annual report are similar signs of new and revived associations to be seen from Wales. While there is a rise which may reflect the higher level of political activity connected with Home Rule, National Insurance and the battle with the House of Lords, as well as the renewed hopes for disestablishment, the 1911 affiliation figure does not come near the earlier peak of the 1890s, and shows signs of almost immediately beginning to decline again. There is some evidence that in this respect women's liberalism also differed from male activity. In the Cardiff (male) Liberal Association, for example, after a period of falling membership from 1897, a rise was clear from 1902.[82] The women's association, on the other hand, had a fluctuating membership in the same period, and showed an overall decline from 1902 to 1911.[83] The story behind the figures was that the Cardiff association experienced seismic change between 1910 and 1912, in its case connected to the destructive impact of the suffrage issue on women's relationship with liberalism, to be discussed in part II; not until the late 1920s were there again to be signs of a large organization of Liberal women in the city.

While most years saw a sprinkling of new associations and some revivals, there were none in 1912–13, by which time there were twenty-eight associations in Wales, only eleven in the south and south-west, and three new societies in north Wales constituencies the following year did not survive the war. The pattern of returns suggests that membership of several of the societies in existence the year that war broke out was nominal, and that they were on the point of expiry. By 1914, the valleys of south Wales had almost no WLAs. Aberdare, which had expired in 1903, was successfully revived in 1910, though with a small membership which reached twenty-seven in 1914. There were no WLAs listed in the Rhondda, and apart from the tiny Aberdare society which struggled on through the war, none outside the commercial and coastal centres of Cardiff, Swansea, Newport, Tenby and Carmarthen. Swansea WLA appeared exceptionally healthy: drawing from the Town and District constituencies, and possibly enrolling some women in the Gower or West Glamorgan constituency too. In the period when Cardiff WLA was tearing itself apart over women's suffrage, Swansea Liberal suffragists were very satisfied with their MP, Alfred Mond. Swansea claimed a membership of almost 1,700 in 1914, rising to 2,075 in 1915. Membership fell, but it remained very large throughout the war. From 1921, the association represented Swansea West constituency only, claiming 420 members, and the constituency became a Labour seat in 1923, after which the WLA disappeared from WLF returns; Swansea East, a Labour seat from 1922, had no WLA.[84] This indicates the impact of the rise of Labour in this hitherto strongly Liberal and Lib–Lab area, and suggests the value of further research in Swansea and west Glamorgan, on the significance of the shift from Liberal to Labour for women's politics after the First World War.

The population imbalance between industrial and urban south Wales and mainly rural mid- and north Wales, and the presence in the figures for south Wales of the huge Swansea association, meant that there were more women members of WLAs in the south and west; membership in Swansea alone was greater than for all of the northern associations combined. But, proportionately, things looked rather better for women's liberalism in the north, where the recovery from the dire position of 1903 was more marked and better sustained. A total of fifteen associations were affiliated to the WLF in 1914, just under a half of those having over one hundred members, and Caernarfon Boroughs having 302. A WLF organizer, Mrs Vaughan Davies, was based in the north in 1912, under the WLF's Area Scheme for reorganization; she was active in forming new associations, where the use of the Welsh language was particularly noted, and in bringing associations together in an area committee. The activity was reflected in regular reports in the *WLF News*, whereas the reports from the south were almost exclusively from the Swansea association.[85] The 'Lloyd George factor' was particularly strong in this period; he embodied the radical challenge to the House of Lords, as well as the national aims of disestablishment; his disagreements with suffragists did him no harm electorally in his own constituency, and with an injection of effective organization, women Liberals in north Wales appear to have made their choice in favour of liberalism and Wales before women's suffrage.

*Conclusions*

The activities and characteristics, and fluctuations in fortunes, of local associations do not reflect only British or Wales-wide patterns, as the local case studies will show. However, a number of general conclusions can be drawn from this analysis, while not necessarily being neatly explanatory of what is a complex picture. Associations came into being in Wales in response to the need for electoral organization, often in constituencies which were not safely Liberal; they shared this origin with associations throughout Britain. However, as we have seen, the origins of some associations were clearly located in 'Welsh conditions': the possibility, thanks to franchise and electoral reform, that grievances might be addressed and ambitions connected to specific conditions of religion and land tenure, as well as more positive political and cultural aspirations, might be realizable. Other associations combined Liberal aims with their own feminist ambitions. The activities of the associations indicated an ethos of earnest, moral-reform liberalism, which did not confine itself to Welsh or British perspectives, and of which many saw suffragism as an essential element. While the overall decline in Welsh WLAs from 1895 to 1905, like that in England, can be linked to the crisis of liberalism of this period, and perhaps to divisions over the South African War, from 1906 differences between women's liberalism in north and south Wales are indicated by the divergent pattern of recovery and decline. The following chapters will, it is to be hoped, contribute to an understanding of those differences. As suggested at the beginning of this chapter, they concern the extent to which associations orientated themselves towards Wales, or towards women.

# 2

# 'Women, Awake!' The Welsh Union of Women's Liberal Associations and the Impact of Women's Suffrage

## Introduction

Having examined the local structures of Welsh women's liberalism, this chapter and the next turn to a wider context at two levels, the Welsh and the British. I begin with a discussion of the contention that the Welsh Union of Women's Liberal Associations (WUWLA), along with many local associations, was created in 1891-2 as a move in the progressive strategy to build a strong body of support within the Women's Liberal Federation (WLF) for placing the enfranchisement of women among the aims and objects of the federation, the successful achievement of which split that body in 1893. This is followed by an examination of the organization and ethos of the WUWLA, through its structures, its relationship to associations and to the WLF, and its publications, propaganda and self-representations. The chapter will also consider the continuing impact of the women's suffrage issue in the context of Welsh national issues and the thorough defeat of the Liberal party in the 1895 general election.

In the history of the WUWLA, and the narrative of its rise and fall, as in the history of the local associations delineated in the previous chapter, the 'politics of place' can be seen in contention with broader ideologies and party loyalty, and the factors of personality, leadership and resources in the making and unmaking of political institutions.[1] In the British context, Welsh politics displayed some of the characteristics of 'a politics of place', in the intertwining of myths of community and myths of party in the making of political identities, in so far as liberalism represented a specific construction of Welsh nationhood. How did women's politics connect to this sense of locatedness? The issue of the distinctive 'Welshness' of women's political organizations, and their independence or otherwise from British/English structures, has been a sub-theme of Welsh women's political history, particularly the history of the temperance and suffrage movements in Wales.[2] Whatever the conditions specific to Wales at the beginning of the 1890s, the evidence of its part in the plans of others – specifically, the suffragist faction in the WLF – cannot be ignored. Nor can the wider picture of the fate of the Liberal party in this period: like the last, this chapter bears out Jon Lawrence's thesis of the importance of 1895 as the nineteenth-century 'nadir' in Liberal party fortunes, but here the focus is on the impact of that on women's organization, interacting with Welsh conditions.[3]

## Preconditions for national organization

In the spring of 1891, there were just six Welsh WLAs listed in the annual report of the WLF. The circumstances of their formation have been discussed in the previous chapter; clearly, neither nationalism nor electoral considerations had been enough to galvanize women into party organization up to this point. The question of why that might have been is difficult to answer, absence being less easily read than presence and activity. Women's organization throughout Britain, particularly after the Home Rule split, was also weak at the end of the 1880s; the WLF, which must be seen as the only potentially British national organization for Liberal women at that time, had not yet impressed women as a vehicle for their political ambitions. When she chaired the inaugural conference of the WUWLA in 1892, Eva McLaren expressed her satisfaction at the 'strong wish of women [in Wales] to come forward and take part in political life'. She suggested that the lack of organization hitherto 'was because the Liberal cause in the Principality was so strong. Perhaps the Liberal cause did not need women's help in Wales as much as in England' – a similar explanation was to be offered for Scotland, perhaps reflecting an understanding of the nature of politics in the 'Celtic' periphery.[4] However that may be, women were entering into pressure group activism in Wales in a variety of ways at the end of the 1880s. As has been shown, in addition to those few WLAs formed during the decade, some women were active in the defensive politics of land and religion. Women in the mixed-sex temperance organizations were gaining the experience and confidence to move towards creating their own organizations.[5] Perhaps more indicative of modernizing trends, a number of women and men had become active in the Association for Promoting the Education of Girls in Wales. These influential women, middle and upper class, a number of them themselves beneficiaries of the first wave of educational reform in Britain which breached the universities and medical schools, lobbied and wrote papers on the position of girls and women, as both students and teachers, in the developing secondary and higher educational structures in the country. The creation of a system of education administered within Wales, and answering to Welsh needs and conditions, was firmly linked to ideas of national progress, and women and their supporters were able to connect this with the widespread notion that the position and condition of women was an indicator of the state of a nation, to mount arguments for women's educational equality which became the consensus position.[6] The skill of those, led by Eva McLaren and Nora Philipps, who developed women's party organization in the early 1890s, was in convincing a number of different single-issue groups (though with much overlapping membership) that the construction of a unified identity in women's liberalism would be a more effective way of achieving their aims, and that these aims must also be tied to demands for women's suffrage: the success of that effort is shown in the work and ethos of the WLAs in the mid-1890s, discussed in the previous chapter. This chapter will look more closely at how that ethos was constructed at the level of the WUWLA, and will also demonstrate the fragility of that construction.

### The progressives in Wales

While any account of political developments must take the broader social and political context into account, the role of key individuals – the right woman at the right time – must also be considered. Almost from its foundation, the WLF had been divided between the progressives, who wished the organization to write women's suffrage into its list of objects, and the moderates, who believed that the role of the WLF should remain primarily one of support for the Liberal party. The issue had been debated and defeated several times at the annual meetings.[7] The difference, in 1891–2, appears to have been made by the involvement of Rosalind, Countess of Carlisle, a forceful woman, who, after standing aloof for some time, joined the WLF in 1890 with a combined 'temperance and suffrage' agenda for the organization, ready to put her considerable personal resources into the effort. The evidence from Wales seems quite clear, and is supported by Margaret Barrow's account, of a 'meticulously planned campaign' by the progressives, headed by Carlisle, and aided by her daughters, by organizer Bertha Mason and by Eva McLaren.[8] In effect, while WLF speakers and organizers worked to build election machinery, the progressives developed a parallel strategy which was to result in the adoption of women's suffrage as an object of the WLF and the election of Carlisle as its president. The voices of such women, prominent in the temperance movement and in campaigns like the Ladies National Association for the Repeal of the Contagious Diseases Acts (LNA), will have found ready listeners in the principality, as the discussion in the previous chapter has shown.

By the spring of 1892, the number of Welsh associations affiliated to the WLF had grown from six to forty, all with voting rights at the annual council meeting; some were large associations, entitled to multiple votes. The evidence linking the campaign in Wales to the progressive campaign does not depend purely on timing, or numbers; it is evident in the politics of the two women most instrumental in the creation of the Welsh body, Nora Philipps and Eva McLaren; in Philipps's written accounts of the period in the Welsh periodical press; in the character of the WUWLA, set up just before the 1892 WLF Council; and in the style of the inaugural meetings of some of the new associations.[9]

### The politics of Eva McLaren and Nora Philipps

As a close ally of Carlisle, Eva McLaren spearheaded the efforts in Wales which culminated in the creation of the WUWLA at a meeting in Aberystwyth on 29 March 1892.[10] Working alongside her was Nora Philipps, while other WLF representatives also played a role, travelling all over Wales in the winter of 1891–2, sometimes holding more than one meeting, and launching more than one association in a day.[11] McLaren was a member by marriage of the leading radical and feminist networks of the nineteenth century.[12] She was prominent in the suffrage societies, the temperance movement, the LNA and in the bodies campaigning for women's enfranchisement in local government. Within the WLF, for which she had been national organizer and honorary treasurer since its foundation, McLaren was a leading member of the progressive faction; after the 1892 decision, she continued to persuade Liberal women to be more active in pursuit of their own enfranchisement, through the Union of Practical Suffragists (1896), and, in the period of growing disillusionment of Liberal women with their own party, the Forward Suffrage Union (1907).

Nora Philipps's career is less well known, but she was 'a committed feminist who reflected the movement's late Victorian preoccupations'.[13] Though raised 'in an atmosphere of Liberal thought and Liberal movements',[14] she appears to have made her first real foray into political activity in support of her husband's successful candidacy in Mid Lanark in 1888. Philipps's subsequent career has close parallels and links with McLaren's, at least until the late 1890s. Philipps may have been connected with the formation in 1888 of the Society for Promoting Women as County Councillors. By the early 1890s she was a member of the Central National Society for Women's Suffrage, a supporter of the Women's Franchise League (which campaigned for the inclusion of married women in demands for the franchise) and later of the Women's Emancipation Union. In 1892, she was invited by Millicent Fawcett and Helen Blackburn to represent the Central National Society on the Special Appeals Committee and, in 1895, she was on the combined subcommittee of suffrage societies for parliamentary action, a precursor of the National Union of Women's Suffrage Societies (NUWSS). She had a reputation as a particularly effective and affecting speaker. Her husband's parliamentary seat (until 1894) gave Philipps a foot in Scottish women's politics too, and she was to be a vice-president of the Scottish Women's Liberal Federation, formed 1892.[15] In Eva McLaren, as their first honorary secretary, Welsh women Liberals were getting one of the most experienced and well-connected feminist campaigners and workers of the period. In Nora Philipps, who was to be their founding president, they had a woman who in a relatively short time had established herself as charismatic and energetic in the causes of the women's movement, and as a powerful, emotional speaker. Most importantly for the progressive agenda in 1891–2, her marriage gave her a political base in Wales that was fully exploited in the drive to form associations.

## Nora Philipps and the history of the WUWLA

Philipps's accounts of women's liberalism in Wales were produced in a series of articles from 1892, in her reports and other writings for the WUWLA, and especially in her articles in the journal of the Cymru Fydd movement, *Young Wales*, when she was editor of a section on women's politics, from 1895–7. In these writings she emphasized the feminist beginnings of the union, making it plain that the aim had been to build support for the progressive position in the WLF, but also that the progressive 'missionaries' seem to have found themselves pushing at an open door. She attributed that to the awakening of an inherent love of freedom and tendency towards democracy amongst the Welsh, a flattering construction of Celticity also deployed during the suffragette period. Philipps introduced the debate between the progressives and the moderates into the Welsh periodical press early in 1892, with an article in which she declared that women who refused to demand their own citizenship while taking on party work were 'pathetic as well as ludicrous'; and that 'Woman's Suffrage is the burning question in the Women's Liberal Federation at the present moment',[16] drawing a reply from Eliza Orme, a leading moderate in the WLF. Philipps's personal and combative tone belied her later reputation as an even-handed conciliator: replying to Orme, she suggested that it was the progressives, rather than the 'Anti-Progressives', who were the best and hardest-working friends of the Liberal party; she emphasized the role of the progressives in the creation of new associations, and the expected victory for the progressives at the annual council. In fact, eighty-four Welsh delegates, about one-eighth of the total, attended the 1892 council of the WLF to record their vote on the progressive side.[17]

The suffragist beginnings of the WUWLA and the links with the progressives were reiterated and celebrated by Philipps in *Young Wales*, in articles written towards the end of her presidency of the WUWLA, and on the point of its merger, as it seemed, with the Liberal national movement. Much of Philipps's writing in *Young Wales* was historical, sometimes taking a long view, but much of it concerned the recent past as she set out to provide and to shape a history of the contemporary Liberal feminist women's movement and its relationship with the Welsh national movement.[18] It is clear that Philipps saw the future of the women's organization in being joined to the nationalist movement; her valedictory articles ruminated on the nature of nationalism and women's relationship to it. However, she wanted to emphasize the feminist origins and the links with a wider British women's movement. Whatever the future for the women of Wales in relation to nationalism, she wrote, their identification with the wider causes of the women's movement, reaching beyond Wales to 'womanhood throughout the country', would 'always be a great thing to remember'.[19] It is arguable that Philipps had done more than anyone to bring women Liberals together with Welsh nationalism in the 1890s (as the next chapter will discuss), but she also ensured that she left behind a feminist history of the organization. There is a suggestion in her writing of regret that Welsh women Liberals might turn inwards towards a Welsh identity, forsaking the transnational identity of 'womanhood'; perhaps she feared that the commitment to women's suffrage which she and colleagues had wrung from Cymru Fydd would weaken – as it had by early 1896.

This is, of course, a history of the movement from a particular perspective, and created at a very specific moment. It is probably not the history which would have been written by the Nonconformist activist Susannah Gee, or the anti-suffragist Mrs Osborne Morgan, both members of the executive of the WUWLA, but each representing other strands in the movement. It should be read in the context of Philipps's ongoing involvement with both Welsh Liberal politics and the WLF and the suffrage movement, and her continuing interest in shaping the outcome of votes in the federation. Newspaper accounts of the same events support the central role of the progressives. Philipps's account, despite her flattering references to the readiness of Wales for the progressive message, minimizes the agency of Welsh women Liberals in the creation of their own political organizations, when faced with an organized and financially well-resourced campaign. The press reports of set-piece meetings and conferences also tend to emphasize the role of the visiting, usually higher-status, speakers, at the expense of local activists. However, the language of the WLAs self-reporting, discussed in the previous chapter, revelatory as it was of local cultures and mentalities, suggests that the progressive missionaries were preaching to the converted; they spoke the same ideological language of moral, social and spiritual reawakening, of the evangelical politics which was what women called liberalism.

*Shaping the Union: 'for Women, for Wales and for Liberalism'*

The task for Philipps and McLaren, and their supporters in Wales, was to unite all strands of Liberal opinion in Wales in 1892 – no easy task – while also creating a strong bloc of support for women's suffrage in the WLF. In two days of meetings in Aberystwyth, on 29 and 30 March, designed as a model in national unity and inclusiveness, women Liberals in Wales formed themselves into an impressive campaigning body, providing the votes which would boost the suffrage party in the WLF. The three main resolutions at the public inaugural meeting approved the formation of the union and its goal of the enfranchisement of women, called for disestablishment and wider measures of self-government and supported Home Rule for Ireland.[20] Speaking to the women's suffrage resolution, Philipps attempted to connect as many elements of Welsh life and politics as possible to the progressive project, including the support for the language, disestablishment, the position of working-class women and the growing north Wales women's temperance movement, emphasizing the commitment of its leaders to women's suffrage.[21] Philipps's speech, while reflecting the importance of temperance campaigning for British women Liberals generally, and for Philipps herself, was also intended to bind into the WUWLA and progressivism a group who might otherwise see their interests as lying elsewhere.[22]

If the aim of the inaugural meeting had been national unity and inclusiveness, the first meeting of the council of the WUWLA the following day, which would prepare resolutions and elect delegates for the WLF Council, was about pragmatism, and reining in resolutions which went further than the WLF council was likely to accept. Calls for the claims of Wales to be put alongside those of Ireland, instead of second to them, while generally supported, were not incorporated into the resolution. An attempt by Elizabeth James of Aberystwyth to amend the suffrage resolution explicitly to include married women was rejected under the combined persuasion of McLaren and Philipps, who thus kept a firm grip on the progressive agenda. The resolution which the meeting carried then read:

> That this conference is of opinion that the Parliamentary franchise should be granted to women on the same terms as it is granted to men, and resolves to use its best endeavours to induce the Women's Liberal Federation to make this reform one of its avowed objects.[23]

The WUWLA now appeared to be committed by its council to supporting the progressive movement in the WLF annual council. In practice, this could only work through the voting instructions to delegates from individual WLAs, since the WUWLA – like other regional unions – had no constitutional role and was not represented within the WLF.[24] It was crucial, therefore, that individual associations should be committed to the progressive agenda, since it was association delegates who voted at the annual council. For this reason, the women's franchise resolutions, and the rousing speeches which accompanied them from Nora Philipps, Eva McLaren and others, at the local meetings which created the associations, were an important part of building that commitment. Equally important were the cohorts of local women and male Liberals, and notably of Nonconformist ministers, who also lent their support to the role of women in politics and to women's suffrage in meeting after meeting around Wales. As represented in the Liberal press, these meetings became suffrage demonstrations, rapidly moving on from the requisite resolutions of support for Liberal principles in general and election victories in particular, to end on a rousing vote for the women's cause.[25] Such events would have created a strong feeling of local support and justification for women, some of whom were moving into public political activity for the first time, when they sent their delegates – or were themselves delegates – to the council meetings in London. The process is clearly seen in the creation of the Aberdare WLA described in part II.[26]

It is clear, then, that the WUWLA was formed in 1891 as a move in the progressives' strategy for dominance of the WLF, and that the surge of creations of local associations which followed was designed to bolster that strategy. However, the time was right for the creation of such an organization from the point of view of Welsh Nonconformist liberalism, with its overriding aim of the disestablishment of the Church in Wales. A Liberal victory in the 1892 general election would mean that a disestablishment bill had a good chance of being put forward by the government. The WLF would provide a forum within which support for disestablishment could be built up across the United Kingdom. Two months after the Aberystwyth meetings, at the WLF Council at which delegates from the Welsh WLAs cast their votes with the progressives, they also presented for the first time to the council a resolution in support of disestablishment, moved by Nora Philipps, seconded by Susannah Gee and supported by a group of women representing a geographical spread of Welsh WLAs, constructing a 'national' bloc in the federation. The resolution was carried unanimously 'amidst a scene of remarkable enthusiasm, and with round after round of prolonged applause'.[27] This support for Welsh national aims was the quid pro quo of support for the progressives, and it may well have been the prospect of thus shaping opinion, in the run up to a general election, which made associations like Denbigh, which had not hitherto thrown in their lot with the WLF, now take an active part in both it and the WUWLA. 'Disunity was the eternal danger to the scattered forces of Welsh Liberalism';[28] the strenuous efforts made to represent Wales geographically, ideologically, structurally and rhetorically were an acknowledgement of that. It is clear that there was lots of potential for such disunity within the WUWLA, both on women's suffrage and the national questions. Male Liberals in Wales might well envy the ability of the leading women to forge a unified identity which endured at least long enough for the achievement of its immediate purpose.

### Structures and ethos

The WUWLA was to encompass all associations with at least fifty members, with a delegate council and an eight-woman executive committee, increased to thirty-six in 1895; Nora Philipps was its first president until 1895, with Eva McLaren as honorary secretary. McLaren's work as secretary was supported by five assistant secretaries who between them covered the country, and who included women who were becoming leading figures in Welsh Liberal circles, like Kate Jenkins, a farmer, of Llangadog, Carmarthenshire, who was later active as Kate Freeman in the Swansea WLA.[29] Philipps was followed by Sybil Thomas as president, with Ada Thomas as secretary. Sybil Thomas was succeeded as president by Mrs Brynmor Jones, who presided over what seems to have been the demise of the union in the first few years of the twentieth century, with the novelist Gwyneth Vaughan (Annie Harriet Hughes) as secretary. The list of almost fifty vice-presidents of the WUWLA in the 1890s linked the organization to liberalism throughout Britain, and reflected its causes: Florence Balgarnie, Josephine Butler and the Countess Carlisle were listed alongside leaders of progressive Welsh movements like the educationalist Elizabeth P. Hughes, suffragist MPs like Thomas Edward Ellis and Walter McLaren, and women who were well known only in their own locality, like Mrs Kelly of Cardiff and Mrs Morgan Williams of Swansea.

Philipps and McLaren relinquished their posts after three years. They had accomplished what they set out to do in Wales on behalf of the progressives in the WLF. For both, other suffrage work was increasing as suffrage societies began to work together again, culminating in the creation of the NUWSS in 1897. They were, however, also preparing a further attempt to make woman's suffrage a 'test question' as a condition of WLF and WLA support for candidates in elections, and this may be part of the reason why Philipps retained the post of honorary secretary for a while after giving up the presidency. Philipps's connection with Wales continued because of her husband's family connections, her presidency of three Pembrokeshire WLAs and, later in the decade, her husband's election as the county MP. McLaren had been president of some short-lived associations formed during the campaign of 1891–2, but retained the honorary presidency of Cardiff for some time.

They were leaving the WUWLA in, it must have seemed, a healthy state. The number of associations continued to increase, from about thirty to fifty-seven, between its formation and 1895. As moves to create a Welsh national party gathered pace in 1894–5, the conditions were created for the WUWLA to be part of the new organization and for the new party to espouse women's suffrage; and Philipps ensured that these things came about: these issues are fully discussed in the next chapter. There was clearly regret amongst at least a number of WLAs that the duo were leaving their posts; even Aberdare, which supported their own president Sybil Thomas as new president of the WUWLA, would have preferred Philipps and McLaren to have stayed in place.[30] The 1896 annual report listed the loss of the two officers amongst the factors in the 'testing time' the union had been through in the previous year:

> A change of this nature always causes much anxious doubt as to the future of any cause, but when we consider that in this instance, it meant losing as leaders the two women who had organized and founded the Union, who had given to it so generously, even lavishly, time and thought and talent of a rare order, whose experience as leaders of other women and as workers of the foremost rank in all matters of Reform, their resignation could not but occasion the deepest regret and the gravest misgivings.[31]

Associations took the occasion of the change of officers to examine the constitution of the WUWLA, in particular in the provision for the accountability of officers, and the representative nature of committees. The president's term of office was limited to three years, a position of acting vice-president was created and all officers were to be elected annually, all moves clearly intended to increase accountability. Provision for the election of executive committee members for three years instead of one seemed to offer more stability, and membership of the committee was increased from eight to thirty-six, which must have been intended to improve its representativeness. The following year, however, Aberystwyth WLA proposed 'that more women living in Wales should be put on the committee of the WUWLA, so that Wales may be more adequately represented'.[32] The lists of the executive, both before and after the 1895 change, showed a large majority with Welsh addresses, though some of those also had London addresses and would be likely to spend a good part of the year there. With just five as a quorum, even after enlargement, it had sometimes been found convenient to hold committees in London. Given the difficulties of bringing people together from all over Wales, it would have been easy for a small group to shape union policy. The changes may be signs of misgivings on this account.

As far as the British structures of women's liberalism were concerned, the WUWLA was a regional union, on an equal footing with others in regions of England – the Yorkshire and Durham Union was the earliest, formed in 1888–9 – rather than an independent federation like the Scottish Women's Liberal Federation. Welsh WLAs affiliated in their own right, directly to the WLF, and the WUWLA had no constitutional recognition within the WLF. The federation's view of the fairly limited role of unions was that they could do 'valuable educational work by the distribution of literature and the arrangement of lectures and conferences at different centres'.[33] Two attempts were made to change the constitutional position. The first came in 1893, soon after the formation of the WUWLA.[34] In the second, in 1901, Gwyneth Vaughan, secretary of the WUWLA, supported by Sybil Thomas and Elsie Jenkins of Cardiff, moved to amend the WLF rules to allow the WUWLA 'to be affiliated as a Union to the WLF'. Vaughan argued that the change would benefit the WLF as well as the weaker unaffiliated associations, by creating or renewing a connection between them; 'they do not affiliate on account of the fee being too large for their resources'. As a model for the change, Vaughan cited the example of the relationship between the North Wales Women's Temperance Union (UDMGC) and the British Women's Temperance

Association (BWTA), in which the UDMGC was allowed three dele-gates for one thousand members, the BWTA having originally wished the branches in Wales to affiliate directly.[35] Vaughan's motion was withdrawn after arguments that such a precedent would weaken the federation; Vaughan gave notice that she would try again the following year, but no such proposal was made again.[36] By this time, the WUWLA itself was greatly weakened. No annual reports later than 1896 appear to have survived, and a further sign of its weakness was the difficulty in arranging an annual meeting after 1897. Evidence suggests that the union failed to hold an annual conference between 1900 and 1903.[37]

### *Writing women's liberalism*

The publications and other records of the WUWLA provide evidence for the identity and ethos of the organization in its heyday. In its first year, the WUWLA published, in Welsh and English, papers by Nora Philipps on poor law guardians and her 'Appeal to Welsh Women', and by Ada Thomas on disestablishment, as well as reprints of speeches by Lady Carlisle, Eva McLaren, John Gibson of the *Cambrian News* and others. In the ensuing years it published papers on disestablishment and temperance, on the education of girls and women and on local government reform. It distributed 15,000 leaflets on Home Rule and other reforms to associations, and arranged tours by federation speakers. It used its funds to subsidize local associations to pay lecturers and organizers, and to build local organization and networks. The union quickly found a role as the representative of women, and women's liberalism, to other bodies – at conferences of the Liberation Society, the Disestablishment Campaign Committee, the North Wales Liberal Federation and the National Liberal Federa-tion. As the first annual report pointed out, the income of the WUWLA was not equal to its activities, and it appealed for support to 'the men as well as the women of Wales': Liberal women activists, identified as middle and upper class, may well have been relatively comfortably placed in life, but many would have had little disposable income of their own.[38] Subscriptions in the first year amounted to just over £100, while expenditure was just over £150; donations and literature sales bridged the gap. In 1895–6, according to the last extant report, both subscriptions and donations had markedly decreased.[39]

Such activities fulfilled the first of the six objects of the WUWLA, to organize and support associations and to publish Liberal literature in both languages. Home Rule for Ireland and disestablishment of the Welsh Church followed, along with, rather more vaguely, support for 'Liberal principles' and 'measures of reform for Wales'. The fifth and sixth objects were support for the enfranchisement of women and the intention to work for its incorporation in the Liberal party programme and to 'protect the interests of children', which was also contained in the WLF objects. The union developed a set of 'model objects' for associations, which had more to say about local activities, including women's role as local government voters and candidates.[40] The ways in which associations adopted and adapted these rules, and the way in which such statements constructed the politics of associations, has been previously discussed. In publications and on the public platform, the list was reduced to three main objectives. When asking for the support of MPs, the union developed a more or less standard paragraph:

> The Liberal Women, for whom we speak, are ardent advocates of Welsh Disestablishment, Home Rule and other Reforms, but they also feel they are entitled to expect from the Liberal and Nationalist Members an equally warm support of measures of justice to women; and we can assure you that nothing will so stimulate women to work in the Liberal ranks, as to see that to that party they may look for the realisation of their aspirations.[41]

In its public meetings, resolutions on Home Rule, disestablishment and women's suffrage were accompanied by stirring addresses, with the women's suffrage resolution being put last, when a head of Liberal steam had been built up.[42]

The aims of the WUWLA were sometimes stated in practical and limited terms, echoing the WLF view of its role, as aiding in the political education of women, their organization and building of networks, and without any distinctive Welsh or 'national' objectives.[43] However, the union was also frequently constructed in more exalted terms. In words which reflected her preoccupation with rousing a broad and international consciousness in women, Nora Philipps began her 1893 pamphlet 'The Aim and Object of the Welsh Union' with a ponderous statement that the object was 'to teach women what women need, what Wales wants, and what the world ought to have, in order that it may be a better place to live in'. It aimed, she said, to help women 'realize their power, and to be reminded of their responsibility'.[44] Philipps had been developing these themes over a number of years, and in 1891 had published 'An Appeal to Women' which was 'an attempt to rouse women to political action' emphasizing 'individual rights and social duties, extolling the concept of service to the state as a social good'.[45] A few years later, 'An Appeal to Welsh Women', published by the WUWLA in English and Welsh, in contrast to the rather plodding opening of 'The Aim and Object', began 'WOMEN AWAKE! You have a political duty to perform', emphasized Home Rule, disestablishment, temperance reform, votes for women and 'justice for all', while presenting women with a 'double duty' to family and 'to the wider family, the world of human beings outside'. 'Womanly duty' consisted in claiming political power in order to fulfil those duties, a constant theme of her speeches and writings. Philipps could be wordy and elaborate in her writings, but the 'Appeal to Welsh Women' was constructed of short exclamatory paragraphs, with lettering in bold face, key phrases leaping from the page and subheadings littered with exclamation marks.[46] Philipps clearly felt she needed to attract attention.

An even more fervently moral and crusading tone was occasionally struck by other voices in the WUWLA. Writing to the women Liberals of Auckland, New Zealand in 1896, on the subject of the Contagious Diseases Acts, the union described itself, in a letter signed by Sybil Thomas and secretary Ada Thomas, as '[o]rganized for the purpose of strengthening the cause of Womanhood, of promoting Social Purity, and of furthering the principles of Justice and Righteousness'.[47] The annual report in the same year ended on a perfervid note, linking the union, in vaguely transcendental prose, to moral progress, perhaps inspired by attempts at temperance legislation during the year, by the moves towards creating a Welsh party, or by the hopeful signs of increasing unity among suffrage organizations in 1895–6:

> During the months that have gone by new light has been given, new thought quickened, new possibilities revealed, new hope inspired. Light which will grow clearer, thought which will deepen, possibilities which will ever widen, hope which will reach yet higher, all tending to promote that 'righteousness which exalteth a nation', and to make an end of sin which is 'a reproach to any people'.[48]

It was an odd note to strike following the disastrous defeat of the party in the general election of July–August 1895, and the now clearly emerging splits in the Welsh party.

The moral fervour of Liberal women was not an exclusively Welsh trait in this period, nor was the religious inspiration and familiarity with biblical language; historians are increasingly paying attention to the deeply religious foundations of much political activity of women in late nineteenth-century Britain.[49] Nora Philipps, the English-born daughter of European Jewish parents, married into the Welsh gentry and buried according to the rights of the Church of England, did not catch her moral earnestness and propensity to dramatize it from Nonconformist Wales. However, she found very receptive audiences for it, and set a tone for the WUWLA which its members, and audiences generally, if newspaper accounts are to be relied on, appear to have found sympathetic.[50] Josephine Butler and Lady Henry Somerset, respectively a vice-president and executive committee member of the union, with all that they stood for, were also greatly admired figures in Welsh reforming circles. In 1893, on the occasion of the Swansea annual council, a letter from Butler was read to the meeting, in which she constructed politics as a 'continuous conflict of principles . . . on behalf of justice truth and mercy' in which women claimed an equal role 'in the name of the God of justice': 'Our cause is just and holy, and God is with us. Let us hold fast, dear friends, in all things to the highest and purest principles, with firm faith in God and in our cause.'[51] This construction of liberalism as concerned less with individual rights than with militant Christianity in a Manichean universe, has been to a great extent credited to Butler, especially as it developed through the campaign to repeal the Contagious Diseases Acts.[52] The letter to Auckland quoted above reflects her language, as do the titles of the WUWLA's publications, many of them originally papers read at annual meetings: *The Duties and Opportunities of Women with Reference to Parish and District Councils; The Duty of Welshwomen in Relation to the Welsh Intermediate Education Act*;[53] and the prize essay on 'The duty of electors to vote according to their conscience, irrespective of worldly advantage',[54] a topic reflecting Butler's construction of political rights as a sacred trust. Welsh women's Nonconformist liberalism was part of a wider British Liberal culture, with which it shared these values. At the same time, however, Wales understood itself to be peculiarly religious and moral, and distinctively Nonconformist; temperance (after the successful passage of the 1881 Welsh Sunday Closing Act) was understood to be a Welsh cause. The WUWLA was able to put itself forward as representing these national characteristics, aspirations and political aims.

As in the discussion of Nora Philipps's history of WUWLA, it is necessary to problematize the sources of this version of Welsh women's liberalism: reports, speeches and letters produced by the hand of relatively few leading figures. They share the ethos of local associations discussed in the previous chapter, but those too, though the product of a slightly larger coterie, were still a minority. How were these papers, with their endless emphasis on the duties, responsibilities and opportunities of women in the social and political sphere received by their intended audience, the membership of associations and, more widely, potential members? There were clearly some misgivings on those grounds; the 1896 annual report had pasted over its title page a 'Kindly Notice', in bold type, reminding secretaries and committees of WLAs to have publications of the WUWLA read aloud for discussion at meetings, and circulated beyond the membership, to 'enable all its members to realise the importance of the work and take an active part in it', and to enlist wider support. Such publications, ideological propaganda, are valuable sources in the attempt to comprehend how women's political organizations understood their own purposes and activities, and how they thought they could effect change. The reception of such literature more widely is difficult to judge. Against the temptation to regard activists as more generally representative, it is important to remember that a large – five hundred members – and effective association like Aberdare was kept going by a core of perhaps eight stalwarts, even at its height, as its records show.

## 'For women'? Women's suffrage and the WUWLA

Such national representations as the WUWLA briefly constructed were fragile. The 1896 annual report was the first opportunity for the officers to report to the union on the April 1895 Aberystwyth meetings to create the Welsh National Liberal Federation, or Cymru Fydd. The account by Philipps, appended to the annual report, related the triumph of the women in ensuring that women's suffrage was made an object of the new organization, and that the WUWLA was given a constitutional role, as a divisional council, within it, but made no mention of divisions which had shown themselves within the WUWLA, or those which rapidly emerged in the ranks of Welsh liberalism. By the time the report was published, before the 1896 annual meetings of the WUWLA at Newtown, Cymru Fydd had effectively collapsed. The annual report gave no hint that any of this acrimony had affected the union, although acknowledging that the year had been a particularly difficult one, 'a testing time'. The resignations of Philipps and McLaren had created uncertainty about the future, perhaps about the viability, of the WUWLA. The defeat of the Liberals in the general election of July–August 1895 had had 'a depressing influence even upon Liberal women, and for a time it seemed as though the whole party were politically paralysed'. In addition, 'the first flush of enthusiasm' for the union had begun to pass, giving way to 'a certain amount of lethargy and apathy'.[55] The report did not speak of the fact that its new president was the wife of the man, D. A. Thomas, regarded by many as having destroyed Cymru Fydd. Nor did it mention that, although its Newtown meetings had been held under a banner declaring 'We <u>Will</u> Have the Vote!', it had been preceded by a couple of weeks of public disagreement between its leading members, and the resignation of one of its vice-presidents, Lady Osborne Morgan. Though one of the original vice-presidents of the WUWLA, Morgan was an anti-suffragist, the only identifiable Welsh signatory to the infamous 1889 'Appeal Against Female Suffrage', views she shared with her MP husband.[56] In April 1896, she had written to the *Pall Mall Gazette* deploring the 'prominence' given to the suffrage issue in the agenda for Newtown: six women's suffrage resolutions had been submitted by associations, five of those, as the press pointed out, from south Wales. Morgan maintained that the prominence given to the question was 'calculated' to undermine liberalism. She noted 'the part which branches in South Wales are likely to play in the matter'. Her salvo was reported in the Welsh press, and was followed in the *Pall Mall Gazette* by a rebuttal from Sybil Thomas, who declared that Morgan's views represented a 'very small minority' of the WUWLA.[57] A further anonymous rebuttal, in the form of an interview with 'one of the best known and most pronounced supporters of the Welsh Women's Union', struck a characteristic Nora Philipps note with the suggestion that the liberalism of those 'who oppose the enfranchisement of their sisters' was 'a sham'; and expressed the discontent of Liberal women who bore 'the heat and burden of the day' only to be 'insulted' by the men they worked to elect. The speaker hoped that Newtown would make women's suffrage a test question;[58] in the event, after 'animated discussion', it did not. Morgan, having resigned her vice-presidency, did not attend, and the argument against women's suffrage (and not just against the 'test question') was put by Mrs Humphreys-Owen, also a vice-president of the union, wife of the MP for Montgomeryshire, on the grounds that it would tend to enfranchise more Conservative voters, an argument strongly contested by Sybil Thomas at the public meeting.[59]

The events of Newtown in 1896 reflect the origins of the WUWLA in support for the progressives in the WLF, and the ongoing campaign in the federation to make women's suffrage a test question. These events demonstrate again the potential of the suffrage issue to disrupt Liberal women's unity: after the 1893 split in the WLF, a small number of Welsh WLAs had discontinued their affiliation to the WLF, including two, Rhosllannerchrugog and Wrexham, of which Morgan was president. Wrexham appears to have kept up affiliation to the WUWLA until 1896, but no lists survive after that date. Morgan's reference to the prominence of south Wales associations in promoting women's suffrage resolutions was a barely veiled suggestion that they had an interest in disrupting national unity, and would have been read in the context of the divisions which had destroyed Cymru Fydd.

## Conclusions

The achievements of the WUWLA and its member associations were considerable: Nora Philipps did not exaggerate when she wrote, in 1895, that

> [t]hree years ago men were asking why women should be political at all, and now there is scarcely a town that has not women running for the Board of Guardians, whilst in many villages women have already been elected as Parish Councillors . . . the Welsh Union has been instrumental in helping to awaken women to their responsibilities and in inducing them to undertake them.[60]

The relationship of the Welsh associations to the WLF reflected that of Wales within the United Kingdom, absorbed into the 'national' structure, without constitutional distinctiveness. In 1890, when the Scottish societies first considered their Scotland-wide organization, they emphasized that 'the nationality' of their organization 'should be maintained in consideration of the distinctive position of Scotland relative to the leading political questions of the day'.[61] The only evidence that the founding meetings of the WUWLA included such a discussion of its relationship to the WLF is in the attempt to raise the matter in the annual council of the WLF of 1893, and then not in terms of independence but of a constitutional role for the WUWLA within the federation.[62] Was the WUWLA not strong enough to contemplate an independent existence at this point? In 1894, when the WUWLA was approaching its peak of fifty-seven associations and 9,000 members, the Scottish Federation included thirty associations, with just under five thousand members. Explanations about the failure to pursue an independent line remain speculative, but can perhaps be found in the bargain made between the progressives and the 'national' element in the WUWLA (though as we have seen, they were by no means completely distinct) discussed in this chapter: it was useful to Welsh political aims to be included in a 'British' forum; it was important to the progressive agenda – led by the president and secretary of the WUWLA – to maintain a strong corpus of support in the WLF.

While an independent federation on the Scottish model was, we must assume, rejected, the WUWLA nevertheless played a role in the Welsh context which was greater than the limited role envisaged by the WLF for regional unions, and distinct from those. Its distinctiveness was embodied in a number of ways: it gave women visibility in the political forums of Wales and more widely; the idea of nationhood was an impetus to organization; the WUWLA was a vehicle for and an expression of national aims; it, and hence its constituent associations, could be seen as representative of, and agents of, national progress, which was always understood in moral terms.

However, the attempt to work 'in the interests of Women, of Wales, and of Liberalism'[63] had proved more problematic than Nora Philipps's optimistic writings and speeches suggested. The reasons for the decline of women's liberalism in Wales, whether traced though the WUWLA as a body, or through its associations, were complex, connected, like the decline between 1895–1902 of the WLF and its English associations, to the fortunes of the Liberal party in Britain and at Westminster, as the 1896 annual report suggests, and connected especially to the problems of Welsh liberalism in the same period. Added to the mixture were the tensions caused by the women's suffrage issue, tensions which were to become all the more destructive in the twentieth century. The following chapter reconsiders a part of the period covered in this chapter, to examine women's relationship to Welsh Liberal nationalism in the 1890s, in which these themes are again to the fore.

# 3

# 'The spoken centre'? The Welsh Union of Women's Liberal Associations and the National Movement in Wales

## Introduction

This chapter explores the relationship of women and their organizations to Welsh liberalism, focusing on the mid-1890s, the high point of women's Liberal politics and of the Liberal nationalist movement, Cymru Fydd. That relationship was forged at two levels. At the level of political events and actors, of cause and effect, it was an issue of women's structural relationship to the party in Wales and the possibilities it offered for achieving their political objectives. At the level of political discourse, this was a chapter in the evolving linguistic relationship of women and feminism to constructions of national identity. The relationship of women with Cymru Fydd, and the discourses deployed in its construction, demonstrated the problematic relationship of feminism and nationalism, identified in recent literature discussed below. However, the period can be understood as a moment when, briefly, women were included in the imagining of nation on their own terms.

This argument will be supported by an examination of the way the originally masculinist language of national self-representation shifted to emphasize equality between women and men; and how, through women's efforts, Cymru Fydd espoused women's suffrage as an objective, and gave women's own organizations representation within the new party's structures. As a result of these developments, at the height of women's Liberal organization in the 1890s, they forged a distinctive politics in which nationalism and feminism were briefly united.

The sources for this history, the surviving documents – discussion papers and manifestos, the periodical press and newspaper accounts

of the meetings, conferences and assemblies, with their speeches, resolutions and votes – have been used to narrate the rise and fall of
Cymru Fydd, and the careers of leading male figures.[1] I will use the
sources to plot an alternative narrative which reveals the politics of
women's relationship to male liberalism, and the tensions between
feminism and nationalism for Welsh Liberals, female and male.

The chapter does not attempt a thoroughgoing discussion of
gendered visions of national identity in nineteenth-century Wales:
there is now a growing literature on this topic, from the mid-century
cultural reaction to the Blue Books controversy to the relationship of
women to language, religion and 'respectability' in the nineteenth and
twentieth centuries.[2] My focus here is strictly on the implications for,
and the impact on, women's liberalism, of this period of national
'rebirth'. Like the previous chapters, this ends by examining decline –
of Cymru Fydd and of women's participation in national Liberal
structures – and suggests that there were signs that a more reactionary
construction of gender was emerging within an increasingly conservative, Celticist nationalism, in the context of a greatly weakened
Welsh liberalism, at the turn of the century.

### *'Rebirth of a Nation' and the historians*

In the 1880s and 1890s, 'the social cleavages of land, religion and class
matched and reinforced one another'[3] in Welsh society and its political
discourses. Cymru Fydd – the attempt to create a national party (in the
Welsh National Liberal Federation, WNLF) and the failure to do so –
was the political expression of those cleavages and their intersections.
The attempted creation of the Welsh national movement was marked,
at the end of the 1880s, by fears from north Wales that it would lead
to a weakening of Welsh claims, particularly disestablishment, at
Westminster and, in the 1890s, by suspicion from the industrial and
commercial south-east of domination by Welsh-speaking and rural
interests.

Despite the fact that the Cymru Fydd moment was short lived – its
end was effectively acknowledged early in 1896 – historians have
understood it as a central issue in the period; it is therefore important
to explore women's relationship to the movement and the gender
culture of Cymru Fydd. Groundbreaking work on the subject was
written from the 1960s to the 1980s, but the 1990s saw a resurgence of

interest, arising from new academic interest in nationalism both in Wales and elsewhere, including revisionist analyses of press and periodical representations of national identity.[4] Despite the growth of interest among scholars internationally in the gendered nature of nationalist discourses, none of these writers on Wales has paid attention either to the role of women in the movement, or their representation in the nationalist newspaper and periodical press.

For political historians, debate in recent years has centred around the 'radical' and 'democratic' credentials of Cymru Fydd and its appeal for the industrial working class of south Wales and their Lib–Lab representatives.[5] Aspects of that debate have relevance for the relationship of women to Cymru Fydd. Emyr W. Williams has discussed the involvement of the Welsh Union of Women's Liberal Associations (WUWLA) in what he called the second Cymru Fydd movement of the mid-1890s, and the inclusion of women's citizenship amongst the objects of the WNLF. Williams argued that in the late 1890s, Welsh liberalism moved from radicalism to conservative, romantic nationalism; the place given to women's claims and women's voices, and the claims of Labour – the 'new radical interests' – tested Welsh Nonconformist radicalism, and the turning away from those claims was one of the signs that Welsh nationalism had abandoned radicalism.[6] This is a useful interpretation, of which I have made some use. However, Williams focused on what the espousal of women's aims, and then their partial rejection by Welsh liberalism, said about the party, a perspective which obscures the active way in which women's organization and individual women shaped both events and language, which this chapter explores. The comparison highlights the different historical chronologies of men's and women's politics in this period for, as we have seen, a British feminist agenda rather than a Welsh national history provides the explanatory framework for developments in women's organization from 1891 to 1895.

### Feminism and nationalism

A number of strands in historical literature are relevant to this chapter. The 1990s saw the growth of a historiography addressing the representation of women in nationalist movements and movements of national self-determination and liberation, and the uneasy relationship to these movements of feminism. This includes work on

Welsh nationalism, though mainly for the twentieth century.[7] The other strand, on the face of it more relevant to modern British history, excluding the case of Ireland, explores radicalism and the language of radicalism in nineteenth-century Britain, in particular analysing constructions of 'the People'. A number of historians have made a notable contribution on the relationship of women to constructions of 'the People' and of citizenship, and on women's own 'efforts ... to speak as members of "the people", and in "the People's" name'.[8] Nineteenth-century representations of 'the People' had a specifically Welsh variant, directly relevant to Liberal women's position in the Welsh 'nation' of Cymru Fydd.

Scholars have identified a number of ways in which women have been represented in nationalist movements.[9] Women have been included in nation-building as mothers, as the biological reproducers of citizens and as the reproducers of the language, culture and values of the nation, through their children, within the home – or as it was often expressed 'at the hearth'; the Welsh language was 'the language of the hearth'. Women have, in addition to their biological and nurturing roles, been identified in the role of active reproducers and 'transmitters' of the culture, though not necessarily as mothers. They have been represented as engaged in national struggles, in the political sphere as well as the cultural. And women have been seen as symbolizing or standing for the nation. In the meetings, political debates and writings produced in the Cymru Fydd period, all of these different identities can be found, though some are more constant and appear to carry more weight than others.

The relationship of movements for women's emancipation and citizenship to nationalist movements and emerging nations has also occupied scholars in recent years. As Charlotte Aull Davies has written, both nationalism and feminism are universalizing discourses, which give primacy to particular differences and collective identities, which may cut across each other.[10] Nationalism has been understood to be inimical to feminism, essentializing femininity in ways which impeded women's emancipation and progress, and hostile to feminism as an alternative, and potentially international and transnational discourse, which might undermine women's identification with the interest of the nation.[11] This approach has in turn been problematized by Third World and black feminist challenges to the 'universalist and totalizing dream' of feminism,[12] and, in the context of the historiography of Irish women's politics, by analysis of the exclusions inherent in understandings of the term 'progressive'.[13] This is a useful point: suffragists within the Liberal women's movement claimed the term 'progressive' for themselves, as previously discussed, while those who broke away from the WLF claimed they did so to concentrate on support for 'progressive' Liberal policies. In the Welsh context, a 'nationalist' WLA, like Denbigh, might be more inclined to hold meetings which combined magic lantern lectures on the radical and progressive causes of Welsh tithe sales and Ireland than on women's suffrage.[14] The perception of similarities between the cases of Ireland and Wales was an important feature of the Welsh national movement, and support for Irish Home Rule was strong amongst Welsh women Liberals as in the WLF more broadly. However, there is no sign – apart from lecture tours by Alice Kearney, who was a generally popular speaker – of WLAs forming special links with Irish women's groups and, ultimately, the Welsh and Irish contexts were not directly comparable: the movement for home rule for Wales was a movement for greater recognition and autonomy within the British state and the empire, not for independence (though the conduct of empire often came in for bitter denunciation by Cymru Fydd writers), and the 1890s provided opportunities for expressions of fervid loyalty.[15] Above all, despite the 'tithe wars' of the 1880s, there was, of course, no militarization of the movement and hence no opportunities for the extremes of gender polarization in nationalist discourses and practices to which militarized movements frequently give rise. There is, therefore, no intention here to compare the position of women in Wales and Ireland in relation to their nationalist movements.

However, nationalist movements and ideas beyond the British mainland had relevance for Liberal and feminist women inside and outside Wales, and for Welsh nationalists. The impact of the Italian reunification movement and its leaders, and in particular the intellectual influence of Giuseppe Mazzini, on British radicals have been explored by a number of historians, and their significance for women radicals and feminists has been convincingly established.[16] Mazzini's writings, including the widely read *Duties of Man,* were available in translation in Britain from the early 1860s, but were republished in different editions in 1890 and 1894, reintroducing them to Welsh radicals and feminists during this key moment in their own movements. Mazzini's emphasis on civic duties before rights, on the family as the school of citizenship and civic virtue,[17] like the moral emphasis of

Josephine Butler previously discussed, would have had great appeal for the earnest Liberal women of Wales. For both women and men in Wales, who might have found it difficult to connect to the British language of radicalism, with its appeals to the ancient constitution and Saxon birthright, the European models provided an alternative.[18] The intellectuals and leaders of Cymru Fydd sought to construct a lineage for Wales amongst the European nations which emerged in the nineteenth century, ideas developed in the periodical literature of the movement. The journal *Young Wales* (1895–1903) was established and named in conscious imitation of the journal *Young Italy*, established in 1831, and of the Young Ireland movement and its journals. Writers in the journal frequently placed Wales in the context of European nationalisms: Ireland, Italy, Spain, Portugal, Holland, Belgium, Bohemia, Croatia, Serbia, Finland, Poland and Hungary were all liable to be invoked for comparison. Mazzini and Thomas Davis were particular heroes of the editor of the journal, John Hugh Edwards, as they were of Thomas Ellis and other Welsh Liberal leaders. Lloyd George and Ellis were compared to these figures as national deliverers. In particular, Mazzini's elevation of nationalism and patriotism to a religious principle, his idea that nations had unique and divinely appointed missions in the world, were attractive to many in Wales in this period: *Young Wales* frequently asked 'What is Wales' mission to the world?'[19] While placing women securely in the context of family, Mazzini also emphasized the essential equality of men and women in all efforts for the progress of humanity.[20] His views could 'accommodate sexual difference while also offering women a breadth of activity within a public setting'.[21] Nora Philipps, too, placed Mazzini in her pantheon of exemplary lives.[22] However, bearing out the discussion of the problematic relationship between feminism and nationalism, Mazzini's writings, as used in *Young Wales*, became a double-edged sword for Welsh suffragists, which will be further discussed below.[23]

Populist discourses of the late nineteenth century in Wales have been dated by historians from the memorable definition of 'the Welsh people' by Henry Richard, at the prospect of their enfranchisement in the 1867 Reform Act. In a much quoted election speech at Merthyr Tydfil, Richard asked rhetorically:

> The people who speak this language, who read this literature, who own this history, who inherit these traditions, who venerate these names, who created and sustained these marvellous religious organisations, the people forming three fourths of the people of Wales – have not they the

right to say to this small propertied class . . . We are the Welsh people and not you? This country is ours and not yours . . .[24]

This construction of the people as an idealized, cultured, pious and historical peasantry, the *gwerin*, (literally 'the folk' or 'the people', though the full resonance of the term is agreed to be untranslatable) was highly developed in Cymru Fydd writings, and by nationalist historians and nation-builders. The significance of this construct to Welsh understandings of nationhood has been explored by historians, but the difficulties for women of associating themselves with this version of the country's past and present have not been examined.[25] This chapter will briefly do so, through the Cymru Fydd journal, *Young Wales.*

### *1888–96: the feminizing of Cymru Fydd*

This first Cymru Fydd movement saw an attempt in 1888 to unite the Liberal federations of north and south Wales with 'the national elements in Welsh life', represented by the Cymru Fydd leagues and the land leagues. Women had taken part in the meetings, but appear to have made no claims of their own, and the final resolution excluded them with its use of the term 'Welshmen'.[26] This movement collapsed when the forces of Nonconformity in Wales saw Westminster as the surest route to disestablishment. The collapse of the London Cymru Fydd society in 1890 left the home rule movement without an organizational base.[27] From 1891 to 1894, local branches of Cymru Fydd were formed throughout Wales, 'under the dynamic stimulus of Lloyd George'.[28] However, a number of national and parliamentary initiatives in the same period came to nothing, and the years 1890–4 have been identified as a period of fragmentation and drift for the movement.[29] As has been shown, however, these were crucial years for the growth of women's Liberal organizations at a local and national level. By 1895, the WUWLA represented the membership of some fifty-seven local associations and 9,000 women. So well before the period of 'the second Cymru Fydd Movement', 1894–6,[30] the organization of Liberal women had been transformed, and they had a clear political programme of their own, discussed in the previous chapter.

In April 1894, in protest at the lack of clear commitment from the government on disestablishment, a group of leading Welsh MPs withdrew themselves from the Liberal whip: 'the situation was ripe for the re-establishment of an organised Cymru Fydd movement'.[31] In May, the Cymru Fydd societies of Manchester and Liverpool issued a joint manifesto, *To Young Wales*. This set out a variety of religious, political, educational, linguistic and cultural objectives which, while including the 'interests' of miners and quarrymen and hopes for Welsh self-government, made no mention of franchise reform; and, while declaring itself open to all sympathizers, it made no specific mention of the membership of women or their organizations. The document deployed masculine forms of language: 'we like yourselves are Welshmen'; 'the strength of a nation lies in its young men'. All the signatories, officers of the leagues, were men, and the endorsements of the manifesto appended to it were from leading male Liberals. Plans for the 'solid national force' proposed by the manifesto, and for local branches, made no mention of a need to include women, but ended by emphasizing that 'this is a Young Wales Movement. It appeals to the coming generation of Welshmen everywhere . . .' Young Wales, the 'rising life of our country' was thus represented as exclusively male.[32]

From that point on, however, the movement's records bear witness to the gradual inclusion of women, both in the language in which the nation was constructed and in the increasing place of women in the structures of the hoped-for national body, a development brought about through intensive work by women behind the scenes. Over the course of a few months, various draft constitutions for the proposed new body moved from purely masculine forms of language which excluded women to a consistent emphasis on the equality of men and women as individuals. By the summer of 1894, meetings throughout the country had enthusiastically endorsed the plan to create a new national organization, with the formation of local branches to which 'women should be admitted on the same terms as men'.[33] A number of draft constitutions produced that year made a point of stating the equality of men and women as members, though with no structural role for women's organizations.[34] At a conference in Neath in August 1894 an intervention by Kate Jenkins, the Vale of Towy farmer and WUWLA secretary, convinced the meeting that a 'truly national movement' must include women, and ensured that some women were to be included as constituency representatives in a new joint planning committee, but there was no sense that there were specific women's interests to be represented.[35] Evidence of the membership of women in the local branches of Cymru Fydd being formed in 1894 and 1895 is hard to find: there were no women among the officers or committee members of the Cardiff branch, for example, and nothing on women's issues in its programme for 1894–5, despite the fact that Cardiff Central WLA had affiliated to the branch.[36] If, as has been suggested, the personnel of Cymru Fydd and Liberal associations were to a great extent interchangeable, there may have been limited scope for women's activity in the branches.[37] However, the achievement to this point should not be underestimated: the language of Cymru Fydd had changed to encompass gender equality and moved away from a purely masculine vision of the nation, and a few women were being elected to the planning meetings. But there appeared to be no consciousness in all this that there might be different interests to be served, that women might have claims as women. Women present at these meetings seem not to have suggested this themselves. However, this was to change when Kate Jones, a leading figure in the Cardiff WLA, reminded the executive of the WUWLA that Liberal women had their own political objectives, and were concerned for their organizational integrity. Following her suggestions, the annual meeting of the WUWLA resolved that it was desirable to affiliate to the league, provided that the league made the obtaining of equal citizenship for women one of its objects, and that the union was adequately represented on the council of the league.[38]

The annual meeting of the WUWLA in March 1895 had emphasized the importance of WLAs in 'the education of women in political independence';[39] why, then, did the women want union with the new body, given the apparent strength and success of separate organization? Union on the terms the women had now laid down would mean that, for the first time, a British political party would have written women's suffrage into its own programme, and would be answerable to a strong women's organization within its structures. In the mid-1890s, Welsh liberalism provided an important group within the parliamentary party and in the National Liberal Federation (NLF), which had so far resisted making women's suffrage one of its objects. Through Cymru Fydd, women would be able to apply pressure on the NLF and the parliamentary party. Union with Cymru Fydd on the women's own terms would therefore suit the feminist objectives of the WUWLA.

There were pragmatic, and even opportunistic, reasons why women might be encouraged by the leadership to throw in their lot with Cymru Fydd. Despite the appearance of strength and vitality, partly a product of enthusiastic propaganda, it is now clear that Welsh women's liberalism was an alliance which took some building and some holding together. Ultimately, the national organization could only be as strong as its parts and, as the previous chapters have shown, many WLAs were quite weak, and there was potential for division. Nora Philipps and Eva McLaren were on the point of disengaging from their leading roles in Wales. Despite her emphasis on the size and strength of the WUWLA in her negotiations with the Welsh party, it may be that Philipps envisaged leaving Liberal women in Wales, and a voice for women's suffrage, embedded in what might be a strong national body, ensuring their organizational survival.

However, there were also ideological reasons why women should join in the attempt to create a national party. As the previous chapter on the work and activities of the associations has shown, these women were enthusiastic Liberals, and the agenda of Welsh Nonconformist liberalism in the 1890s was particularly close to the aims of many Liberal women inside and outside Wales. While intent on maintaining their autonomy, Liberal women in Wales also welcomed the increasing closeness and cooperation with the men's party which was taking shape in the mid-1890s; they saw this as part of a 'greater recognition of women's position'.[40] Women Liberals were also, to varying degrees, nationalists, in the ways in which Welsh Liberals were nationalists in the 1890s: at the 1895 annual conference, the Llanelli WLA proposed a resolution in favour of self-government for Wales, which would 'tend to the highest development of the powers and resources of the country, and be in harmony with the national aspirations of the people'. The conference approved a resolution on similar lines, adding support for disestablishment and disendowment of the Church in Wales and land reform.[41] While this nationalist programme was supported by the WUWLA and the associations, women were actively involved in contesting the definitions of nation, of Welshness and of Welsh womanhood in this period. The tensions between divergent definitions emerged in the debates during which women's entry into Cymru Fydd was negotiated at the Aberystwyth convention of April 1895.

### *'Forward . . . hand in hand with the women'*

The convention was the beginning of the end of Liberal national organization in Wales. The culmination of the many meetings, proposals and draft constitutions of the past year, it was intended to dissolve the existing federations and leagues into one Welsh National Federation. Over two days, the convention agreed on the objects and the constitution of the new party; and, during those two days, the WUWLA obtained a commitment to women's suffrage and separate representation for itself in the structures of the new body. The press reported that the organization had been 'cleverly captured by the ladies'; but the end of these hopeful developments was already contained in the boycott of the conference by the South Wales Liberal Federation (SWLF) under the presidency of D. A. Thomas.[42]

Accounts of the rise and fall of Cymru Fydd have revolved around questions of class, language and rural versus industrial interests.[43] However, it was the woman question which transformed the convention. The first debate was aroused by Nora Philipps's proposed inclusion among the objects of the new body of the clause 'To secure for women equal rights of citizenship with men'. Similarly, on the second day, the question of the representation of the Welsh union in the Welsh National Federation was the only question which was seriously contested. The *South Wales Daily News* reported that the conference had particularly enjoyed the fact that women were divided amongst themselves. Despite that and other trivializing comment, it seems clear from the reports that it was in the context of the debates on the women's proposals that different conceptions of nation, nationalism and the role of Cymru Fydd were able to emerge.[44]

Despite her standing as the first president of the WUWLA, and experience on political platforms, Philipps exhibited some lack of confidence in presenting herself to the meetings. Notwithstanding the presence of women, she addressed the gathering as male, and invoked the protection of her absent husband, representing herself as standing in for him. 'Had he been present', she said, 'he would have spoken to them man to man in favour of women's suffrage'. At least some of Philipps's unease may have come from the fact that, despite her continuing involvement in Welsh politics, she was herself not Welsh, her connection having come through her marriage. But, given her experience and her acknowledged skills as an orator, her diffidence can also be read as a calculated appeal to the chivalry of the male majority of the audience, as she flattered male Wales on its 'good work for womanhood, greater than any part of the kingdom'. This suggestion that Wales had been particularly supportive of the equality of women, and that women were in a better social position than in other parts of Britain, was common at this time and into the Edwardian period. The best evidence for any truth in it is probably, briefly, in developments in secondary and higher education, while as a discourse it had its roots in a romantic construction of Welsh egalitarianism and justice.[45] It should certainly also be regarded as a strategic rhetorical device. Philipps continued in more typical vein, describing Welsh national aims as a moral example to the world. She represented Wales as an organic community, a family composed of 'the people in the homes of Wales'. The use of familial language was and has been common in conceptions of nation, contributing to the construction of gender-specific roles and identities in nation-building.[46] In this case, Philipps used the familial trope to ask for an equality which, paradoxically, it was in the gift of men to bestow. This was to be reciprocated by support from women for the men's aims, for she suggested (as reported in the press) that she understood men's and women's aims to be different and separate: if the men helped the women to bring about women's suffrage, then the women 'would help the men in all the noble objects on which they had set their hearts'. Thus the programme of Welsh liberalism was represented as that of Liberal men only. This was unlike Philipps: in her speeches and writings elsewhere, she laid claim to the whole world of politics for women.[47] Philipps's rhetoric shaped the course of the discussion over two days; her presentation of the case in the form of a bargain between the women and men of Wales, a notion which was to be sustained by other speakers, meant that no one needed to declare for or against women's suffrage, only to weigh up what they would get from the compact. It also suggested that men and women would have different forms of Welsh citizenship, 'gender-specific involvements in nation building and in the construction of national identities',[48] reflected in the interjections over the next two days in support of Philipps's proposals. In the suffrage debate, none of the reported arguments was based on the justice of women's claim to the vote. Most speakers concentrated on the consequences – the danger of dilution of the idea of nation by single issues, or the strengthening of Cymru Fydd by the accession of a large body of workers. Similarly, in the debate on the way the WUWLA should be represented in the WNLF, neither side of the debate had much to do with the merits of the women's case, but with other political, ideological and tactical considerations.

The desire that nationalism should express one collective identity, which overwrote differences and single issues ('specialization' of demands, in the language of the conference), be they of class, religion or gender, made the acknowledgement of women's specific need for enfranchisement, or for separate representation, a dangerous one for nationalists like Susannah Gee and those who supported her in the debates. Nationalism should present, in Gee's words, 'a clean sheet', a blank page on which everyone who could identify themselves as 'Welshman or Welshwoman' could inscribe their name. Significantly, the other single issues she feared would swarm into the breach made by the feminists were all working-class and trade union struggles, class being the other major universalizing and potentially transnational concept. On this occasion, though, other ways of conceiving of the nation, and women's role in it, won the day. For Lloyd George the very acknowledgement of difference would make Cymru Fydd more open to the other desired allies, working-class organizations. The image of women as a strong band of activists and companions in the struggle was evident in the remarks of several speakers, including the president, Thomas Gee; the size of the WUWLA was frequently mentioned, and it was likened to an army of evangelists. A religious and potentially conservative view of the nature and role of women, as guardians of national purity, was linked to their public role in a religious nation. For a gathering which had already made up its mind, an appeal by Miss Carpenter, women's warden at Aberystwyth University College, to the Liberal concept of 'rights' and to the aspirational symbol of the University of Wales, with its (theoretical) equality of the sexes, clinched the debate. As Councillor Moses Walters of South Monmouthshire put it, despite the desertion of the South Wales Liberal Federation, 'their watchword was still "Forward", and hand in hand with the women forward they would go'. The Welsh National Federation became the first party organization in Britain explicitly to include women's suffrage amongst its objects. It was to be warmly congratulated for its courage and radicalism by the WLAs.[49]

The conference also endorsed, again by an overwhelming majority, the constitutional committee's proposal that the Welsh Union be regarded as a separate division of the national federation, with its own divisional council.[50] In the absence of Sybil Thomas, recently elected president of the WUWLA, it again fell to Nora Philipps to put the case. Like Philipps, and most married political women, Thomas was inevitably identified with the politics of her husband, and Philipps had to address this point when she rose to reply, suggesting that, despite being opposed to the creation of Cymru

Fydd, Sybil Thomas, as president of a democratic organization, would carry out the wishes of her members. The debate was a lengthy one, with Susannah Gee again leading the opposition, but in the end all the conditions set by the Welsh union for its cooperation with Cymru Fydd had been met.

So, to some opposition from its own members, including at least one of the executive committee, the WUWLA had got what it wanted. The *South Wales Daily News* expansively declared: 'henceforth the Liberal Women of Wales will be admitted to the inner councils of Welsh Nationalism, and the new organisation stands pledged in black and white to aim to enfranchise "the weaker sex".' Just three women representing the WUWLA were elected to the provisional executive of the new organization, joined by three more elected as constituency representatives.[51] Clearly, if women's interests were to be represented in the organization, it would not have been safe to rely on their theoretical equality with men. Equally clear was the potential for fractures in the leadership, and probably in the membership, of the Welsh union, along the fault lines occupied by Philipps, Gee and Thomas.

Two further conferences that year modified the constitution of the WNLF, but left the women's clauses intact. However, in November 1895, the executive of the SWLF accepted all but the women's suffrage clause, which it deemed to be included in a clause on promoting the political, social, industrial and educational interests of the Welsh people. The decision was effectively endorsed at an infamous January 1896 meeting at Newport, which has been seen as marking the end of hopes for a Welsh liberalism united in one organization around national objectives. Cymru Fydd's programme of separate organization and home rule for Wales gave way to a return to 'the old radical programme' of disestablishment and disendowment.[52]

The opposition of the SWLF to an explicit clause in favour of women's suffrage in 1895–6 may be significant for the feminist aims of the Welsh union, but the evidence regarding the federation's attitude towards feminism is contradictory. It has been suggested that in rejecting the suffrage clause (and Cymru Fydd's wider programme) the SWLF was protecting the 'existing power structures of the party' threatened by the democratizing potential of the women's movement and the labour movement.[53] While this makes sense of the deletion of the women's suffrage clause, the evidence for the anti-feminism of the SWLF is uncertain. Women and their associations were increasingly linked to the structures of south Wales liberalism in this period; D. A. Thomas, SWLF president, who led the opposition to the united programme, and became the villain of the piece as far as nationalists were concerned, was a suffragist in good standing. Feminists at the time may not have interpreted the rejection of the clause in this way. At its annual meeting in March 1896, Cardiff WLA passed a resolution thanking the SWLF 'for promoting women's suffrage in the objects of their association'.[54]

## Young Wales *and the imagining of nation*

Women were actively engaged in contesting definitions of nation in the 1890s, in the face-to-face context of the meetings and conferences of Cymru Fydd and in the daily press reports, with immediate political implications. But the debates, and the imagining of Wales, also took place over a longer time span, and in a more considered fashion, in the periodical literature of the movement. The nationalist periodical *Young Wales*, published from 1895 to 1903, provided a context in which notions of Wales and Welshness were constructed, often in relation to European nationalist philosophies. No other political journal of the period in Wales gave as much space to issues of the position and status of women. While only a brief examination is possible here, the writings of both women and men in the journal, and the way their representations changed over time, provide an invaluable insight into notions of nation and gender in the Welsh context. The rest of this chapter concerns in particular the uses of history in nation-building, and the ways in which visions of Wales's history were gendered.

As previously discussed, feminist scholars have identified a variety of representations of women in nationalist movements. Some have examined particularly women's relationship to a national past, and the gendering of the nation that occurs in nationalist historical narratives. Recent scholarship in this area has seen women appearing in nationalist histories mainly as representative of a 'timeless national memory' and as 'symbolically constructed as the bearers of the nation, but . . . denied any direct relation to national agency'.[55] For a time, more diverse representations of women were constructed in *Young Wales*, including women as social and political agents. However, the dominant version of the history was of a Wales from which women and their experience were absent. In addition, the development of the journal was symptomatic of the fate of the national movement, its decline from 1896 and the turn to a less optimistic view of the present and future of Wales. This is reflected in a diminishing voice for women in its pages, and also in the more frequent appearance of articles which found in the lessons of history a more reactionary view of the place of women in the movement and in the nation.

Literary representations of women in relation to national identity have received increasing attention in recent years. Representations of 'the true Cymraes' (Welshwoman) were an important part of the attempt to rebuild national self-respect in the aftermath of the Royal Commission Report on the State of Education in Wales.[56] Just as the commissioners had identified the depravity of Welsh women as a source of national barbarity, so the subsequent attempt at national self-definition focused to a large extent on producing women as ideal figures of Welsh virtue and respectability. The reception of such models and images amongst their target audience is difficult to determine. A point of relevance to this chapter, however, is to note that the content of such representations appears to be very distant from those of women in *Young Wales*, a reminder that models of national womanhood were class specific. The new opportunities in education, and for a greater part in public life, signifiers of the progressive new Wales of Cymru Fydd, were mainly available to middle-class women, and it was those women who were the contributors to, and the probable readership of, *Young Wales*. The relative absence from its pages of what are understood to be the dominant images of nineteenth-century Welsh womanhood – devout, pious, immured in home and chapel – reflects this class difference.[57] Perhaps the weakest representation in *Young Wales* is that of the mother as biological reproducer of future citizens, though the assumption of a childbearing and child-rearing destiny for women underlay the social Darwinism of some writing in the journal in the late 1890s.[58] Similarly, the role of women as reproducers of language, culture and values tended to be found in the more conservative versions of nationalism in the pages of *Young Wales,* but could also be read in the potentially more progressive attempts to write a Nonconformist history for women, and to argue for the equality of women within nationalist organizations.[59]

Historians and theorists of nationalism agree on the importance of the construction of a common past, 'a usable past', as evidence of historical continuity and distinctiveness in nation-building.[60] In the Welsh context, scholars have analysed the way history-making functioned in the 'rebirth' of the nation in the second half of the nineteenth century.[61] The role of the Liberal press in this process has also been examined, with debates centring on the use of newspaper sources by historians, the engaged nature of the press and the extent to which the press provided a coherent model of national identity in this period.[62] However, these analyses have not included the periodical press, nor the representations of women and gender in the versions of Wales and its history being constructed.

## *Women in* Young Wales

From the start, the journal endorsed the equality of men and women in the hoped-for new Wales, and approved their 'growing power and influence'. The women's movement and the labour movement were claimed as part of the same progressive, democratizing force as Liberal nationalism.[63] The decision to set aside a regular space for women in the journal was a sign of this general acceptance of the idea of the political equality of men and women; it was also recognition of the existence of a distinctive political women's movement and of separate women's interests to be served. At the same time, however, the fencing-off of space for women also carried with it the possibility of marginalization and the perpetuation of gendered forms of national identity.

Liberal women appeared in the journal in a number of ways. They contributed as fiction writers and as polemicists on issues relating to women's position or interests, and, more rarely, on the causes dear to Welsh nationalism, not necessarily in relation to women. One of the most written-about subjects by and about women was education; the relationship of women and religion/the churches was written about from a historical perspective and in terms of the contemporary position; under the editorship of the novelist Sara Maria Saunders, the women's column also explored women in fiction. The women's section of the journal was pioneered by Nora Philipps's 'Notes on the work of Welsh Liberal women' in 1895, which became a regular feature, entitled 'Progress of women in Wales', edited by Philipps and her sister-in-law Elsbeth Philipps. After the resignation of the editors in March 1897, the representation of women's interests became intermittent, and of women's politics very little more was to be found. In 1897, two columns called 'The women of Wales circle', edited by Saunders, appeared, and in 1901 the column appeared twice, edited by novelist Alis Mallt Williams. In 1903, the last year of the journal's publication, the section was relaunched as 'The interests of women in Wales'.[64] The changing titles, as well as the diminishing frequency, of these columns was surely significant.

## Nation and history in Young Wales

A plurality of Liberal voices and visions of nationhood was expressed in the journal over the years, bearing out the contention that the articulation of national identity in the Welsh press was 'diverse and contested'.[65] However, a number of dominant voices and motifs emerged, provided by the editor, John Hugh Edwards, and the regular columnists, reflecting the concerns of the national movement, and embodied in the nationalist heroes of the journal. Just before the Aberystwyth convention of April 1895, Edwards printed without comment a long extract from the writing of Mazzini, which (*inter alia*) envisaged: 'the people, one and indivisible, recognizing neither castes nor privileges save those of genius and virtue; neither proletarian nor aristocracy . . . but simply an aggregate of faculties and forces consecrated to the well-being of all . . .'[66] Such inclusiveness in the national ideal was a recurring theme of the columnists, as they addressed the accusation that nationalists wanted 'Wales for the Welsh'. However inclusive, such ideas showed a belief in the possibility of unitary identity around commitment to the idea of Wales. The potential problems of this universalizing nationalism for separate demands for women's emancipation have already been noted. Edwards took his understanding of the historic development of nations from Mazzini, with implications for feminism, as will be further discussed below.

### Historical narratives, representative lives and lessons from abroad

The need to create a usable past, on which to build for the future, and the need to embody that past in a national museum, art gallery and a 'national architecture', were promoted in the journal from the beginning, and leading writers and political figures returned to the idea.[67] The persistence of the idea of nationhood, from ancient times into the present, was frequently asserted; Thomas Davis, the Irish leader, was quoted, stirringly evoking the survival of 'that race which stood under Llewellyn, and rallied under Owen Glyndwr', while Llewelyn Williams evoked 'an unbroken succession of minstrels, bards and writers . . . from the time when the struggles against the Saxons raised the Welsh people to a consciousness of their nationhood'.[68] The more recent myth of origin, the coming of religious dissent to Wales, and its founders and early struggles – the myth of foundation of those who were 'the people of Wales' in Henry Richard's sense – was also reiterated.

One of the most frequent forms of historical writing in *Young Wales* was the biography. Lives of Welsh and European nationalist figures were used to construct emblematic and inspirational models. The biographies of Welsh figures were central to the national idea: they were never just stories of individual promise, achievement and leadership, but a metaphor for the progress of the nation; two of the most vivid examples of this were the profiles of Thomas Ellis and Lloyd George, published in April and August 1896.[69] The use of the biographical form to embody the story of the nation had gender implications: women were not seen as suitable subjects for this treatment; a series of articles under the title 'Rising young Welshmen' was just that. Women were not absent from *Young Wales*, but they did not function as emblematic figures, whose life stories contained within them the story of Welsh nationhood. While nations might frequently be symbolized by a female figure, or personified as female,[70] individual women did not, in the pages of *Young Wales*, carry representativeness in the way that individual men might do.

The other kind of historical narrative presented in the journal was that of the European nationalist movements and their leaders. In 1897, John Hugh Edwards returned to his hero, Mazzini, in two lengthy articles. The second was the more strictly biographical, with Mazzini's life and the progress of the Young Italy movement being recounted in ways which pointed up lessons for Wales.[71] The first was a discussion of types of nationalism. In it, Edwards distinguished between small nations, struggling 'to secure full recognition of their national individuality', and confident great nations.[72] In the latter, wrote Edwards, there was agitation for 'the claims and conditions of labour or the rights and fitness of women for a greater sphere and deeper influence in the life and activity of the nation'. The implications were clear, but Edwards spelled them out: 'Thus . . . among the powerful nations of the world one hears the piercing cries of *"The Rights of Labour"* and of *"Woman's Rights."*'[73] For smaller nations, however, the cry was not for women or for labour, but for the *'Rights of Nation'*: 'The smaller peoples have to struggle hard lest they become absorbed by the more powerful nations. They have to strain every energy to retain the mother-tongue, the treasury of their national traditions and of their most cherished memories.'[74] Rights of labour and of women had, therefore, to be sacrificed, to wait for national self-determination, a familiar response of nationalist ideologies to pressure from women's separate claims for emancipation.[75] This retreat into a nationalism which supposedly transcended class and gender, what Edwards called 'this religion of the fatherland', reflects in the journal the developments discerned in the crisis of Welsh liberalism after 1895 and 1896, the move towards a more conservative form of nationalism. It was echoed by other articles in the journal at this time, written by both men and women; in the nation's struggle against absorption, women had a clear role: to maintain 'tradition' and to ensure the survival of the language.[76] As far as the journal was concerned, the 'cry for Women's Rights', was barely to be heard again.

Why, after a relatively short time, did the political voice of women in the journal become faint, giving way to a more conservative, even reactionary tone? The explanation, as suggested, must lie in the pessimism of Welsh Liberal nationalism at the end of the 1890s; in a long period of Tory government, Welsh liberalism had no hope of achieving its aims for Wales, and was bitterly divided internally. The failure of anyone else to take over where Nora Philipps left off, as a clear voice for Liberal women, may well reflect a loss of faith and energy amongst women too; there is plenty of evidence for that in the records of the WLAs. Many women, like Philipps, would now have become more involved in the reunited and revived suffrage movement.

A tension has been identified within nationalisms which looked to the past, sometimes dim and mythical, for narratives of foundation and authenticity, and simultaneously stretched out to the future of progress and emancipation; a tension which has frequently been resolved by a kind of gender division of labour, where women 'are represented as the atavistic and authentic body of national tradition

... embodying nationalisms' conservative principle of continuity', while men represent active, progressive makers of the future.[77] That gender dichotomy, and an 'atavistic' role for women, can be found in a number of the approaches to the past in *Young Wales*. It is possible to read the journal as resolving the tension between past and future, by the restatement of gender difference, as Welsh nationalism moved from radicalism to a conservative and romantic, Celticist, identity, epitomized by figures like Alis Mallt Williams. The 'Progress of Women' had been represented by Nora Philipps, Llewelyn Williams and others, as a sign of the progressivism of nationalist Wales. The intermittent, and progressively weakening, voice for organized political women in the journal, as well as the authorship and content of the articles as time went on, may well reflect the fragmentation of women's organization, but it can also be read as a mirror of their relationship with the national project.

## Women Liberals and the end of Cymru Fydd

In 1898, the idea of national organization was embodied in the Welsh National Liberal Council (WNLC), a coordinating body formed to unite the movement after the rift of 1896, but which subsequently failed to revive either the spirit or function of Cymru Fydd. There was no express commitment to the interests of women, but the WUWLA was granted ten places on the council and sixty delegates to its annual convention.[78] Maria Richards of Aberdare WLA, at a women's suffrage meeting in the town, acclaimed the inclusion of so many women on the national council as 'recognition accorded for the work done by the various Women's Liberal Associations in Wales'.[79] This, at a time when 'local Liberalism ... showed a consistent picture of disintegration of organization and morale',[80] was probably a fair statement: Welsh liberalism needed the women's organizations, even if those organizations were themselves dwindling.

Women now had a place in a national organization judged by historians to be to be toothless: real power lay with the parliamentary party.[81] The WNLC was considerably longer lived than Cymru Fydd, but in the period when it could have been useful for women to have influence in a national political organization – the period of Liberal government 1906–14 – the council was particularly ineffective. This was despite an attempt, in 1907, to revive it by greatly widening its membership, increasing women's representation and drawing in the leagues of Young Liberals, Labour organizations, the Free Churches and temperance organizations.[82] By 1907, there was no WUWLA, and local organization, as shown in previous chapters, was weak. Women appear never to have taken up their full allocation of seats on the national council. As the Edwardian suffrage campaign reached its height, in 1908, a Grand National Convention which included resolutions on adult suffrage, but not on women's suffrage, had no noticeable involvement of women. The following year, a Disestablishment Convention in Pontypridd seems to have been conducted without a visible or audible presence of women.[83] This is a depressing record which certainly reflects the lack of dynamism in Welsh women's liberalism which had been evident from the later 1890s, but also just as certainly the deteriorating relations between women and the Liberal party, in Wales as in England, more fully examined in part II. The breadth of the WNLC and its convention has been read as 'a nation in a nutshell'.[84] Women's inclusion in this version of the nation was tested almost to destruction in 1910, as the following chapters show.

## Conclusions

There has been an assumption that the fate of women's Liberal organization was tied to the fate of Cymru Fydd:[85] that assumption involves others, about the nature of women's Liberal politics – that it was essentially Welsh and auxiliary in character, rather than, perhaps, 'British', autonomous or feminist. Any one of those characterizations would be a simplification. This chapter has demonstrated the extent to which identification with nationalism amongst women, like their identification with party, was created out of a variety of alliances and compromises. The virtue of the women's movement in Wales, as described by Nora Philipps – '[t]he breadth of the basis on which the Welsh women reared their edifice of social and political endeavour . . . the diverse interests and individualities that linked themselves together'[86] – could also be its weakness. The judgement that Philipps's attempt to unite feminism and nationalism in Wales was largely expedient probably has much truth in it,[87] and her successor as president, Sybil Thomas, was certainly more of a feminist than a nationalist, and perhaps more of a feminist than a Liberal. There were others who put country first and, like Susannah Gee, maintained women's representation in Welsh liberalism to the end. Amongst the leadership, the figure who was most dedicated to both her national and her feminist identities and their expression in political and cultural activities, was probably the novelist Gwyneth Vaughan. In the period after the collapse of Cymru Fydd, Vaughan was more likely to be feted for her attachment to a purported heritage of bardic and heraldic trappings, than for her still active suffragism.[88]

Part I of this book has examined the rise and decline of women's Liberal organization in Wales, its characteristics and personnel, its ethos and the sources of strength, as well as of tension and weakness. It is easy to overemphasize the latter, and to see the story as part of what we now know as the longer narrative of Liberal decline. This would be at the expense of understanding the strength and uniqueness of the movement in its time. Part II develops the understanding of the local movements, begun in chapter 1, by close study of two south Wales associations, Aberdare and Cardiff.

# PART II

# POLITICS, PLACE AND GENDER: TWO CASE STUDIES

# 4

## 'Life in earnest': Aberdare Women's Liberal Association, 1891–1914

### Introduction

As in part I, my aim in the second part of this book is to construct a narrative of women's politics, here set in the context of the local dynamic. This chapter and the two following examine the characteristics and ethos of two south Wales Women's Liberal Associations (WLAs), Cardiff and Aberdare, formed in February 1890 and November 1891 respectively, through close analysis of their structures and personnel, their social and class positions and their self-representations in speech and writing. The interaction of the WLAs with the wider networks of women's politics and with the local male Liberal organizations is explored, along with the impact on the WLAs of wider political events and social and political change. In the 1890s, the participation of WLAs in local government contests sheds light on the themes of gender, party and electoral politics, of 'womanhood' and public service. In the period 1900–14, and especially from 1906 onwards, the focus shifts to the impact on women's Liberal politics of the suffrage movement, the rise of militancy and the crisis of liberalism. Throughout, two strands are constant: women's conception of their own place in the public political sphere; and, linked to that, 'what women called Liberalism'.[1]

The value of local studies, which bring small groups and individuals to the centre of the stage, has been discussed in the introduction. In these chapters, the approach allows a deeper examination of the narrative of rise and decline which part I has provided: the two case studies show that there is more than one such narrative, for while, of course, the Liberal women of Aberdare and Cardiff and their organizations had aims and ethos in common and much that they pursued together, the local contexts were different and perhaps increasingly diverging. Aberdare was the Welsh Nonconformist Liberal industrial town par excellence: enfranchised by the reform acts of 1867 and 1884, its political culture was shaped in that period by a middle class who recognized themselves in their MP Henry Richard's definition of the 'people of Wales'. It was part of a constituency returning the biggest Liberal majorities in the United Kingdom in the 1890s, but experiencing in the twentieth century the political changes which were to transform coalfield politics, with the rise of Labour. Cardiff was increasingly cosmopolitan, marginally Liberal and insecurely 'Welsh'. Those were the conditions in which Liberal women shaped their politics. The WLAs, and their histories, reflected those differences.

## The sources

Aberdare WLA was formed in the autumn and winter of 1891–2. At its peak in the middle of the decade the association had approximately six hundred members. In Wales, only Cardiff was then larger, though there were also some very large associations in Pembrokeshire; Aberdare's sister association, Merthyr Tydfil and District, was about half its size. Sixteen years later, the last committee meeting was recorded. There was an attempt to revive the association in support of a women's suffrage bill in 1907, and evidence of vestigial life after that, until a revival and reaffiliation to the WLF in 1910. Unlike many associations, Aberdare struggled on with a small membership, rising to thirty, through the First World War and into the new political terrain of the post-war period.[2] The main source for the history of its WLA is what appears to be a rare thing in Welsh political records, a continuous handwritten minute book covering the whole of the association's active life, from 1891 to 1903, with a number of entries on the attempted revival of 1907.

Assiduously compiled over sixteen years, the minute book includes the minutes of executive and general committee meetings, recorded by six different secretaries; newspaper accounts of public meetings and events organized by the WLA were collected and pasted into the book. Such a record contains material which allows us to speak about the self-representation of political women, to each other, and through their resolutions, letters, appeals and memoranda, to the political world. The minute book is a vivid illustration of the understanding of 'the local' as previously discussed: it reveals the networks of women's Liberal, reforming and suffrage politics covering the United Kingdom, and with international dimensions, to which local women belonged, while also showing that broad culture to be rooted in a local identity. Its pages record indignation at the treatment of women – by the criminal justice system, by Parliament, by the ancient universities, by the military and colonial powers. There are notes of exasperation at the behaviour of their MP, or at their own president's neglect of them; at such times the book's voice is not that of a docile servant of the Liberal party but of a collective with a strong sense of its place in the world, and the value of its contribution. While the press reports of public meetings, with their long lists of names, and reports of enthusiastic audiences, can create an impression of energy and momentum, the minutes, along with the attendance registers in the back of the book, also reveals the absence of most members of the committee from most committee meetings, showing that a small dedicated group kept things going.[3] This reflects the picture of WLAs around Wales in the 1890s seen in chapter 1: energy and zeal expressed in written reports, masking weaknesses which contribute to decline.

There are limits to the interpretations and conclusions which can be based on such a source. Typically, the discussions or debates which led to the adoption of resolutions were barely recorded, so a sense of collective identity was constructed, at least within the pages, at the cost of the silencing of dissenting voices. The tone and content of debates is very difficult to infer from the bare recording of resolutions and decisions, arrangements for future meetings and speakers and the catering for teas and suppers. The minute book, therefore, cannot stand alone, but needs to be set in the context of wider events, ideas and issues of the period. An important, though problematic, source for this wider context is the press of the day.

The question of the representation of political women in the newspaper press is complex. The press played a significant social and political role in nineteenth- and twentieth-century Wales, and sections of it had a symbiotic relationship with the Liberal party.[4] The owners, editors and journalists were activists, as were women of newspaper-publishing families, and the space allotted to women's politics, the importance attributed to them and the editorial stance on such question as women's enfranchisement and role in public life were shaped by the broader political context, which, of course, changed over time. The political organization of women in south Wales was welcomed by the Liberal press, particularly in the context of the coming general election of 1892 and of activity in the area by the Primrose League. 'Now shall it not any longer be said', the *Aberdare Times* declared, 'that the Primrose Dames are having it all their own way'.[5]

The dominant imagery in reports of this period was of women as workers and fighters in the cause of liberalism and temperance, and the coming election, with use of mock-military language of recruitment, enlistment and brigades. At the same time, a specifically 'womanly' role was constructed, with the understanding that, on welfare matters, '[t]he obligation and necessity of women's participation in political work are becoming more and more clearly realised'.[6] This appears to have been the more comfortable position from which to view women's activity, when satire and mockery, even by the supportive, could be dropped; women's presence in the public, male, world of elections and campaigns was most acceptable when understood in terms of difference, of distinctive, gender-specific contributions to the community good. Women themselves made increasing use of the press, submitting reports of their meetings, ensuring that the press were invited. Quite early on, Aberdare WLA discovered the penalty for excluding a male reporter from the women-only monthly public meetings: the result was a slightly flippant account of Maria Richards's very serious paper on 'The position of women in all ages', and a decision by the association to open the meetings to men.[7] Liberal women also made use of the letter columns and interviews, including those of the 'anonymous representative' variety, to put disputes over policy and tactics into the public domain (see chapter 2). Women were learning the essential dark art of modern politics, exploiting the interest of the press in novelty and conflict, though their control over the representations which resulted would have been limited.

### The social and political context

The Aberdare town and district is situated in the northern hinterland of Cardiff, at the head of one of the converging lines of valleys – Rhondda, Cynon and Taff – which made up the central coalfield. The town was the commercial centre for the series of iron and coal villages which by the 1880s had made 'a long urban sprawl' on the bank of the river Cynon.[8] A population of over 38,000 by 1891 continued to rise to a peak, just after the First World War, of 55,000.[9] It was an overwhelmingly working-class population in terms of numbers, but one in which nevertheless the middle class of clergy, shopkeepers, teachers, solicitors and others stamped its values on the town and organized itself politically at the earliest opportunity, in response to the 1867 Reform Act, to ensure the representation of those values in Parliament.[10] By coalfield standards, Aberdare was a town with a substantial commercial life, and 'a numerically significant, self-confident middle class', a class which was moreover growing proportionately in the expanding town after 1880.[11] Historians have noted a shared ethos of the middle and working classes of the town, in 'a rich Welsh-speaking culture based on the chapel and all its institutions'.[12]

The political counterpart of perceived cultural harmony was Lib–Labism; in the 1890s the constituency was to become the safest Liberal seat in the country. As in other parts of the coalfield, leading figures in the miners' union were also active in the Liberal party. This picture, of a 'superficially conciliatory Lib–Labism', cultural and political, has been called into question.[13] The 1890s were to see the beginning of the end of Liberal hegemony, and of Lib–Lab cooperation, with the creation of some struggling and short-lived socialist organizations, the increasingly militant politics of coal culminating in the strike of 1898, the jailing of some miners' leaders and the election of the first Independent Labour MP, James Keir Hardie, in 1900. The next decade saw the growth of the ILP to become 'a powerful force in local politics', but in parliamentary terms, Liberal dominance was maintained up to 1915.[14]

With regard to specifically feminist politics, before the 1890s evidence for support in Aberdare for women's suffrage is sparse. More is known about the support of men, middle and working class, for women's suffrage, than that of local women. Interestingly, in 1868, the year when the male Nonconformist electors of Aberdare and Merthyr had organized so effectively to ensure their representation by Henry Richard, one woman in the town seems to have succeeded in placing her name on the parliamentary electoral register.[15] She appears to have been the sole Welsh participant – or the only successful one – in a national campaign in which thousands of women attempted to exploit an uncertainty in the 1867 Reform Act, by placing their names on their local registers. In 1872, Aberdare's then MP, H. A. Bruce, was one of the opponents of women's suffrage in the House of Commons and, after losing his seat in 1869, as home secretary in Gladstone's government, was responsible for introducing a controversial bill to replace the Contagious Diseases Acts, which was opposed by the Ladies National Association (LNA) and the NVA. In the 1880s, however, both of the constituency's MPs, C. H. James and Henry Richard, were supporters of women's suffrage, and Mrs C. H. James was one of a number of Welsh 'dual activists' for women's suffrage and the repeal of the Contagious Diseases Acts. In 1884 Richard was one of seven Welsh MPs who put their names to a women's suffrage memorial to Gladstone. Later in the same year, a meeting of the Aberdare, Merthyr and Dowlais District Miners' Association called for the enfranchisement of women and supported a series of meetings by a suffrage speaker, Miss Jeanette G. Wilkinson.[16] So there appears to have been a basis of support for women's enfranchisement in the town and constituency, located in the body of opinion, radical Nonconformity, represented by Richard, and including male working-class support, even though that support as yet lacked organizational focus. It is perhaps indicative of the extent to which women were without representation in the town, as well as, perhaps, of the poverty of Liberal organization in the 1880s, that it was the Miners' Association that arranged the meetings for a visiting suffrage speaker.

The evidence suggests that interest in women's emancipation, rooted in the dissenting and reforming communities, had a social base in south Wales, which responded to the British movement, through organizational links and the stimulus of visiting speakers. There does not appear to have been any manifestation of a 'nationalist' or localist antipathy to imported ideas and itinerant propagandists, such as was to be evident in the militant period. On the contrary, the speakers were welcomed by the Liberal community, as representatives of shared values and common social and political goals. This was the context from which the Aberdare WLA emerged. The women who formed it recognized that women had an interest in politics, wanted to be active, but lacked 'a groove to work in'; the association aimed to provide that groove.[17]

### What women called liberalism

In March 1899, the committee of the Aberdare Women's Liberal Association (WLA) recorded the death of one of its founder members,

Ann Griffiths Jones.[18] Jones, forty-seven years old at her death, serves as an important representative of the values and ethos of the association, and of local liberalism. After her death she was presented as a distinctively Welsh type, when the cultural nationalist journal *Cymru* carried a long, eulogistic obituary, entitled 'One of the daughters of Wales'.[19] The obituarist devoted several column inches to her splendid Nonconformist pedigree, embodied in the patriarchal line of father, grandfathers and uncles who had contributed to the religious and cultural life of the nation and the town. Her life as the 'happy help-meet' of her husband, a prominent Unitarian clergyman, was described. So far, so predictable – a woman's life described in terms of the men to whom she was connected; but Mrs Jones was not so easily explained. His subject's public persona and active intellect both inspired and unsettled the obituarist, who wrestled with notions of womanliness, the public and domestic spheres, national progress and piety on the one hand, and social and political impatience on the other. Mrs Jones, he averred, was 'an all-round woman, a manly woman without being masculine . . . one of the most womanly women I ever met . . . a woman on the public platform as she was on her hearth at home'. In fact, Ann Jones burst irrepressibly out of the categories of wife and mother: she was a linguist, with Welsh, English, French and Latin at her disposal; a reader, a thinker and writer, publishing her first article on 'International arbitration' at the age of twenty-one. A teacher and a preacher, she taught in the Trecynon Seminary alongside her husband, as well as in Sunday School, and when her husband was unable to conduct services in the Old Meeting House she took his place. In the 1890s she began a career of clearly political public work, but long before this, according to her obituarist, 'Mrs Jones had seen that the tide of women's rights and duties had risen too high for her to ignore it'. In 1891, she 'found herself on the crest of the first wave' as a founder of the Aberdare WLA.[20] Mrs Jones was clearly remarkable in many respects, but she was not unique amongst the women who founded the WLA. Far from being confined to a domestic or private sphere, these were women who had helped to create the public culture of the town and its surrounding villages in the previous half of the century. In the WLA such women founded an arena of activity in which they were able to bring together Liberal ideas of rights and progress with the Nonconformist conscience and the familiar rhetoric of 'woman's mission', and above all an overriding sense of duty and responsibility to their 'sisters'. Thus, 'life in earnest', as the obituary described it, acquired a political purpose as the notions of rights and duties were brought together to create a model of citizenship which empowered women to demand a full share in the life of their communities and their nation.[21]

The history of the Aberdare WLA and its leading women provides a vivid example of these developments. It was also a relatively brief history: the timescale of development, growth and decline in the association corresponds to that for women's liberalism in Wales as a whole, described in part I. The stresses of the militant suffrage years can be seen at work in Aberdare; and the local circumstances, its position in the coalfield, in a town with a Labour movement which gained influence after 1900, make it possible to raise questions about the significance for women's politics of the transition from Liberal to Labour, not all of which questions can be answered within the scope of this book. The shift 'from Liberal to Labour' has been pre-eminently the framework within which the political history of Aberdare has been set.[22] The records of the WLA allow us to raise questions about the extent to which this provides a useful understanding of women's political history. At the very least they remind us that, despite the torpor of male Liberal organization in the town and constituency,[23] there was a functioning and active Liberal association in Aberdare for about ten years, provided by an earnest and energetic group of women.

Its formation took place in the context of heightened public and political activity by women throughout Wales. The local press had also reported on the creation in the town of a branch of the National Vigilance Association (NVA); on the activities of the Primrose League and on the annual meeting of the Cardiff branch of the Charity Organisation Society (COS). In addition to the association at Aberdare, branches at Mountain Ash, Merthyr, Cardiff, Swansea, Carmarthen, Tenby, Pontypridd, South Monmouthshire 'and a few other places' were reported.[24] The odd one out, in these reports, is the Primrose League, with its jolly evening of music-hall style entertainment, including a ventriloquist, a conjurer and dancing. All the other events can be linked to a characteristic strand of women's politics in the period 1880–1914, which had the aim of civilizing and purifying public life and culture, and represented political activity in the earnest language of morality and duty. The list of events indicates the extent to which, in so far as women were active in the public and social sphere, it was Liberal women who predominated. That presence of Liberal women was achieved through the wide, and closely interlinked, networks of organizations and pressure groups to which so many of them belonged. The NVA and the COS were two among many such organizations, which included the Women's Guardians Society (WGS), the Women's Local Government Society (WLGS), the British Women's Temperance Association (BWTA), the suffrage societies and the Women's Liberal Federation (WLF). The guest speaker at the launch of the Mountain Ash WLA, Laura Ormiston Chant, exemplified these political forms and their ethos. A prominent member of most of these organizations, she put enormous energy into her mission to purify the social and cultural spheres.[25] As a member of the executive of the WLF, she was a colleague of Nora Philipps, Eva McLaren, Sybil Thomas and Newport WLA president Evelyn Pelham. With McLaren, she shared membership – in some cases as a founder – of most of the other organizations. McLaren had also had her early training in public work with the COS. McLaren, Chant and Sybil Thomas were all members of the executive of the Central National Society for Women's Suffrage (CNSWS). As the names suggest, these networks involved elite, and often London-based, women,[26] but these reports in the south Wales press in 1891 and 1892 indicate that the networks were then increasing their penetration of British society. One of the things that united them, along with other organizations, was support for women's work in local government, where such matters as regulation and licensing of pubs and theatres, supervision of the poor, education of the working class and sanitary and housing reform could be achieved. Temperance and women's suffrage were to be the key to a new society; ultimately members of these organizations believed that, until women had the parliamentary vote, the transformation of society which they desired would never come about, but that, once women did have the vote, the world would be duly transformed. Hence, in the person of Laura Chant, the repressive social and sexual attitudes of the NVA were united with the radical aims of disestablishment and home rule, and with the progressive plan for the WLF. To what extent were these characteristics of women's politics at the end of the nineteenth century represented in the Aberdare WLA?

## Constructing political identities

The creation of the Aberdare WLA involved meetings in the town and in the industrial villages up and down the valley, from November

1891 to February 1892. The accounts show that, like the formation of the association, the construction of a collective political identity was a process rather than a 'given' inherent in the membership; that identity was to some extent expressed in the 'Rules and Objects' presented to the inaugural meeting. The inclusiveness of the opening statement of the rules, that the association would consist of 'Women of all classes', was entirely in keeping with Welsh liberalism of the period, with its still fairly safe assumption of the possibility of class harmony around national and Nonconformist aims. Whether it was more than a pious hope for the Aberdare WLA will be discussed below. The second section of the rules, which set out the association's political stall, contained a mixture of statements on Liberal principles, electoral work, the organization of the association and the political, social and educational advancement of women. Its opening statement, that 'The Objects of the Association shall be – (a) Quiet work for the Liberal Party', is redolent of the period:[27] 'quiet work' was a phrase designed to reassure those men and women who saw the incursion of women into politics as dangerous and improper. Such anxieties were acknowledged by speakers at the public meetings;[28] the promise to do 'quiet work' signalled that there was to be no shrill or competitive activity, that most of the work would be safely out of the public gaze and behind the scenes – in a word, ladylike.

Along with these reassurances, a discourse of duty – the 'double duty' of women – could also be mobilized to bring reluctant women into politics. The activities of Conservative and Unionist women in the Primrose League were cited as creating the unpleasant necessity for Liberal women to become active, and Ann Jones described herself being reluctantly dragged from her domestic retirement to combat the danger to the Liberal cause by a stern reminder of her selfless duty from her clergyman husband.[29] The close connection of Welsh liberalism with religion, with temperance and with the just cause of Irish Home Rule, and the identification of Gladstone with those principles, made it possible to invoke duty and morality in this way. For women, this provided a framework which, while acknowledging gender difference and the appropriate boundaries of male and female activity, nevertheless enabled them to cross those boundaries. Political work for women was far from new: it was almost a decade since the formation of the first WLAs and, throughout the 1880s, speakers on women's suffrage had increasingly toured the country, appearing on platforms often alongside local women. Yet the Aberdare women entered the local political arena preceded by disarming apologies and explanations, as though new ground were being broken. They clearly felt the need, as Eileen Yeo has suggested,[30] repeatedly to acknowledge the boundaries, even as they stepped over them. This exemplifies one of the contradictions in the history of women in nineteenth-century Britain, where an increasing presence of women in public life was paralleled by persistent use of the language of separate spheres, by both women and men. The language acknowledged that, while women appeared in the public sphere, they did so on different terms to men. However, the language employed in this case is also amenable to a more empirical explanation: in this period party organization was reaching wider and deeper into provincial community life, and especially into the lives of many more women, than it had done before. For some of the women now being mobilized, this was, indeed, new ground.

If the Aberdare Liberal women were as yet rather tentative in their aims, others had plans for them. For the party and its MPs, this was an attempt at a much greater mobilization of constituency workers. As far as the WLF progressives were concerned, it was a strategy to create votes in favour of women's suffrage at the annual council. This may have been a risky strategy. There is nothing in the tentative appearance on the public stage of Ann Jones and her colleagues to suggest they could safely be counted on to vote with, rather than against, the progressives; they offered a modest vision of their role, both in their meetings and in their rules and objects. The intention, expressed in the rules, to support 'equal justice and political rights for all sections of the community', was broad enough to accommodate almost all positions on franchise reform. The statement on women's work on elected local bodies, and on women as local government voters, was perfectly compatible with the position taken by, for example, the signatories to the 1889 'Appeal against Female Suffrage', in which local government work was presented as offering women the fullest desirable measure of active citizenship.[31] However, the association was drawn safely inside the suffrage tent at the inaugural meeting, in the Temperance Hall on 4 February 1892, in time for the formation of the WUWLA at Aberystwyth at the end of March and the WLF Annual Council in London in mid-May.

The formation of the Aberdare association was part of the efficiently executed campaign by suffragists during 1891–2 to create a power base in the WLF, discussed in part I. Since the WLF was a democratic organization, it was the votes of delegates from the associations which would provide that base. It was crucial, therefore, that individual associations should be committed to the progressive agenda, and, in achieving this, the meetings which launched the associations were crucial. The inaugural meeting of the Aberdare association was representative of this process. This was the moment when the association, after a series of district meetings in the villages up and down the valley, presented itself to the public of the town. It was an occasion which appears to have been professionally reported, rather than relying on a secretary's summary, and the effect of the language and the length of the report is to construct the evening as groundbreaking but unthreatening, a wholly welcome development. The speakers reported at greatest length will have been those judged most interesting or important by the editors. Beyond that, it must be safe to assume that the association committee will have put some thought and effort into creating an event which would be impressive, soundly based in ideas, values and an ethos with which people could identify and which would attract members. While the lists of names in the report were headed by the political leaders and visiting speakers, the platform was freighted with local men and women who represented the core of Nonconformist liberalism and Lib–Labism in the town. There were speeches from women and men, in English and in Welsh. But the meeting had also to move beyond the local and the familiarly Liberal. Beginning with the resolution of support for Gladstone, it was to end on a triumphal note of support for women's suffrage, expertly delivered by Nora Philipps.

Philipps was considerably more radical in her address than Aberdare had heard before, paying scant attention to pieties about 'womanhood' in a speech which challenged the notion of separate spheres in politics, in morality and in family life. In an expansive vision of women's place in politics, Philipps ranged widely, drawing in employment law, cruelty to children, Home Rule for Ireland, local politics and temperance, qualifications of voters and industrial conditions for working women to depict a society in need of women's intervention in the defeat of power and privilege and defence of the powerless. The resolution she put to the meeting supported the enfranchisement of women in the usual terms – 'as it is or may be granted to men'. More important, it resolved to 'support the progressive suffrage party in the various Liberal Federations'. Progressive speakers toured the WLAs again a couple of months later, and in

Aberdare the speaker was then supported on the platform by no fewer than four Nonconformist ministers.[32] As at Cardiff in 1881, local radical respectability was represented, supporting the women as they moved into the public political sphere.

At the beginning of 1892, then, the AWLA was, according to its rules and objects, committed to a liberalism which was expressed in terms of principles ('Absolute religious equality') rather than programme. It had set itself a number of tasks in relation to women's welfare and political education and participation and representation at the local level. It was loyal to Gladstone and the party he led. It had also, however, in its committees and public meetings, committed itself to working for women's suffrage. The association maintained this commitment during the 1890s, through public and membership meetings, petitions, memorials, letters and resolutions to MPs and ministers and by questioning election candidates.[33] Despite such activity, the terms in which the association claimed the vote were cautious, a retreat from the larger vision of Nora Philipps. The idea of women's 'double duty' remained a useful one for local speakers. Women, they said, could be 'better wives and better women' through an understanding of politics, placing the emphasis on women's work, capabilities and duties in the public sphere, rather than their rights. Active citizenship could be understood as a Christian as well as a womanly duty, an essentially conservative and religious view of the nature and role of women utilized to propose radical change.[34]

While it had allied itself from the beginning with the progressives in the WLF, the association distinguished between national and local tactics in support of women's suffrage. This need not be read as a simple desire to maintain an auxiliary and supportive role towards the local party and MP. In June 1892, the committee decided that the association should not affiliate to the CNSWS, 'this year'. This may have been because of the expense involved, or for political reasons, or in the fear that direct connection with the suffrage movement might undermine broad local support, which was then being created. Many associations did affiliate to the society, a demonstration of the belief that the enfranchisement of women was an essentially Liberal reform, a belief which was certainly shared by the Aberdare committee.[35] In February 1900, the association supported a proposal by the Union of Practical Suffragists (UPS) that the WLF executive should withhold election help from candidates who did not support women's suffrage.[36] This resolution (eventually adopted by the WLF in 1902, as the

'Cambridge Resolution') still left local associations free to make their own decisions, and so was potentially less divisive, but nevertheless would withhold from candidates the help of the experienced organizers employed by the federation.[37] Aberdare remained reluctant to adopt the 'test question' tactic in the constituency, though evidence of the minutes suggests that discussion on this point was sometimes at least lively; however, the committee remained unanimously supportive of the Cambridge Resolution, which was threatened with a challenge at the 1903 Annual Council, and instructed their delegate, Sybil Thomas, to vote accordingly.[38] There was consistency, and political sense, in these apparent contradictions: the Aberdare women supported the application of the 'test question' principle as far as official WLF help to candidates was concerned, but at a local level, they wished to keep their own options open, to allow freedom to individual members and maintain a broad base of support. From 1900, both the MPs for the constituency, D. A. Thomas and James Keir Hardie, were supporters of women's suffrage. Hardie, whose name appears nowhere in the deliberations of the association, was one of the staunchest supporter of women's suffrage in the Labour Party and in Parliament. But the Liberals had hopes of regaining the second seat from Labour, and no doubt at least some of the WLA membership would wish to be free to work for the election of whomever the party selected; to forbid them to do so might risk losing more of the dwindling membership. It is entirely possible that some of the 600 women who formed the membership in the mid-1890s were now among the ILP and Labour women who canvassed, leafleted and organized meetings in support of Hardie during the 1900 election.[39]

Support for the suffrage movement was not the only political and social aim of the Aberdare WLA. They supported the aims of Welsh Nonconformist liberalism, the programme set for the Liberal party by Gladstone and the Newcastle Programme of the 1891 National Liberal Federation (NLF) conference. The conference had committed the party to a wide range of reforms, including free elementary education, Welsh and Scottish disestablishment, a 'direct popular veto' on the drink trade, the creation of parish councils, home rule all round, free trade and reform of the franchise and the House of Lords.[40] This translated into a set of objectives which featured again and again, in the minute book of the AWLA, in the form of petitions, memorials, resolutions for WLF and WUWLA annual conferences, and in the speeches, by local women and visiting speakers, at the many public meetings large and small which the association mounted in the district.[41] Of all these issues, apart from women's suffrage, it was perhaps temperance reform, in various guises, about which Liberal women felt most passionately. In the late nineteenth century 'temperance work had become almost endemic among the Nonconformist middle classes'.[42] For Liberal women, the distinctiveness of their temperance campaigning was in its connection with the cause of women's suffrage, and sometimes women spoke as though they wanted the parliamentary vote chiefly as a means to temperance legislation.[43] Amongst the national leadership and the local grass roots, the major temperance organizations shared common membership with the WLF and the WLAs. The British Women's Temperance Association (BWTA) had many active members in south Wales, including leading members of the Aberdare WLA, as did other major temperance organizations.[44] Liberal women were urged to use their local government votes to ensure that the publicans and brewers and their supporters were kept off boards of guardians and local boards of health. Temperance, they believed, was 'above all a women's question, as women suffered most in consequence of intemperance', which was seen as the cause of numerous social ills, including poverty and domestic violence.[45] Temperance provided the link between Welsh Nonconformist liberalism and late nineteenth-century feminism and, allied as it often was with a broad social purity agenda, it created support within the Nonconformist communities for women's role in public life and for their enfranchisement. The shared culture can be seen in the similarly worded letters from the Aberdare WLA, Aberdare BWTA and the Dowlais Primitive Methodist Society to their MPs, protesting at the regulation of prostitution in India for the benefit of British troops, as 'immoral, cruel and degrading'.[46]

As the Aberdare minutes show, a temperance and social purity agenda was allied with a sense of duty towards other women, especially those who were seen as vulnerable in the male-dominated worlds of work, the criminal justice system and medicine. Like women reformers throughout Britain, the Aberdare WLA believed that women could best look after women, and that it was more appropriate that they did so. Thus they supported the employment of women as inspectors of lunatic asylums and factories, as police court 'matrons' and as sanitary inspectors. They also wanted to open up these and all fields of public and professional work to women. When it came to economic activity, protective instincts towards their own sex gave way to egalitarianism which resisted protective legislation on conditions and hours of work which did not apply to both men and women workers. Improvements in the hours and conditions of shop-workers, promoted by the trade unions, were supported since they applied equally to both sexes. They supported 'Equal Work, Equal Pay'. The equal rights approach extended to women's right to recognition in higher education, and to the equalization of the divorce laws, the latter also being part of the attack on the double standard of sexual morality which had been a feature of British feminism since the anti-Contagious Diseases Acts campaigns.[47] These welfare, economic and social purity issues had additional significance in the context of the class position of Liberal women, and their identification with imperial Britain, which is further discussed below.

If they shared this familiar woman-centred agenda with Liberal women all over Britain, the Aberdare WLA, like the majority of associations in Wales, shared with male Liberals an interest in specifically Welsh causes, above all in disestablishment. From 1892, resolutions on disestablishment were sent annually to the WLF Council. Other international issues arose from time to time which united female and male Liberals. The association took the initiative in organizing meetings, bringing in visiting speakers and collecting relief funds in support of persecuted Armenian Christians under Turkish rule in the 1890s.[48] During the period of Conservative government from 1895 to 1905, attempts, finally successful in 1902, to introduce an Education Bill which would provide for the funding of faith schools out of the rates, united Nonconformist Liberals and led to the 'Welsh revolt' of 1902–5, when some local authorities refused to implement the act.[49] Again, the WLA appears to have taken the initiative in organizing local meetings on the subject. The divisions amongst Welsh Liberals over the South African War have been discussed; the town was subject to those tensions, particularly around election time.[50] Aberdare WLA, or at any rate its committee, shared the WLF's opposition to the government's prosecution of the war and ventured to organize a meeting, with a visiting speaker on 'Chamberlain and His Policy'. Originally planned for the Temperance Hall, advertised in three local papers, and with 500 handbills and 250 WLF leaflets on 'the war question', in the event, the meeting on 8 February 1900 was, perhaps because of fear of disruption, a cautious and low-key affair, an essentially 'private' meeting, in the reading room of the Liberal Club, with no resolutions reported as being passed.[51]

It is difficult to know to what extent Aberdare women participated in the many regional meetings and conferences which led to the formation of the WNLF (Cymru Fydd), since the press only sometimes reported the presence of women.[52] In October 1894, Maria Richards took part in a meeting at Hirwaun to inaugurate a branch of Cymru Fydd, at which she was reported as making 'a spirited defence of the new Forward Movement among women'.[53] But during the whole period of the formation and demise of Cymru Fydd, no discussion of the organization, or of the WLA's relationship to it, took place in the meetings of the association, or in any of the public meetings organized by it. This is in contrast to the creation, two years after the failure of Cymru Fydd, of the Welsh National Liberal Council (WNLC), which was roundly welcomed by the Aberdare women. Maria Richards's resolution to a public meeting in February of that year particularly welcomed the recognition for women's contribution to liberalism in Wales which the WNLC constitution provided.[54] Maria Richards was to be one of a few long-serving WUWLA representatives on the WNLC executive.

## Local government

Until 1894, no women had won election to any of Aberdare's local government bodies, and the WLA had only limited success in its objective of increasing women's participation. There were opportunities for work by women on local bodies which did not depend on election: Mary Lloyd recommended the satisfactions of poor law visiting,[55] while both she and Ann Jones had their turn as Liberal representatives as school governors, later also joined by Labour women. Despite their eligibility from 1894, there were no women candidates for the new urban district or parish councils: the first woman district councillor in the town was elected in 1920.[56] Nor were school boards fertile ground for women in Aberdare: there appears never to have been a woman on the local board during its whole existence from 1870 to 1903. It is not immediately obvious why the 'representativeness' with which women might be endowed in the context of the new parish councils could not carry over to school board work; or why, on the other hand, the strong arguments based on gender difference which helped them into poor law work were less useful for education. More research into local electoral politics is needed to answer these questions, but it may have something to do with the hierarchy of political importance of local government bodies, and the gendered nature of status. Hollis suggests that while there were more seats to go round on boards of guardians, they were also of lower status compared to school board work, which was a part of the male political career structure. In the case of Aberdare, it has been suggested that the school board elections were increasingly important sites of contest between different class and sectional interests.[57]

In the 1894 elections for the Merthyr Board of Guardians, which included Aberdare, the WLAs in both towns were keen to nominate and support women as candidates.[58] In Aberdare, the names of seven women were proposed as nominees of the association, but most declined to stand, including women like Mary Lloyd, who were not otherwise afraid to take on public work. It may have been that the electoral contest, and the public scrutiny involved, were unattractive or intimidating to some women. In the event, the WLA sponsored three candidates, and staged some large public meetings, with visiting speakers; arguments in support of women's fitness for the work were aired and the candidates made brief electioneering speeches in a supportive setting.[59] The outcome was that Maria Richards topped the poll in Gadlys ward, Mrs J. A. (Margaret) Williams, a school mistress, was returned third in the poll in Aberaman, while Mrs Miles, their candidate for the Town ward, was unsuccessful. In Merthyr, too, two of three women candidates were successful. The successful running of two candidates was a matter of great satisfaction to the Aberdare association. They could now feel, said Ann Jones, 'that their work had not been in vain'. She added that she 'hoped the two Guardians would act in a ladylike manner', reflecting residual anxiety, despite the celebration, about the impact on femininity of a competitive and abrasive local politics.[60]

The return of so many new women guardians throughout Wales in December 1894, the majority of them Liberals, was seen as a historic breakthrough, and Maria Richards was one of a number of the new guardians who wrote brief but revealing accounts of their view of the work in the journal *Young Wales*. The accounts are full of confidence and a sense of the possibilities of the role the writers were taking on. Generally, they saw their work in the conventional way, as 'domesticity enlarged and enlightened', envisaging the transformation of the chaotic world of pauperism, under women's influence, into something resembling a well-ordered middle-class household where everyone knew their place and behaved well, sure of the warm but unsentimental care of a good woman. They were convinced that they had a responsibility for the moral development particularly of children and young women. While caring and domesticity were dominant themes, they also used the classic Liberal language of retrenchment and reform, while gender solidarity was muted by consciousness of class difference.[61]

We know very little about how women in Wales fared on the boards, whether they were able to undertake the whole range of committee work or whether they suffered the hostility of male board members which Hollis has shown was the fate of many on the English boards.[62] The number of women on the board ranged from four in 1894 to seven in 1913; despite these miserable numbers, the board remained women's best hope of elected office for some decades. As far as education was concerned, in towns like Aberdare, women were better represented when, with no right of election, they were coopted to the LEAs after 1902, when each party nominated one woman representative.

### *'Women of all classes'? Social and political identity in the Aberdare WLA*

This section will explore the social characteristics of the association, as far as sources permit, and its position on class-related issues. After 1900, despite the continuing support for D. A. Thomas from the working-class voters of Aberdare, it seems unlikely that the Aberdare WLA could wholeheartedly claim to represent 'women of all classes'.[63] In the absence of membership lists, it is difficult to know whether, and to what extent, the claim had ever been true. The names of more than sixty local women can be identified in connection with the association, as members of the executive and general committees, as correspondents, or as speakers and performers in public meetings and entertainments. That number is approximately one-tenth of the peak membership in the mid-1890s. The submerged nine-tenths is a reminder of how fragmentary is the evidence for the political identities of women in nineteenth-century Wales.

To some extent, the claim to represent all classes can be tested by the extent to which working-class women were able to take leadership positions in the association. It was and is frequently asserted that working-class women in mining areas had their work cut out for them in managing a home and family.[64] If so, absence of active involvement need not be read as lack of support for an organization, or lack of interest in politics. However, the tenor of any organization was likely to be determined by its most active or dominant group. The association might also claim to represent women of all classes through its position on issues affecting working women and working-class women.

Analyses of class in nineteenth-century mining communities have mainly been concerned with areas of male domination, work and party politics. Women have occasionally, very briefly, featured in the histories of Aberdare politics, when their gender and their marital status rather than their class has been seen to shape the nature of their involvement. Indeed, the political and social spheres have been presented as a kind of marriage, in which women held a complementary conception of the roles of themselves and their menfolk, seeing themselves, in the case of Liberal women, 'as responsible for the social welfare of the general population while their husbands governed political life', or, for Labour women, seeing their function as servicing the male organizations.[65] The evidence does not suggest that Aberdare Liberal women accepted this gender symmetry in local or national politics; on the contrary, they claimed the political as well as the social spheres for their own, as the range of issues addressed in the minute book demonstrates. Conversely, despite the rhetoric of separate spheres, men had not surrendered their control of 'the social' to women, as the discussion of local government has demonstrated.

However, liberalism (and politics more generally) in Wales at the end of the nineteenth century was a family business. It is difficult to know how far apparent unity of political aims in the public sphere reflected real political as well as conjugal partnerships; or how far spousal or family duty – especially at leadership level – placed women at the head of local WLAs, or on the public platform. The assumption is that this kind of duty operated on wives rather than husbands, perhaps a fair enough assumption when elections and male careers were at stake; but the level of activity pursued by many women in the rich associational culture of the late Victorian period demanded a great deal of support from husbands in return.

In Liberal constituencies, the wife of the MP usually took on the role of WLA president, as did Sybil Thomas, wife of the senior member for Merthyr and Aberdare. The elevated social standing of the president did not reflect that of either the association or its committees, though the local women might have found the social confidence and entrée of their president useful on the national stage. The role of the president was not to attend every committee, but to represent the association at the national meetings of the WLF and the WUWLA; to preside over the annual meeting and other major public events, particularly when there were guest speakers or important resolutions on the agenda; and to dip fairly frequently into her private purse to subsidize association activities. All of these, as the records show, were included in Sybil Thomas's work for Aberdare, and were one part of a bargain between the association, the MP and the MP's wife, another side of which was electoral work by the association. The association could expect to see rather more of their president, and their MP, when an election was in the offing, and the work of the WLA for the candidate needed to be secured, but her attention could be harder to get at other times: in April 1897, the committee instructed the secretary to write 'a strong worded letter' to Thomas, requesting her attendance at the annual meeting. However, they loyally re-elected her each year, and supported her presidency of the WUWLA (though they would have preferred Nora Philipps to stay on) and for the executive of the WLF.[66]

A small, dedicated core kept the Aberdare association going. From the beginning, of some thirty-two women who were listed as committee members, seven or eight could be described as regular attenders at meetings, and this continued to be the case.[67] The committees, and in particular this active core, were dominated by the religious, educational and commercial leadership of Aberdare, the middle and lower middle class of white-collar workers, Nonconformist ministers, teachers, journalists, solicitors and, of course, shopkeepers. The majority of members of the executive committee belonged to these social groups, but such an identification fails to convey the extent to which many of these women were woven into the Nonconformist history of the town, were shapers of its culture and were connected to each other in this milieu, independently of, and pre-dating the formation of the WLA. Three figures can be taken as representative: Mrs Mary Smith (Walter) Lloyd, Mrs Ann Griffiths (R. J.) Jones, and Mrs Maria (D. M.) Richards.

Mrs Jones's character has already been discussed at the beginning of this chapter. Like her, Mary Lloyd also belonged to the group of small cultural entrepreneurs, businessmen and ministers, who had done so much to create a civic life in Aberdare over the previous half-century or so. Her husband had been one of the group of local businessmen and ministers who composed the Nonconformist Election Committee of 1867 which persuaded Henry Richard to represent the constituency.[68] A Scot by birth, Mary Lloyd appears to have arrived in Aberdare in the 1850s as a missionary for the Tract Distribution Society. After her husband's death in 1883, Lloyd carried on the family printing and publishing business at *Y Gwladgarwr* (The Patriot) offices, with her adult children. In the 1890s, she involved herself in Liberal and temperance politics with gusto, as a vice-president of the WLA and as founding president of the local branch of the BWTA, a position she held for eighteen years.

Maria Richards was undoubtedly one of the most dominant figures in the WLA and, like Mary Lloyd, a force in the life of the town over a long period. She exemplified the first generation of 'public women', produced by the Liberal women's movement, who blazed a trail (though they might have preferred not to) for the socialist and Labour movement women who replaced them in the twentieth century. Her family was active in politics: her husband, David M. Richards, was a journalist, a local historian and acted as agent or secretary for a number of societies and associations in the town, including D. A. Thomas and the ILP.[69] Richards's Welsh cultural and linguistic identity was important to her: she and her husband completed their 1891 census return in Welsh. As with other women profiled here, Nonconformist and temperance principles formed the continuous core of her life, and her political work grew from that.[70]

These women, and most of the other committee members and correspondents were clearly members of the religious, political, cultural and commercial leadership of the town, as it had shaped itself since the middle of the century.[71] It is perhaps significant that the most socially exalted local woman invited to join the committee declined.[72] However, at the other end of the social spectrum, working-class women appear to have had a fragile tenure on the committees. Four women listed as early committee members were working to support themselves, but they included Mrs Lloyd as head of the family printing firm, her daughter Bella and Mrs Margaret Moses, the widowed mother of five children who had a grocery business. This was to change in the Edwardian period, when young career teachers took leadership roles. One of the few named women clearly identifiable as working class in the early days was Mary Edmunds, the correspondent for Trecynon, a dressmaker who lived with her family of three collier brothers and two younger sisters who were both 'servants'. Mining families were also represented in the early committees by Ruth Morgan, wife of the miners' agent and prominent Lib–Lab figure David Morgan, who had her five daughters and two sons, miners, dressmakers, milliners and servants, living at home; and Anne Davies, wife of Henry Davies, checkweigher and Lib–Lab activist, a vice-president of the Aberdare Liberal Association and a member of the executive of the South Wales and Monmouthshire Colliery Workmen's Federation. Mrs Davies died in 1892, just thirty-four years old. Ruth Morgan died in December 1899, her death being understood to have been caused by the strain of her husband's imprisonment for his role in the 1898 strike and lockout.[73]

The minimum annual subscription of 1*d*. had signalled the intention of the Aberdare WLA to make membership accessible to any woman who wanted it. In addition, there was clearly an understanding that the audience at public meetings included the wives of miners and colliery workers, and women who were used to heavy domestic work (though this would be true of most women at this time as, apart from the draper's establishment, of thirteen households of committee members identified in the 1891 census, just four had one domestic servant living in).[74] As the peak membership of about six hundred was reached in the mid-1890s, there must have been a number of working-class women among the membership. And, while the consistently active membership may have been small, there appears to have been an attempt by the founders to give the association a broad social base, through invitations to join the committees, or to act as village correspondents. However, it seems clear that, despite the good intentions of the founders of the WLA, its committees were far from embodying 'all classes' in any effective way. The presence of a young working woman like Mary Edmunds indicated that for any woman interested in reform politics in the early 1890s the WLA was the only resort, and was to remain so for more than a decade; but it remained dominated by the social group – in many cases by the same individuals – who had emerged as the religious and civic leaders of the district in the 1850s and 1860s. Could the members of this group surmount their social identity to develop a politics relevant to the working-class women of Aberdare?

On issues of class, and in their economic beliefs, the Liberal women of Aberdare expressed positions comparable to those of Liberal feminist women throughout Britain. There was an assumption that all women shared the same inequalities and oppressions, and that all sought the same remedies. In the area of paid work, for example, it was believed that what all women needed was greater and equal access to waged work, which led the Aberdare WLA to oppose all protective/ restrictive legislation on hours and conditions of work which did not apply equally to both sexes,[75] an individualist orthodoxy increasingly questioned by organizations like the Women's Co-operative Guild (WCG), and the Women's Trade Union League (WTUL).[76] This had some relevance locally for the small number of women who still worked sorting coal at the pithead, whose occupation had been the target of a determined attempt at abolition in the 1880s, headed by miners and coalfield MPs including Henry Richard.[77] The proportion of women in paid work in Aberdare by 1911 was high in comparison to other coalfield areas – 18.9 per cent, compared to just 14.4 per cent in Rhondda. The workers at the pithead and the brickyards, who tended to be portrayed by artists and photographers in search of the exotic, occupied just 0.2 per cent of working women locally, a proportion which declined over the next two decades.

Far more important was the growing 'professional' category, mainly made up of teachers. As recent analysis of this category has shown, the professional status of many women teachers, themselves low paid and with minimal qualifications or career prospects, is questionable.[78] In class terms, too, their position was ambiguous:[79] the pupil-teacher route provided a way in which working-class children could escape the labouring jobs, or the more traditional domestic service and needlework, or the years at home as mother's helper, which were the lot of so many, but this did not necessarily provide middle-class income, status or lifestyle. The WLA's support for 'equal pay for equal work' would have appealed to the growing number of women teachers in Aberdare, and the record shows that a number of them found a home in the WLA in the 1890s, just as they were to do in the Labour movement in the 1900s.

However, the association had less to say for the major employment groups for women, the highly segregated domestic service and dress, which accounted for two-thirds of the town's wage-earning women. Nor is there any evidence of the association's addressing itself specifically to local working conditions for women. Above all, they had nothing to say about conditions for working-class families, wives and mothers, either locally or more widely. There is no sign, for example, of any interest in housing conditions and tenancy issues, which came to the fore of local politics about the turn of the century.[80] The WLF joined the campaign for the regulation of midwifery which resulted in legislation in 1902, but nothing of this makes its way into the minutes or public meetings at Aberdare, despite continuing high infant mortality rates in the poor and overcrowded local housing. One can only speculate on the reasons for silence on such issues. It is possible that the temperance and religious perspective of many of the leading women encouraged them to view social problems as arising from personal weakness and 'sin'. In addition, the Liberal approach to 'retrenchment and reform', and economy in spending, may well have seen any moves towards municipal spending on behalf of the working class – as in a housing programme, for example – as too socialistic. The influential Maria Richards was described as having 'a healthy contempt for Socialism as preached and practised by many in the town', which was shared by the Nonconformist clergy, increasingly concerned, as their hold over sections of the population weakened, with temperance, sabbatarianism and 'godless socialism'.[81] Such a world view militated against any inclination towards New Liberal ameliorative perspectives.

## Twentieth-century change

The Aberdare records reflect the difficulties experienced by women's Liberal organizations in the changed political environment at the end of the century, discussed in part I. Indicative was the failure of attempts, over a number of years, to bring the annual meetings of the Welsh Union to Aberdare.[82] It was not a reflection on the association, or on women's commitment more widely, that the meetings had to be cancelled when a general election was called for the autumn of 1900.[83] However, the weakness of women's liberalism in Wales was now suggested by the difficulty encountered in attempting to reconvene the meetings.

The collapse in membership and activity of the Aberdare association took place against the background of the growth of Labour and socialist organization in the constituency, particularly following Hardie's 1900 election success. This is not the place to attempt a history of Labour women in Aberdare. What is relevant, however, is to try to assess how the political conditions for women were changed by the gradual and faltering appearance of other kinds of politics, and other possibilities for activism. What did the rise of Labour politics in the constituency mean for the Aberdare WLA?

There appears to be no evidence of any women's names associated with the short-lived socialist groups, often affiliated to the ILP, formed in the Aberdare valley in the 1890s and early 1900s. There are signs of activism among women in support of Hardie during the 1900 election,[84] but there are no signs that the ranks of the ILP in Aberdare were swollen by an influx of former Liberal women. The Aberdare Valley ILP was reorganized in December 1905, gaining strength over the next few years. No women were listed in the only surviving subscription lists, for 1906–7 but, after the formation of the twenty-strong women's branch in 1908, three women joined the twelve men on the executive committee.[85] Other labour movement organizations for women emerged in these years, including the Women's Co-operative Guild and the Railway Women's Guild.[86] It is not known whether Social Democratic Federation (SDF) activity in the area involved any women.[87] A branch of the Women's Labour League was formed in Aberdare in 1917, in time for the post-war reconstitution of the Labour party, when the league branches were the basis for the creation of Labour party women's sections.

Three areas of activity may have brought Liberal and Labour women into contact, competition and, sometimes perhaps, cooperation with each other. They were membership of local government bodies, electoral organization and the suffrage movement. In each of those areas, and particularly the first two, the present state of historical knowledge is such that it is only possible to suggest areas which would benefit from further research. This is especially the case in the area of local government. The clean sweep of local government in the area made by the Labour movement in the years just before and after the First World War was not accompanied by the opening up of careers for any but one or two women, as during the period of Liberal dominance. Rose Davies, secretary of the ILP women's branch, was co-opted onto the education committee in 1909, was a candidate for the council in 1919 and eventually won a seat in 1920.[88] Did the old Liberal feminist desire to see women progress in public life extend to welcoming socialist women to share the work? That kind of sisterhood was perhaps easier to encompass when the other party was not snapping closely at the heels of one's own. However, in the area of suffrage activity, there are clear signs that Liberal and Labour women, and constitutional and militant suffragists, were able to find some common cause locally.

### Liberal and Labour suffragists in the age of militancy

Aberdare WLA's constant support for women's suffrage since their inauguration had reflected their belief that their enfranchisement would simply constitute 'the application of Liberal principles to womanhood'.[89] Much of the suffrage activity in Aberdare in the period 1906–1912, however, marked the deteriorating relationship between the Liberal party and suffragists, while also indicating that young Labour party women were beginning to bring feminism and socialism together in their political lives. There were also signs that the anti-suffrage movement, achieving a degree of organization in this period, may have had a local presence.[90]

The most active suffragists among Liberal women had begun to feel that they needed to concentrate more fully on their own enfranchisement, even if at the expense of the party. Something of this spirit, and the prospect of another women's suffrage bill in March 1907, appears to have led to the attempt to revive the Aberdare WLA. The association had hoped to have its revival meeting the evening before the second reading of the bill on 8 March, but were unable to get their speaker, Alyson Garland, until 11 March, by which time the bill had been talked out.[91] The disappointment of the meeting, in Carmel Hall, was evident. Three of the longest-serving members of the WLA, Maria Richards, Mary Lloyd and Mrs Miles, reminded the meeting that the association 'had been working quietly' for all that time, and that they 'were still as zealous, if not as active as ever'. But a revival of the association appears to have been a vain hope, at least for a few more years.[92]

Not much is known about the activities of the Liberal suffragists of Aberdare between the 1907 meeting and their 1910 revival. That revival came in a period of a rapid deterioration in relations between suffragists and the government, and between women Liberals and the party, as it became clear that the enfranchisement of women was not a priority for the government. It was claimed that women were abandoning Liberal work 'in shoals'; it has been estimated that from 1911 to 1914, sixty-eight local WLAs and some 18,000 members were lost, attributable to the 'demoralization' of Liberal women, and forming 'a major reason for the party's protracted decline during the post-war period'.[93]

The change in Liberal attitudes to the suffrage question, in response to the heat engendered by militancy, can be seen in November 1909, in the reception Aberdare gave to D. A. Thomas's daughter, Margaret Mackworth (Margaret Haig Thomas, later Viscountess Rhondda), secretary of the Newport WSPU, and her guest, WSPU organizer Annie Kenney. Mackworth had been invited to speak at the Aberdare Liberal Club but the invitation was withdrawn, as was the advertised chairman for the meeting, when it became clear that Kenney would also speak. The meeting was instead held in a public hall, and the chair taken by Maria Richards. It proved beyond her skills to keep order in what rapidly became, in the words of the *Aberdare Leader* editorial, a 'hooligan carnival', with a distinct threat of violence, and the speakers were forced to flee. Liberal Club members and male letter-writers to the *Leader* expressed, in the main, satisfaction with the events of the evening; their feeling was that the suffragettes had got a taste of their own medicine.

It was indicative of the unshaken support for women's suffrage of the old members of the WLA that Maria Richards stepped in to chair the meeting at the Memorial Hall, despite the fact that she would certainly have disapproved of escalating militancy, and of the attacks on the Liberal government which were now WSPU policy.[94] This was a gulf of difference between Liberal women and men: Liberal men, for the most part, may have supported the enfranchisement of women in a general sense, but failed to comprehend how much Liberal women suffragists wanted the reform. These divisions were exacerbated in the autumn of 1910: as Lloyd George led the crusade against the power of the House of Lords, he alienated suffragists by reiterating his opposition to the Conciliation Bill, and by his dusty answers to constituency women at his home in Cricieth.[95] To add insult to injury, the chancellor decreed that no women were to be admitted to the annual convention of the WNLC, to be held that year in Mountain Ash, in the Aberdare district. A number of women, including Maria Richards, were members of the WNLC council, and women on the Hospitality Committee were vital to the arrangements for the meeting. 'A number of resignations' from women followed, and the Hospitality Committee rather timidly requested of the chancellor that women who were hosting delegates might be admitted.[96] In this context, the old Aberdare Liberal suffragists took part in the national meeting of Welsh women Liberals convened in Cardiff in November, the first resolution to the conference being put by Mary Lloyd, as an impeccable representative of Nonconformist Liberal suffragism. The conference, as discussed in the following chapters, went on to carry with near unanimity a resolution that Liberal women would abandon election work in favour of suffrage campaigning, supporting only Liberals who supported the bill and refraining from opposing candidates of other parties who supported it.

However, if those events mark the alienation of women from liberalism, clearly some women still had some faith in party as a vehicle for their enfranchisement. Before the end of that month, in anticipation of the January 1910 election, a new Aberdare WLA had affiliated to the WLF, with forty-five members, soon to be reduced to fewer than thirty.[97] The new WLA was probably the same organization as the 'women's section' of the newly formed branch of the League of Young Liberals, which was attempting to ginger up Liberal organization, with branches forming throughout south Wales.[98] The league appeared to be to the fore in anti-suffrage disruption at this time, and only in Aberdare and Hirwaun was any involvement of women reported. Even before the inaugural meeting of the branch, in February 1911, the women's section had met to pass resolutions in support of women's suffrage and to appeal for the support of the candidates for the Conciliation Bill in the forthcoming election.[99] In the following March, the section organized a public meeting addressed by Lady Laura McLaren on the subject of the Women's Charter.[100] The well-attended meeting heard the arguments McLaren would put to the WLF council the following June, and the impeccably constitutionalist meeting went off without a heckle, in the post-general election calm.

It is significant that the new president of the WLA, Ann Gwenllian George, was a local woman, not a member of the London political class. The lack of involvement in the revived association by national leadership women or WLF personnel is in strong contrast to the mighty effort of organization mounted by Liberal suffragists twenty years before. In many ways, George was a very familiar type of political leader in the town, with her connection through her family to the religious and political history of the town.[101] Otherwise, as a teacher and later school head she represented something newer and, as an independent professional woman, may have had more in common with some of her young counterparts in the ILP women's group than with Mary Lloyd and Maria Richards. What they all shared was an interest in their own enfranchisement.

For some years before this, the initiative in suffrage campaigning in the town appears to have passed to women associated with the Labour movement. Despite the strength of the South Wales Federation of Women's Suffrage Societies between 1910 and 1914, there was no branch of the NUWSS in Aberdare, nor of the WSPU, which had perhaps five branches in Wales. There was, however, a branch of the Women's Freedom League (WFL). Wales has been described as a 'relatively strong' area of support for the WFL, with seven branches in 1911, though most were short lived; Aberdare was one of five branches still in existence in 1913.[102] In the same period, there is evidence of cooperation between Liberal and ILP women in suffrage meetings and debates in the town. In February 1906, the Aberdare Debating Society pondered the question 'Should the parliamentary franchise be extended to women?' Among those who took part was Mary Lloyd, the veteran of the moribund WLA, now in her seventies, and its former secretary, her daughter Bella. However, the proposer of the suffrage argument, put 'with vigour and eloquence', was Miss Jenny Phillips BA, a teacher at the Aberdare Girls Intermediate (County) School who, a couple of years later, was to be chair of the ILP women's group and two years after that the secretary of the Aberdare WFL.[103] There is evidence that other local ILP women were also members of, or sympathizers with the WFL.[104] The Aberdare branch of the WFL was probably formed in November 1910, with ILP women's support and leadership. The cooperation of Liberal and Labour women in WFL meetings during this period suggests that they were able to work together in this militant suffrage organization and, together with the 1906 suffrage debate and Maria Richards's willingness to chair the Mackworth/Kenney meeting, supports the claims of suffrage historians in recent years that the divisions between 'constitutional' and 'militant' suffragists which have shaped the histories since the 1920s were less important than has been thought, particularly at the local level.[105] The same events suggest that Liberal and Labour women were also able to make common cause in local suffrage activity in Wales, even as Lib–Labism disintegrated.

## Conclusions

As suggested at the beginning of this chapter, Aberdare WLA represented important aspects of Welsh women's liberalism: its leading members displayed Nonconformist earnestness about public service, woman centred in its concerns, seeking women's enfranchisement as an opportunity to enter into wider duties. Broad in their ability to look beyond their own locality and nation, they nevertheless shared the focus on temperance of their class and generation of women, which may have narrowed their view of the possibilities for New Liberal approaches to the work of local government. This may explain a contradiction in the minutes and other records: for all the detail of organizations, meetings and speakers, and the strong sense of the locatedness of the association in the warp and weft of the town life, there is also an absence of certain local social realities: of local conditions for working women, of housing, health and infant mortality in working-class families; no comment on the often bitter industrial relations of the district in the 1890s which had enormous social and political impact in south Wales, directly contributing to the rise of Labour in the constituency. The weakness of liberalism and the rise of Labour were experienced by the Aberdare WLA in their own decline, as a generation which had created a civic culture in the town, but who seemed to have nothing to say on the pressing social and political issues of their time, and who now saw a new generation of women Labour activists moving into some of the spaces they had themselves created – few as those spaces still were.

As the working-class population of Aberdare increasingly identified the remedies for their grievances with socialism and Independent Labour representation, the WLA, despite its support for women's emancipation, appears to have failed to create a form of politics which would attract the young working-class women who were to find their way into Labour politics during the first decade of the twentieth century. Wedded to the old ideals of temperance and disestablishment, they were to find that in the new political landscape, with the rise of Labour on the one hand, and of militant suffragism on the other, and with a Liberal government apparently indifferent to their claim for citizenship, they had little firm ground on which to build. It is difficult not to read these events of the early twentieth century, and the social and political changes from which they arose, in terms of what we now know was the beginning of the decline of liberalism, and the rise in its place of the Labour party. However, women's suffrage changes the picture. It is clear that, in Aberdare, Liberal and Labour women shared an interest in their own enfranchisement, and were able to cooperate in that aim, which – for Liberal women at least

– put them in conflict with the men of their own party, locally and nationally. In the early twentieth century, all thinking women had to make up their minds, one way or another, about their own enfranchisement. In south Wales, in communities like Aberdare, Merthyr, Cardiff and Swansea, political women found themselves pulled by the often competing loyalties of family, class, party and feminism. This was particularly true for Liberal women in the period 1906–1914. The following chapters on Cardiff WLA will explore that further.

# 5

## Out of 'villadom': Cardiff Women's Liberal Association, 1890–1900

### Introduction

This chapter has two main themes. The first may be summed up as 'continuity and change in women's urban politics.' The background to the foundation of the Cardiff Women's Liberal Association (WLA) demonstrates continuity of political, social and religious identity, and to some extent of individuals and families, between the association formed in 1890 and an earlier history of suffrage campaigning, temperance activism and opposition to the Contagious Diseases Acts. As in that earlier period, links with the broader British movement, and specifically with the south-west of England, are clear; but, also as in the earlier movement, the association is seen to be firmly based in local, Nonconformist urban society. Such a narrative of continuity is itself an important contribution to the understanding of women's political history in Wales in the nineteenth century, and it can be established with more certainty in Cardiff than in Aberdare, thanks to previous research on women's reform movements up to the 1880s.[1] However, the urban society evolving in Cardiff differed in important respects from Aberdare: aspects of those differences were to be embodied in the membership and characteristics of Cardiff WLA, and enable examination of an association in a growing, and increasingly important, commercial and civic centre. An examination of the social position, class, religious and 'ethnic' affiliations of the membership, as far as records allow, is intended to show the extent to which women's liberalism reflected or represented the society and communities in which it was formed, and the extent to which different categories of women were involved in Liberal politics. The chapter demonstrates the extent to which Liberal women were part of the creation of a civic society, through their membership of organizations and social agencies: this extends the conception of Cardiff's urban politics to show women active on a number of fronts, their Liberal identity a broad one. In some cases different women's co-membership of these societies serves, to some extent, to complicate the neat divisions between old and new liberalism, between the puritan sabbatarians and the proponents of a rational Sunday, previously detected in Cardiff politics; an analysis which takes a gender perspective, and includes support for women's emancipation alongside other markers of Liberal progressivism, changes the picture.[2]

The second theme of this chapter concerns the way in which episodes in the life of the association bring to the surface contradictions and tensions inherent in women's party organization in this period. In the 1890s, in Cardiff, the participation of women in the election of poor law guardians provides a rich study of the organizational forms produced by women, of the way they conceived of women's role in local government and in urban society and of the difficulty of being both 'Liberal' and 'women' in a time when elections to local bodies were becoming increasingly partisan. The analysis of the elections is intended as part of an examination of Cardiff WLA in terms of the relationship between party and feminism, and party and 'women', and between the WLA and the Cardiff Liberal Association (CLA). This is not a contribution to a history of women in local government work, but instead is more narrowly focused on the electoral politics of these events, and on the gendered representations to which they gave rise. This extends the discussion provided in the Aberdare context for a number of reasons: far more women took part in the election in Cardiff than in Aberdare, and two major newspapers covered the events extensively, providing a meaningful basis for social analysis of women in this area of public life; women in Cardiff attempted to some extent to disengage from party during the election, instead promoting a non-partisan and highly gendered argument for their suitability for the work; there was a high level of organization on behalf of the women, with a branch of the Women's Local Government Society (WLGS) being established for the purpose; and the controversies generated by their electioneering and the results shed light on what female and male Liberals understood to be the relationship of women to the party. An appendix to this book provides biographical data on which some of this analysis is based.

## Context and sources

The growth of Cardiff and its economic development arose from the exploitation of deep mines of coal for export; Cardiff became the chief shipping point for coal, replacing Bristol as the main commercial centre for the region.[3] Its scale increased with its commercial importance, the population increasing by 100,000, to reach 182,259, between 1881 and 1911, bringing into being a 'complex and diverse society of wealthy shipowners and coalowners at one extreme and the casual waterfront workers at the other'. This was a richer social mixture than that of most coalfield towns, with a large middle class and a more diverse range of working-class occupations.[4] Following the franchise reforms and redistribution of the 1880s, Cardiff, a single member seat, increased from an electorate of 12,605 in 1885, to 22,361 in 1900, outstripping the declining electorate of the only two-member constituency in Wales, Merthyr Tydfil Boroughs, which included Aberdare. Cardiff Boroughs constituency was Liberal from 1848 to 1895, when it fell to the Conservatives. In 1900, it reverted again to the Liberal party, until the election of December 1910. In municipal politics, Liberals controlled the council for most of the period from 1888 to 1904.[5] The Liberal association in the city dated from 1869; like other urban associations, it was reorganized in the late 1870s on the model of the Birmingham association, with a structure of wards and central committee, and affiliated to the National Liberal Federation (NLF), in 1878. According to Martin Daunton, liberalism in Cardiff from the early 1890s was marked by two competing strains, structural reform versus social reform, the former identified with the old radicalism of Nonconformist rights, temperance and sabbatarianism; the latter with progressive or New Liberal approaches, favouring a greater role for labour representation and a more open or libertarian urban culture. The old Liberals remained dominant in Cardiff, as in Wales as a whole.[6] In terms of political change in the town, the dominance of the old radicals meant that the Liberal organization resisted selection of labour representatives, and separate labour representation took longer to develop in Cardiff than in, for example, Merthyr Tydfil, Swansea or Aberdare. Not that Liberal organizations in those places were any more inclined to select labour men, but in Cardiff the heterogeneous and fragmented nature of the workforce also militated against early labour independence. There were active branches of the Social Democratic Federation

(SDF) and the Fabians, as well as ILP activity in the early to mid-1890s, and the emergence of progressive Lib–Lab organizations like the Cardiff Radical Democratic Union, but independent Labour representation on the council emerged only after the First World War, as did independent parliamentary candidature.[7]

One question for this section will be the extent to which the members or leadership of the Women's Liberal Association can be identified with these positions, or whether other issues defined women's politics in the town. It is just noteworthy at this point that historians' discussions of progressivism in Cardiff politics have encompassed class and urbanization, but not gender or the woman question. It may be that to introduce, for example, support for women's enfranchisement into the equation would produce a different understanding of where the lines were drawn between the progressives and the old guard. The investigation of women's political culture in Cardiff further explores these questions.

A contributor to the development of 'civic' rather than a merely 'urban' society was the presence in the town from 1884 of the University College of South Wales and Monmouthshire; to the commercial and clerical middle class of the town was added an academic and intellectual middle class.[8] One result of this in the 1890s was support for socialism in the form of the Fabians and the ILP (in women's politics, Professor Millicent Mackenzie represented that trend), but more broadly the academic class in Wales was firmly linked to the Liberal national project, producing civic and political leadership 'which was to perpetuate the values of Liberal Wales for a new generation and a new century'.[9] This presence in the town was a significant one for women's political organization and culture, and an important source of difference from the Aberdare association, as later analysis will show.

Cardiff Women's Liberal Association (WLA) was formed in early 1890, in the parlour of the Charles Street Congregational Church in the centre of the city. Starting with a membership of thirty-five, the high point was a nominal membership of 1,163 in 1901. From 1901–11, membership hovered around nine hundred. After 1911, the association affiliated to the WLF was a rather different organization: following a destructive local split, the suffragist Cardiff Progressive Liberal Women's Union was a much weaker affair; the organization which continued, for a short time, to call itself the Cardiff Women's Liberal Association was more or less identical in personnel with the

Social Committee of the Cardiff Liberal Association, shortly becoming absorbed by it, and dedicated itself to support and fund-raising for the party.[10] As the association in Wales's largest city, Cardiff WLA received good coverage in the major newspapers for the region, and especially in the Liberal *South Wales Daily News*. While routine ward and public meetings were reported, the coverage was, of course, most voluminous at times of controversy and crisis. The story of Cardiff WLA which then emerges, mainly from newspaper sources, tends to be an episodic story of crisis and drama, connected to the great historical questions in late Victorian and Edwardian feminism.

Cardiff WLA appears to have made no bid for leadership amongst Welsh WLAs. This may be the result of a number of factors, including the social and political characteristics of the membership and leadership of the Cardiff society, the nature and development of the WUWLA and the evolving relationship of women's organization in Wales to the Liberal party. The first will be further discussed in this chapter. As for the last two suggestions, it has already been made clear that the impetus to the formation of the WUWLA – while finding the right historical, national, moment in Wales – came from a British suffragist faction. The fact that the leaders, Philipps and McLaren, had not previously been involved in politics in the principality may have defused the potential for competition for leadership from different parts of Wales. There was also, in the foundation of the WUWLA, an explicit determination to overcome the entrenched political geography of 'north' and 'south'. In later years, the recovery of women's Liberal organization after 1906 was greater in north Wales, unifying energy had been lost, with little national organization of women worth the name; the WUWLA survived mainly as a small group of representatives – a largely unchanging group – on the Welsh National Liberal Council (WNLC). There was then no 'national' women's political arena in the country in which to exercise, or attempt to exert, leadership.

In a region of Wales which was to become rapidly anglicized, Cardiff was already predominantly an English-language town at the beginning of the period, though migration from the Welsh counties had created a strong Welsh-language religious culture in the town.[11] The contrast in this respect, for women's political culture, with Aberdare and district, in the heyday of both associations, was clear: there appears to have been no attempt by Cardiff WLA to hold meetings in Welsh, or to reach out to a specifically Welsh constituency (though sections of it were enthusiastic about Cymru Fydd), whereas both languages contributed to the political activities of the Aberdare Association. In Cardiff, anglicization was linked to the development of a specific form of Welsh identity, but was to have deeper implications for liberalism in communities like Aberdare, where, however, it did not stand alone as a cultural shift: Nonconformity, the old political force and the preserver of the language, was weakening, while English was 'the primary language of the new political force, socialism'.[12]

## Women and politics in Cardiff before 1890

This section examines the extent to which, before 1890, the Cardiff community provided a context of support for women's enfranchisement and involvement in the public sphere. It argues that in south Wales women's Liberal politics, support for temperance, social purity and suffrage were the background to independent political organization in the 1890s. Stimulus to organization from outside Wales came together with an ethos of social and moral reform provided by Nonconformity to validate women's role in public life.

In Cardiff, the two causes, suffrage and a woman-centred social purity agenda, emerge onto the public platform at the same time. They were clearly linked, both in terms of female and male personnel, and in the belief of campaigners that women voters would 'purify' politics; that temperance legislation would be more quickly achieved if women were voters; and that, had women had the vote, the Contagious Diseases Acts would never have found their way onto the statute books.[13] These connections can be clearly seen at work in the women's suffrage activity in Cardiff in the 1870s and 1880s. These factors, the visiting speakers and the local suffrage, temperance and repeal elements, can be seen together in March 1881, at an overflowing meeting at the Town Hall in support of a House of Commons resolution for extending the franchise to women householders and ratepayers. The meeting was organized by the redoubtable Gertrude Jenner, of a local land-owning family, a member of the General Committee of the Bristol and West of England society and secretary of a Cardiff society formed in 1873. It was addressed by Jessie Craigen, Helen Blackburn and Harriet McIlquham, all well-known speakers on the national women's suffrage circuit, who had been involved in the series of 'Demonstrations of Women' in the major English and Scottish cities from February 1880 to November 1882. In these meetings, conceived as 'women only', men were admitted only as paying spectators.[14] The Cardiff meeting may have been an attempt by local suffragists to bring to the city something of the buoyant spirit of the demonstration, but it was very differently conducted. Jenner addressed the meeting in a speech which combined the notion of women's duties in public life with their rights as taxpayers, but apart from Jenner, no local women appear to have spoken, while a prominent role was taken by local men, including a former local Chartist and temperance campaigner, the editor of the *South Wales Daily News*, and Nonconformist ministers connected through their own activity and that of their wives to the early suffrage committee and the Contagious Diseases Acts repeal campaign. They connected women's enfranchisement to 'all matters of truth, righteousness and peace . . . of right and justice', the purification of public life. While the Liberal arguments of rights and representation were heard, the link between the early campaign for the vote, and social purity and temperance in Cardiff, were most in evidence. If there was a danger that the women on the platform could be caricatured as a professional 'shrieking sisterhood', as they were in the Conservative *Western Mail*, radical and Nonconformist respectability as it was best understood in Cardiff was embodied in the line of male speakers and supporters.[15] The threads – temperance, social purity, suffrage – were to come together again in the 1890s in the formation of the Cardiff WLA. The pattern persists into the Edwardian period: in March 1908 the Cardiff WLA held a series of meetings on the life and work of Josephine Butler, and explicitly linked social purity and the protection of women to the vote; in the autumn of 1912, the Cardiff and District Women's Suffrage Society (C&DWSS) invited speakers on 'the White Slave Traffic' to the town, because 'it is the existence of such problems . . . which makes many of us suffragists'.[16] By that period, however, as the following chapters will show, the characteristics of Cardiff feminism also strongly reflected newer elements in the city's social make-up.

### *Historical continuities: foundations, structures and personnel*

Party electoral and organizational needs, usually seen as the motive for the creation of the women's auxiliaries, can certainly be shown to have pertained in Cardiff. It was becoming the largest single-member constituency in Britain, and had a large lodger population, the kinds of conditions which needed many willing and effective political workers.[17] However, the origins of Cardiff WLA suggest that it was linked not just to party exigencies, but to a history of activity for women's suffrage and to the organized opposition to the Contagious Diseases Acts, stretching back to the 1870s, and previously described, which situates it in the longer history of nineteenth-century women's movements. Aspects of those movements brought them into close alignment with the moral-reform strain of Welsh Nonconformity, expressed most consistently in the temperance movement.

Two meetings in February and March of 1890 inaugurated the association, the first a large meeting of women only, the second smaller one attended by male Liberals who took a prominent role. Visitors from Bristol WLA attended and spoke at both. Donations and expressions of support were received from Lady Reed, wife of the MP, and from Lady Aberdare, the campaigner for temperance and for secondary and higher education for women.[18] Press reports of the two meetings were brief, providing mainly the names of some of the women and men in attendance, very little of political substance being reported. However, the second meeting passed a women's suffrage resolution. As this demonstrated, the new association was not conjured out of nothing. Despite the sparse details of the newspaper accounts, the reports revealed, in the names of those prominent in the meetings and on the first WLA committee, the links with the earliest women's suffrage committee and the March 1881 suffrage meeting discussed previously (in chapter 4), with the campaign for the repeal of the Contagious Diseases Acts and with temperance activism.[19] The association brought together support for women's suffrage with the moral-reform strain in the town's politics,[20] which saw in what was understood as women's culture a way forward for the moral reform of the town and the nation. The links with this old liberalism can be seen to continue in the 1890s, through the extant annual reports, dating from 1894 and into the twentieth century. The significance of this continuity, into the period of a crisis in relations between women Liberals and the party, will be further discussed in the following chapter. Also present at the inaugural meeting of the WLA in March 1890 were representatives of the progressive 'New Liberal' strain in Cardiff politics. The meetings reflected the dominant characteristics of Cardiff liberalism: in terms of social standing or class, there were no unambiguous representatives of the stratum of leading industrialists, shippers and coal owners, who, with one or two exceptions, were not very active in Cardiff social and political affairs;[21] Nonconformity was well represented (the meetings were held at the Charles Street Congregational Church, in the centre of the town) though not, as far as one can tell, other Christian denominations or other faiths; both the old and new strains in liberalism were evident, but there was no one who can now be clearly identified as Lib–Lab or trade unionist. Overwhelmingly, then, the meetings of 1890 presented a group portrait of the Cardiff WLA which corresponded closely to the dominant municipal liberalism of the city, in which a middle class and lower middle class of tradesmen, professionals and ministers of religion exercised political power.[22] However, the association did not remain frozen in that moment; as it grew and established ward associations, its base appears to have become broader and more diverse, reflecting to some extent a more working-class population, at least as far as subscribers were concerned, and amongst its activists a younger and newer urban society was also represented. Over time, the personnel changed, and the politics came out of new circumstances. This will be explored further in what follows.

### Out of 'villadom': organization and reorganization

From its formation, the association was primarily a Cardiff society, rather than constituency based, though women resident in Penarth (who formed their own WLA in 1896) and outlying districts were listed among subscribers. Its first president was Lady Reed, wife of the MP. From 1894, following a relaunch of the association in which she was active, Eva McLaren was president – though the position was essentially honorary – until 1901, with Kate Jones as 'local' president in the late 1890s.

One of the striking things about this period of organization is the extent to which the WLF and some of its leading individuals were willing to dedicate resources, time and energy to local and regional organization. Just a year after its creation, the Cardiff association was judged to need an overhaul. The model of efficient local party organization created by the Birmingham Liberal Association, and copied in Cardiff and other large urban centres, was also promoted in the WLF where appropriate, and in March 1891 Cardiff was visited by Miss

Martin Leake, a WLF organizer. She was blunt about Cardiff's ineffectiveness: the association appeared to have 'no clear idea of the useful work which could be done', and its shortcomings included backwardness in promoting and exercising the political power of women 'in local and imperial matters'; failure to reach into the working-class districts of the city, and to include working women in the organization, instead confining itself to 'villadom'; general inactivity, and failure to undertake methodical door-to-door canvassing. The audience applauded her remarks, suggesting that at least a section of the membership was keen to create a more active association. Following her advice, the association was divided into ten ward associations, with the officers of the wards forming the central executive, followed by a relaunch at which the new rules were adopted in February 1892.[23] For two or three years, each of the ten Cardiff ward associations was separately affiliated to the WLF, but the 1895 report showed single affiliation by Cardiff, which suggests that ward membership may have fallen.[24] In 1893, the association took on a paid secretary and organizer, Elsie Mary Jenkins from Tenby, at a salary of about £60 a year. Her arrival was the cue for further gingering up of ward organization, revision of the rules and an inspirational series of meetings with Eva McLaren, from April 1893 to January 1894, on political organization, women's suffrage and women's citizenship;[25] other WLF figures visited to speak on similar topics. So the indications for the early to mid-1890s are of a series of relaunches, suggesting that enthusiasm, activity and effectiveness had its peaks and troughs, and needed to be whipped up periodically in preparation for national and local election campaigns. Reorganization successfully reinvigorated members, at least for a while: Cardiff – like the similarly reorganized Newport association – effectively supported women candidates for the 1894 poor law elections. Park ward reported that members had 'gradually awakened, and now take great interest in all political questions . . . there are hopes for a very bright future'.[26]

Ward organization provided the basis for regular committee, membership and public meetings, in which local leadership now took over from the visiting speakers. 'Educational work' and 'education and social reform' are phrases that recur in the annual reports, suggesting the way the association saw its role, both in relation to its members and to the wider society. Autumn and winter meetings were leavened with social and cultural activities, and in the summer seaside outings or garden parties were stiffened with political speeches. From about 1896, it is possible to read in the annual reports signs of a falling-off in ward activities, and it is clear that there was a decline in these years which was to lead to much soul-searching in the association after the turn of the century. Once again, the timetable of decline – though nowhere near as absolute as in Aberdare and many other associations – matches the national trends discussed in part I, but Cardiff, as a marginal seat, had its own problems, being held by the Conservatives from 1895 to 1900.

### A WLA in a changing urban society

Cardiff WLA developed in the 1890s to become more representative, in its membership profile, of the social composition of the town: it enrolled as members many working-class women, while increasingly its activists included women who were highly educated, professional, independent and, in many cases, not the product of Welsh Nonconformist liberalism. Many of both the working-class membership and the 'new women' were born outside Wales. This made the association a coalition of diverse groups and individuals, and of different conceptions of liberalism and of women's relationship to it. Some of the strains which resulted can be seen at work in the 1894 guardians' elections, but the full implications were to be seen in the Edwardian period, discussed in the following chapter.

The new structure created in 1891 got the association out of 'villadom' and established a strong presence, at least as far as subscriptions were concerned, in working-class areas of the city, in Adamsdown, Canton and Grangetown, in Splott and Roath, and in the South ward, around the city's docks, the area of smallest membership. This expansion brought into the executive committee of the association women like Mrs Chappell, whose husband was a former coal trimmer at the docks, president of the Coal Trimmers' Union, a Fabian-sponsored candidate for the school board election in 1893, and later Lib–Lab councillor; Mrs and Miss Fisher, wife and daughter of another Coal Trimmers's Union official; and Mrs T. Roberts of Railway Street, Splott, whose husband was a carpenter: clearly, their husbands represented the town's Lib–Lab alliances, though we cannot say whether such a term defined their own political identities.[27] In terms of the general membership, the working-class streets of Adamsdown, Roath and Splott yielded a large membership which included the wives of small shopkeepers, commercial travellers, insurance agents, but in greater numbers the wives and daughters of coal trimmers, plasterers, carpenters, steel workers, railway wagon builders and various categories of railway employees – unionized workers who might themselves be members of their ward Liberal associations, or linked to Lib–Lab politics through their trade unions and the Trades and Labour Council. While a small number of members can be identified as the wives or daughters of a 'general labourer' or 'dock labourer', these appear to have been the exception in a membership which now, nevertheless, reflected not a narrowly middle-class Nonconformist section, but a broader swathe of the social base of the city.[28] Comparison of the 1897 subscriptions lists and the 1901 census reveals that many of these women had large families, and in some cases extended households of relations, lodgers and boarders. The lists include a number of widowed heads of household, some supporting themselves by taking boarders, or taking in washing. There were young wives and single women living within the parental home, but these were a minority; where it has been possible to identify individuals, the majority of members were over forty, reflecting the ageing membership which was seen as a weakness of the association after the turn of the century. In a sample of twenty from the Adamsdown ward subscription list for whom entries could be traced in the 1901 census, half had been born in Cardiff or Glamorgan, while seven of the remainder had been born in the south-western counties of England which supplied so many immigrants to south Wales at the end of the nineteenth century.[29] In the absence of ward or central committee minutes, it is impossible to know how active the members were, but the regular payment of subscriptions (which might be as low as 4*d.* a year) suggests a degree of commitment to politics, which it has generally been assumed was not to be found among Welsh working-class women in this period.[30] We should, however, bear in mind the evidence of Aberdare, where a large membership was politically and ideologically represented by a small group of activists. Cardiff's ward structure created more opportunities for wider participation but, as we have seen, that structure could be weak in times when political enthusiasm was low.

Cardiff's diverse society was also embodied in the WLA by individual women who represented, or were perceived as representing, specific social, religious or ethnic groups (though none identifiably from the growing black community of Bute Town). A number of such figures can be identified during the guardians' elections, when they came under the scrutiny and comment of the press and public. Mrs Annie Mullin, ward secretary for Cathays, a vice-president of Cardiff WLA from 1898, was connected to the Irish and Home Rule politics of which Cardiff was an increasingly well-organized centre. In the 1890s, the leaders of Irish Home Rule nationalism in south Wales and Cardiff were firmly integrated into liberalism, though Irish voters 'did not operate as a single, unified, electoral bloc'.[31] However, the distinctive identity of the Irish Catholic in public life in a city in which political leadership was predominantly Nonconformist, and in which there was some militant protestant activity,[32] might prove a problem. An attempt was made to undermine Mullin's candidacy for the board of guardians in December 1894, with the suggestion that 'she had been brought out as a Roman Catholic'. She was forced to 'indignantly repudiate' the allegation, to emphasize her standing as an official Liberal candidate, 'and that her religion had nothing whatever to do with it'.[33] Relations between Catholic voters and the Liberals were damaged by the Nonconformist opposition to state support for faith schools which Cardiff liberalism reflected strongly. The mounting tensions on this issue, culminating in Liberal loss of the city council in 1904, might be expected to have undermined membership of the association.[34] However, the association's 1897 subscription lists for the Adamsdown ward, which was regarded as the stronghold of the Irish vote in the city, show few recognizably Irish names, and the sample analysed above suggests that women of Irish birth, extraction or connection did not subscribe to the WLA in significant numbers.[35]

Educational developments in the 1890s brought into Wales and Cardiff a new professional and intellectual middle class which made its mark on the politics and culture of the nation and the town. The involvement of women teachers in both Liberal and socialist politics was seen in Aberdare. It is clear that levels of feminism amongst the new generation of women teachers were high, both in terms of their dedication to widening opportunities for girls and in terms of their consciousness of their own value to the community and their invidiously unequal position in relation to men.[36] In Cardiff, the High School for Girls, opened in January 1895, provided a core of active support for suffrage organization in the town.[37] Its first head, Mary Collin, was a member of the Roath ward WLA, (though 'an appreciation', published just before her retirement in 1924, claimed that she 'had taken no share in party politics'[38]). Collin took no executive role in the WLA, but in the new century would take a leading role in suffrage activity, both inside the WLA and as chair of the executive of the Cardiff and District Women's Suffrage Society (C&DWSS). In the Welsh context, Mary Collin represented a new Liberal woman, and even perhaps the New Woman, professional, independent and mobile. English born and educated at Bedford College, London, a graduate of London University, she was, like Annie Mullin, unconnected to the old Nonconformist liberalism of the town which had been so apparent at the beginning of the association; she might well have been one of those for whom the old goals of disestablishment and land reform may have meant very little, and who, as their choice of activism in the Edwardian period suggests, put feminism before party.[39]

The siting in Cardiff of the University College of South Wales and Monmouthshire, in 1883, was central to creating a modern civic identity for the town, academics and others associated with the college contributing significantly to the political and civic life of the city.[40] Women associated with the university – academics like Millicent Mackenzie and Barbara Foxley, graduates and the successive wardens of the women's residence, Aberdare Hall – provided a leaven in the political life of Cardiff in a number of ways.[41] The most prominent representative of the university college in the Cardiff WLA in the 1890s was Kate Jones, wife of the principal, John Viriamu Jones. Deeply involved in the cause of women's education, Kate Jones had been secretary of the committee which worked to establish Aberdare Hall and to raise funds for books and scholarships, activity she wrote about in the *Women's Suffrage Journal*.[42] In this and other efforts for the education of girls and women she continued to work alongside those who had been prominent in the Association for Promoting the Education of Girls in Wales (APEGW). A temperance campaigner, not Welsh born, she took a leading role in the formation of the new Cardiff Progressive Liberal Women's Union (CPLWU) after the split of 1910. Like a number of the women named here, while her values at a number of points are entirely in tune with those of Welsh Nonconformist liberalism, she may have lacked a visceral attachment to its traditional programme, and had pursued a woman-centred and feminist position in her active adult life, producing the logic of her 1910 position.

In the 1890s and the first decade of the new century, as one would expect in a city (as Cardiff became in 1905) reaching the peak of its commercial and civic development, there was a plethora of associations and societies concerned with the moral, social and cultural condition of Cardiff, in which women were able to play an active role alongside men. Liberal women were part of a matrix of social action: over time membership in common can be traced between the WLA, the influential Charity Organisation Society (COS, formed in 1886), the Cardiff Society for the Impartial Discussion of Political and Other Questions (the Impartial Society, 1886), the Women's Local Government Society (WLGS, 1894), the University Settlement, established in Splott in 1901, Cardiff and District Educational Society, the Literary Society and the Cardiff branch of the British National Peace Congress and, in the twentieth century between these organisations, the suffrage societies and other political groups, of which more in the next chapter. Some sense of the character of this public service ethic can be gained by looking at the place of the COS in this matrix. The COS has generally been associated by historians with a repressive and punitive approach to charity and the poor, but in Cardiff the society has been linked with 'those who proposed a "rational" Sunday',[43] meaning the opening up of parks, the provision of sober and respectable entertainment, instruction and refreshment in place of the narrow, teetotal sabbatarianism of the old Nonconformist establishment. The Thompson family, proprietors of flour mills in the city, have been cited as exemplifying this position, in contrast to the Cory family, coal owners and shippers, who are seen as exemplifying 'the attitude of those who "rejoiced to be a Puritan"'.[44] However, the COS in Cardiff contained members of both families, and the Cory family itself was not entirely homogeneous; the shipowner philanthropist John Cory was a vice-president and Mrs Richard Cory was on the managing committee, as was Charles Thompson. By 1891, H. M. Thompson was chair. The COS committee also included representatives of a range of social and religious positions, as well as 'a significant sprinkling of academics and their wives'.[45] Women of both the Cory and the Thompson families were active in the WLA. Mrs John Cory was a subscriber; Mrs Charles Thompson was president of the Grangetown ward WLA in the mid-1890s and her sister-in-law, Mrs Herbert Thompson, was also listed as a speaker at meetings; both were members of the executive committee for Cardiff at this time, while Mrs Herbert Thompson continued on the committee at least until 1902, was at the founding meeting of the Cardiff WLGS, was involved on the suffragists' side in the 1910 split and was a vice-president of the C&DWSS. The University Settlement also represented the New Liberal, 'rational Sunday', end of the Cardiff political spectrum, derived inspiration from socialism as well as from moralizing aims and had a 'strongly political and "progressive" tone'.[46] The Thompson family were its supporters, and the settlement house in Splott had women's and girls' clubs, and a labour agency to help place women in work, in which Lilian and Mabel Howell, members of the family who owned Cardiff's leading department store, were active; each being in turn secretary of the settlement. Mabel Howell was to be secretary of the C&DWSS and in the 1920s of Cardiff WLA.[47]

As all this suggests, Liberal women – and it was clearly a broad term – were enthusiastic participants in, and creators of, the urban culture of Cardiff in this period. Through their work and participation in such organizations, they contributed to the creation of a local civic society, and at the same time shared a culture with women throughout Britain which was to enable them to articulate a special role for themselves in the life of their communities.[48] In the 1890s, the paramount opportunity for this version of women's role to present itself to public opinion came in the 1894 elections to the new boards of guardians.

### Gender and electoral politics in 1894

The year 1894 was a busy one for Liberal activists everywhere in England and Wales, preparing for elections to the new and reformed local government bodies created under the Local Government Acts of that year; but, as far as Cardiff WLA was concerned, since its local authority was a city council for which women were not eligible, the new authorities were of less relevance than the abolition of the property qualification for poor law guardians, which opened up the boards to the membership of married and other non-householder women. Before 1894, no women had been elected to the Cardiff Board of Guardians or the School Board. It is possible that some of the women who stood in 1894 may have been eligible before that time, but the public interest in and support for the changed conditions may well have encouraged more women of all sorts to stand. The Cardiff Poor Law Union was a huge body with, from 1894, eighty-six elected members.[49] A Ladies' Workhouse Visiting Committee had been formed only a few months before, at the prompting of the Local Government Board. While women had done 'good service' in this work, it was suggested that their effectiveness was limited, being 'swathed in red tape'.[50] The visiting committees were a bridge between the public and the social or philanthropic spheres, but reproduced the gendered division of responsibility and authority in the creation of the public sphere in the late eighteenth and early nineteenth century, which middle-class feminists of the second half of the nineteenth century 'attempted to conquer'.[51] Cardiff's late development as a major centre of population meant that its urban culture was in the process of being created even as the women's movement came into being,[52] but, despite women's involvement in many of the important religious, charitable, social and cultural organizations of the town, as described earlier, the centres of political power remained entirely male.

Early in October 1894, the WLGS began to organize in Cardiff in support of women candidates in the poor law elections to be held in December. A temporary committee was created which was clearly an outgrowth of the WLA, though the later elected WLGS committee was to be broader. It is not clear that the WLA had taken any decision before this to run its own candidates. At a garden party in September, a number of the ward branches had pledged to work for the election of women. According to 'A Liberal Woman' writing to the *South Wales Daily News* in October, there had been 'a good deal of talk some months ago' but now the association seemed to be inactive, the initiative passing to 'the new non-political society, formed for the purpose of placing women who renounce politics on local bodies', something to which 'Liberal Woman' was strongly opposed.[53] Once the WLGS was established, the nomination of women and the announcement of their candidatures gathered pace. Of the total of twelve women candidates, all but two were to be successful (see Appendix).

Patricia Hollis has identified the common background of many 'local government ladies', and the Cardiff candidates conform on important points with her analysis, but also diverge in some ways. This is partly because Hollis's generalizations appear to be largely based on analysis of women who were members of boards before 1894, when a relatively high property qualification meant that the women guardians were drawn from a more prosperous, even elite social stratum, and were more likely to be single women. The differences also arise from the nature of the political and civic leadership of

Cardiff, as already discussed. In aggregate, the Cardiff women were probably less socially exalted, less highly educated and prosperous than those identified by Hollis as 'the wives, widows, daughters, and sisters, of a town's civic and social élite, of its industrialists and its professional men':[54] in Cardiff, civic leadership, as we have seen, was provided from lower down the social scale, from professionals, ministers of religion, academics and educationalists and the shopocracy, and the majority of the women candidates for the Cardiff board was drawn from this leadership group. Only one candidate, Agnes Jane Gridley in Splotlands, was identified as working class, or as 'the wife of a working man'.

Cardiff fits Hollis's generalization that women were more likely to be candidates in cities with a strong women's movement, based on suffrage societies or – as in Cardiff – women's liberalism. As for Hollis's characterization of her sample as 'nonconformist, suffragist and liberal, with their menfolk already on the town council',[55] the picture was more mixed than this in Cardiff, perhaps thanks to the early involvement of the WLGS. Seven of the candidates were identified as Nonconformist and Liberal and, of those, four were members of the WLA executive committee. One candidate was Liberal and Roman Catholic, one Liberal and 'Church', and two Church and Conservative. They included one widow and three 'spinsters': the shift brought about by the 1894 reforms is seen in the preponderance of married women. In the case of 'unattached' women, the Liberal press liked to be able to link them, where possible, to a male Liberal lineage, their dead husbands and fathers being enlisted in their support.[56] As a group, then, the Cardiff candidates present themselves as embodying some variations from Hollis's characterization, in terms of the local social strata they represented, and their religious and political affiliations. Despite the essentially Liberal networks of the WLGS, its intervention in the contest had enabled women from a broader section of Cardiff society to come forward. However, while the WLGS laid claim to the majority of the candidates by announcing them at their meetings, it is not clear that this was always their route into the contest. It appears that the initiative in promoting women's candidacy generally, and supporting individual candidates, may have come from the WLGS and the WLAs, with other meetings at which women were confirmed as candidates, including Liberal association meetings, following later.[57] As for the feminism of the candidates, none of them was reported as having linked the issue of women's parliamentary enfranchisement directly with the election campaign, though a series of meetings addressed by WLF speaker Gertrude Southall during the campaign ranged over women's suffrage, trade unionism and their employment as sanitary and factory inspectors, as well as their role in local government, thereby placing the issue of the election of women to local bodies in the context of feminists' wider concerns about women's employment and place in public life.[58] There was, however, a dominant discourse of 'womanliness', distinguished from and set above partisan politics, which was used by the candidates, and endorsed by their supporters and the press, particularly in the context of experience in charitable work among the poor.

Experience in philanthropic activity, identified by Hollis as a central common characteristic of local government women, was emphasized in the newspaper profiles and election addresses of the Cardiff candidates, and was the characteristic which all the candidates shared, or claimed to share, to some degree.[59] Cardiff had seen a rapid increase in the scale of philanthropic activity from the mid-century, a response to the town's rapid development, anxieties about poverty, vice and crime, combined with 'an evangelical sense of responsibility'.[60] Activity by women in this social sphere both prepared them and made them eligible for poor law work. They were involved, variously, as adjuncts to their husbands' religious ministry, through the visiting committee, in three cases through the COS, and in a number of other philanthropic efforts to befriend, rescue or improve the poor and fallen. There was a class dimension to the possibility of exercising these womanly duties: such formalized opportunities for charitable work were less available to working-class women, who were usually seen as the objects of good works. This may be reflected in the way that Mrs Gridley, the 'wife of a working man', was described, rather vaguely, as having been 'a kind of good genius' among the many poor of Splott. Experience outside Cardiff was mentioned in a number of cases, in most detail in the case of Mary Jane Williams of Canton. Such wide experience and evidence of life-long devotion to the work was clearly thought a good thing to mention, but did not help Mrs Williams to get elected. It might have been the ambiguous caveat appended to her portrait by the *South Wales Daily News* which did for her chances: 'Although an ultra-Liberal, she is a woman of broad and generous views towards those who may differ from her opinions.'[61] Just as ambiguously, Annie Mullin was described as 'having spent a great deal of time on the continent' and, therefore, having her views about the treatment of the poor 'based on a broad basis'.[62] Despite this, she came second in the poll in Roath.

Three candidates had been members of the committee of the Cardiff COS. The society sponsored the candidacy of Mabel Thomas as their representative on the board, where they hoped she would use 'kindness and judgement' in the interests of 'both of the poor and the ratepayers'.[63] The COS ethos has been associated by Hollis with ambitions 'to rescue and remoralize the urban derelict', its training producing workers wedded to the 1834 principles. She describes them as 'often heartily detested' for their hard-nosed approach to the poor, and likely to lose their seats after 1894, when such attitudes had fallen out of favour.[64] The records of the Cardiff branch display the COS concern with discriminating between 'classes' of applicants for relief, and for detecting the undeserving.[65] However, as we have seen, historians of Cardiff have identified the Cardiff COS with a rather different ethos, and membership of the COS does not appear to have harmed the chances of candidates in Cardiff in 1894; Mrs Harriette Charlotte Thompson and Marion Thomas were among the five women who headed the poll in their parishes.

Experience in philanthropic work, and its significance as a marker of the appropriate womanly attributes, provided the single most important justification for women's entry into poor law work. The women stood for election in an atmosphere of keen support for the idea of women guardians, as reflected in the Liberal and Conservative press.[66] By the eve of the election, the *South Wales Daily News* was urging the 'absolute need' of women's intervention, in terms of the state of the poor law system, and the opportunity to humanize it. Thus women were welcomed into public life in strictly gendered terms, but in ways which were progressive for the recipients of poor relief – women would be able, as men had not been able, to humanize the system; women would 'do better than men . . . more judiciously, more tenderly, and with prudent womanly tact'.[67] Other supporters spoke in the same vein, and linked their support to a view of women as generally able to purify and reform social life.[68] The entry of women into local government bodies was thus represented not as contributing to women's progress towards citizenship, but in terms of the old moral-reform liberalism of the town.

These were just the kinds of arguments made by women themselves during the election campaign, and the activity of the BWTA in the town during the election period also connected women's local government work with temperance. The language of women's rights, or of local government work as a demonstration of women's fitness for parliamentary enfranchisement, appears to have been entirely absent from the campaign. Instead, service and duty, the contribution of women to the welfare of others, were emphasized. The women who stood for election should be 'inspired by womanly, sisterly and motherly desires' on behalf of the poor, wrote 'A Liberal Woman', and other women echoed her ideas, emphasizing love, motherliness and household skills, as did campaign posters.[69] Such arguments could happily be made by women from across the political spectrum in this period, including some actively opposed to the extension of the parliamentary franchise to women, a vision of active female citizenship based on an essentialist view of gender roles which emphasized duty and contribution rather than rights or emancipation.

There was a strong feeling that this kind of womanliness was incompatible with party politics, that non-partisan caring was what was required of women, and what they were peculiarly capable of; for many commentators, they were most acceptable 'simply as women, and not as political women – to take their share in a work of beneficence and usefulness'.[70] However, in the Liberal organizations, national and local, this endorsement of the role of women created problems. For many women and men, caring about the poor and their treatment under the poor law entailed a determination to ensure that boards were dominated by progressive Liberals. Long before the Cardiff campaigns had begun, the executive committee of the WLF had pronounced cross-party cooperation amongst women undesirable: the object was to secure the election of progressive candidates, men and women, across the country.[71] That might have been clear enough, but Eva McLaren, national organizer and honorary treasurer of the WLF, so presumably party to the pronouncement of the executive, had written to Cardiff WLA in the autumn on the formation of the local WLGS, emphasizing the importance of women working together: 'We shall never achieve what we set out to do unless we can find a common ground on which to meet.'[72]

This was the view of the executive of the Cardiff WLA, as its prominence in the formation and management of the WLGS shows. The policy was as contentious locally as it was nationally; divisions emerged at meetings in support of women candidates and led to some bitterness within Liberal organization and amongst Liberal women, which was aired in the press. As it transpired, a number of the women candidates were taken on to the official Liberal ticket in their respective wards, but not before some damage had been done as far as opponents of the non-party policy were concerned. Candidates who put themselves forward as 'Independents' were in fact, according to such opponents, Tories in disguise, representing Church, brewers and publicans. According to 'A Liberal Woman', one might 'as well look for a rose in an ice-house as expect administrative reform and even-handed justice from the Tories. It is agin' their principles.'[73] The split amongst Liberal women, at any rate, was clear. There were those, supported by the executive, active in the WLGS, who saw the election of women as paramount, and argued for it in terms of the greater humanity that women would inject into the administration of the poor law. It is likely that some of these also saw the campaign as an attempt to penetrate the male-dominated public bodies on behalf of women's greater emancipation, and understood a concerted women's campaign as the way to bring this about. If so, those were not the terms in which the argument was conducted, at least as reflected in the press. On the other side, there were those who wanted not any women, not even any charitable women, but Liberal, progressive reforming women in public life. The differences were fudged by the WLA, and the non-party policy – for women candidates – was supported by the chairman of the CLA, Robert Bird, while the Conservatives may not have entered into the contest in the same non-partisan spirit.[74]

The local press, Liberal and Conservative, had thrown its support behind the non-party policy of the women, though all the women candidates were, nevertheless, identified in print by party and religious affiliation. But, by the election, only four or five of the women, including two women identified as Conservative, had not been adopted as Liberal party candidates.[75] On polling day, women canvassers were busy whipping up voters in support of women candidates. The dire predictions of 'A Liberal Woman' that to stand as an Independent and cooperate with Conservatives meant sure defeat were not born out: apart from the two women rejected by the voters, all had made a very good showing at the polls, and all four Independents came top of the poll in their parishes. The results clearly showed that the voters liked women candidates; in only one of the Cardiff wards where a woman stood did a man head the poll. The results also seemed to show that the voters liked women who represented themselves as above the party fray, with a disinterested, non-ideological and compassionate approach to welfare questions.[76] Women who came top of the poll had been able to mobilize cross-party support.

Given these results, why did some women lose? Mary Jane Williams, the Canton candidate, coming twelfth in a field of sixteen, seems to have fallen victim both to the confusing policy of the WLA and to the poor organization of the Liberal Association.[77] Writing in the *South Wales Daily News*, Williams complained bitterly about lack of supporting organization from the male Liberals, while members of the ward WLA, of which she had been previously secretary, had canvassed in her ward on behalf of the Independent (Church and Conservative) Florence Watson, leaving their own outraged member high and dry. In the post-mortems which followed the election, 'the sick giant' of liberalism in Cardiff, the 'inertness' of party organization and the non-party policy of the women were all indicted.[78] The problem was that the women's campaign, on behalf of themselves rather than any party, had been too successful. But there was clearly some confusion in the broader Cardiff liberalism represented by the *South Wales Daily News*, arising from the need of many to see poor law matters as above or apart from ideology, and to see women as embodying that disinterested position.

Having made the breach in male dominance of this important area of public work, women maintained and increased their position on the Cardiff board. The board elected in 1904 included fifteen women, by the mid-1920s there were nineteen. Some, like Mrs Norman, had very long careers. Women made little headway as committee chairs during the history of the board, despite the suggestion in 1894 that they should be offered some chairing positions in recognition of their popularity with the voters. Despite the rhetoric of women's peculiar fitness for this niche in society, men maintained their dominance of this work to the end.[79] Nor, as seen in Aberdare, were arguments that could be made for women's fitness for certain kinds of public work easily extended into all areas of local government. One year later, WLA speakers were making the same kinds of claims for women's suitability for school board work, as elections for that body approached. However, education was an area riven with rival ideologies particularly in the Welsh religious context; from 1896–8, the Welsh Liberal party at Westminster and in the country was united against the introduction of two bills on the funding of elementary education which increased the grants to voluntary or faith schools.

The *South Wales Daily News* this time emphasized the importance of voters' sticking to the Liberal list of candidates. Rather than organizing as women, with women of other parties, Cardiff WLA threw its organization behind the election of Liberal candidates for the board. The WLGS appears not to have been active in the election campaigns, and only one woman, Kate Jones, entered the field, as one of a slate of Liberal candidates whose platform was opposition to the bills. Voter behaviour in these elections was different from the poor law contest: the 'unsectarians' headed the polls in their wards, and Kate Jones was successful, but despite instructions to Liberal voters to give her two of their votes, she got the smallest number of votes on the slate. The efforts of Liberal women during the campaign, and especially those of secretary Elsie Jenkins, in canvassing for the party, organizing ward meetings and in bringing out women voters, was praised in the newspaper columns, in contrast to the post-mortems which had followed the guardians' elections – while once again Liberal organization more generally in Cardiff was decried as 'inert and apathetic'.[80] While this was clearly an election fought on religious lines, one should not read into it any simple anti-Catholic or anti-Church position on the part of the WLA. A few months before, at the end of 1895, Elsie Jenkins and her workers had been heartily thanked by the Irish National League for their help in electing their nominee, a leading Catholic, to the city council.[81] The school board elections of 1896 provided one of those occasions when Liberal women were able to demonstrate their solidarity with, and usefulness to, the party, even if it meant abandoning their own well-developed, and hitherto fiercely fought, position on the need to feminize the public sphere.

### *Conclusions*

This chapter has examined a WLA in a large urban community going through a period of growth and diversification. It has demonstrated some continuity of political identity with early support for women's suffrage, connected to temperance activism, and the campaigns to repeal the Contagious Diseases Acts. This narrative of continuity has a value in the context of Welsh women's political history, in which the nineteenth century has barely been explored.

The history of urban growth and change to which Cardiff was subject and the evidence of women's participation in the development of a civic society suggest further scope for research contributing to the developing field of urban history in Wales.[82] The chapter has demonstrated Cardiff WLA's roots in a form of Nonconformist liberalism which was to remain dominant, but also its ability, to some extent, to reflect and accommodate the social change around it. However, the campaign for women's election to the Cardiff Board of Guardians demonstrated the association's connections outside the local, to the wider British movement working to insert women into social and political structures, reflected in the activity locally of the WLGS and the prioritizing of gender over party. The Cardiff women's campaign on their own behalf in 1894 presented a danger to a united Liberal front and the electoral fortunes of the party. It must, therefore, have seemed desirable to bring women inside the party tent, and early in 1895 thirty-eight representatives of the Cardiff WLA were elected to the previously all-male 'Liberal 1000', as the committees of the CLA were called. They would now, it was optimistically declared, 'have a practical voice in the choice of Parliamentary and other candidates in the town'.[83] However, the tensions which resulted from the election campaign, while not doing lasting damage in the 1890s, prefigured quite closely – in terms of the positions taken by individuals – the more damaging split between women and party in the Edwardian period, suggesting that the potential for division was now inherent in the membership of the association. The following chapter further explores these issues.

# 'Are not women to be included in the people?' Cardiff Women's Liberal Association, 1900–1914

## Introduction

This chapter focuses on the relationship between Liberal women and the party in the period of Liberal government 1906–14. This was also the period during which the suffrage movement reached its height. The narrative and analysis which follow are not an attempt to provide a history of suffrage activity in Cardiff at this time, but to concentrate on those aspects which reveal the relationship between suffragists and liberalism, and to suggest some of the implications for women's Liberal organization in south Wales in the longer term. The escalation of suffragist militancy, as it became increasingly clear that a Liberal government would not introduce a women's suffrage bill, is well known, and constitutional suffragists, within and outside the Liberal party, also became increasingly disaffected. Cardiff supplies a vivid case study of events hitherto seen in national perspective. All the most bitter lessons of the period were to be learned by the Liberal suffragists of Cardiff, as their loyalty and their electoral workhorse skills were to be outrageously exploited and betrayed. The resulting split in the local party forces came in the middle of the crucial December 1910 election campaign, followed by the loss of the seat to the Unionists, a fatal division of the forces of local women's liberalism and the creation of a large and influential suffrage society. In the process, the last remains of the old Welsh radicalism, now effectively reduced to the single demand for disestablishment, were abandoned by a significant body of women. The local dimension puts flesh on the statistics of declining membership of the Women's Liberal Federation (WLF), and its 'steady decline into irrelevance',[1] in a period of multiple crises for party and for suffragists. A society with a large membership, Cardiff Women's Liberal Association (WLA), if well organised and united, should have been a force to be reckoned in the city, able to exert influence over choice of candidates, as promised in 1894. The destructive impact of the suffrage issue after 1906 is therefore all the more evident as the coalition of interest and identities, built up over twenty years, as described in the previous chapter, was rapidly dismantled.

A number of linked historiographical strands provide the context of debates on this period. One strand has constructed the long, ambivalent relationship between the Liberal party and feminism: in the Edwardian period especially, Liberal women have been found wanting as feminists, following a policy of 'father knows best'.[2] Cardiff provides an example of a significant number of Liberal women who, having been let down by 'father' once too often, turned their back on the dysfunctional patriarchal family of Welsh liberalism. A second historiographical strand focuses on the impact of the National Union of Women's Suffrage Societies' (NUWSS) electoral pact with the Labour party, under the Election Fighting Fund (EFF) from 1911–14. South Wales and Cardiff, and the faithful liberalism of the region's suffragists, have been identified as sources of opposition to the policy. I have contributed to these debates, but have now revisited the material, as a postscript to the history of Cardiff WLA.[3]

A third historiography with a bearing on this chapter is the increasingly rich literature on the relationship of women to radical languages of populism and national identity.[4] This chapter returns to the exploration of chapter 3 of understandings of nation and nationhood, the relationship of feminism to national identity and of women to 'the people of Wales'. During the constitutional crisis of 1909–10 the language of government and its supporters, including the Liberal press, became increasingly populist, as they conjured up the 'coming struggle between the Peers and the people'.[5] A language traditionally used in oppositional discourses by radicals and reformers to claim a wider citizenship and a voice for the unenfranchised was now being used in support of government policy – albeit a radical policy – in a way which attempted to silence and exclude half the population. This language was used in the context of a 'politics of disruption', in which male control of the public political spaces of Cardiff and other towns was sometimes violently reasserted.[6] The effect was increasingly to delegitimize, as Cardiff suffragists protested, the participation of women in the public political sphere. As Helen Fraser, NUWSS organizer, protested at a south Wales meeting, 'Men were not "the people", men and women together were "the people" . . . It was a farce, and the sooner men talked less of the will of the people the better'.[7] In this process, concepts of 'decency', of 'freedom of speech', of localism and of Welshness were used, both against and in defence of the suffragists.

A specifically Welsh dimension to the use of this language was injected by the central role in events of David Lloyd George, the chancellor of the Exchequer: in addition to the meanings of 'the People' traditionally expressed in British radical discourses, Lloyd George was able to draw on the understanding of 'the people of Wales' formulated by Henry Richard in the 1860s, and nurtured in Cymru Fydd in the 1890s. In that period, as we have seen, Liberal women had made determined, and partly successful, efforts to reshape the masculinist language of nationalism and ensure the inclusion of women. Support for women's political and social aims, represented as 'rights and duties' in the nation, had, for a while, become integral to Liberal visions for Wales.[8] As we saw, this version of national identity weakened as Cymru Fydd lost momentum, and feminists and suffragists continued to have an awkward relationship to 'Welshness'. For the Edwardian period, this has been explored by Angela V. John,[9] who has examined the way that '[n]ationality, language, history and a claim to the proverbial high moral ground were drawn upon to distance suffragettes from the true Welsh'.[10] John has explored issues of masculinity and the disruption of gender relations, in response to 'the transgressive nature of [militant] female activists', and, briefly, the Lloyd George 'factor' as an issue for Welsh supporters of women's suffrage, in a period when the chancellor was a member of a Liberal Cabinet with other overriding priorities.[11] I argue that this deployment of 'Welshness' against women was again a product of a period of crisis, but that in Cardiff, and south Wales more generally, it did lasting damage to the party and to women's party organization.

### Cardiff WLA in the twentieth century

Cardiff WLA emerged into the post-Boer war period with only cautious optimism about the future for liberalism and women's organization; there was a feeling of emerging from a very dark period for liberalism, of divisions in the party and loss of faith, and of looking forward to a renewal of 'faith and vigour for the cause of peace retrenchment and reform'.[12] The nostalgic use of the old slogan suggested perhaps a wilful ignoring of the changes signified by the rise of Labour, and the turn to New Liberalism; and, with historians' hindsight, it reflects blissful innocence of the impact the suffrage issue would have on women's relations with liberalism in a few short years. Cardiff was regained by the Liberals in 1900, and in 1901, with electioneering work and public meetings on women's suffrage and famine in India, the association reached a record membership of 1,163. A year later, however, this had fallen to 818 paid-up members, with significant decreases shown in some of the largest wards and in the more working-class areas.[13] The association's secretary, Mary Ellis, had investigated falling ward membership, and identified among the causes a trade depression and poor ward organization. However, the achievements of the association were also enumerated. Thanks to the WLA, Ellis wrote, Cardiff now had women on the board of guardians and school board, had carried out valuable electoral work, getting women voters to the poll for municipal elections and 'helping to return good men to the council', had contributed to the political education of the city by bringing to the town 'first rate political speakers', and had worked for temperance reform and social purity. But the membership was an ageing one, and Ellis appealed to young women to come forward in 'the cause of righteousness and justice'.[14] In the years which followed, membership in Cardiff WLA was to fluctuate, with an overall decline to just over eight hundred until the split in 1910–11.[15]

In the course of the decade 1900–10, a new context for women's political activity developed in Cardiff. In the 1890s, as we have seen, women were involved in the mixed-sex, but male-dominated, institutions and societies which aimed to moralize and civilize the growing town. The WLA had been one of the few female political organizations in the town, along with (briefly) the Women's Local Government Society (WLGS), at bottom a Liberal organization, and the British Women's Temperance Association (BWTA), also closely connected to Welsh Nonconformist liberalism as well as to British nonconformity and feminism. In the first decade of the new century, a specifically female political culture grew up, much of it now coming from the new radical forces, the left and the suffrage societies. Some indication of the breadth of the new forces was shown in the united campaign to get a municipal working women's hostel established in the town, which began in 1910, and brought together religious organizations, social purity and vigilance groups, trade unions and the labour movement as well as women's political organizations including the WLA, the Cardiff and District Women's Suffrage Society (C&DWSS), the Women's Freedom League (WFL) the Women's Labour League (WLL), the Women's Co-operative Guild (WCG), the BWTA, the Association of University Women, the University Settlement, the Ladies Association for the Care of Young Girls (headed by the wife of the bishop of Llandaff) and the Women's Auxiliary of the Cardiff Free Church Council. The groups cooperated in large meetings, in joint statements and in lobbying the city council. The leadership of the group seems to have come from within the WFL, and the approach to the issue was decidedly New Liberal or municipal socialist, explicitly rejecting the argument for the charitable or religious model of provision and instead looking to the example provided by Manchester, one of the models of municipal government for New Liberals and socialists in this period.[16] The Women's Social and Political Union (WSPU) was also present in the city, though not identified as a society with the hostel campaign. In the same period, the WLL, along with the National Federation of Women Workers and the Workers' Union, were involved in attempts to unionize women in the town and to organize support for striking women elsewhere, while women workers in Cardiff's breweries, flour mills, laundries and the sweet-making industry came out on strike, attended meetings and joined trade unions.[17] What was the significance of this new context for the WLA? It may be reflected in the difficulty for the WLA in recruiting young women, who could now find other ways to fight for 'righteousness and justice'. While some of the new organizations reflected an old philanthropic and reforming tendency, the suffrage and labour organizations raised the bar of 'radicalism' and set a new standard of activism. In the national context, militancy made all suffragists think hard about what they were willing to do for their own emancipation. In the new local context, while the issue of leadership, or lack of it, from the WLF was important,[18] Liberal women in cities like Cardiff found themselves in a supportive female political culture which endorsed their independence.

*1906–1910: decency and indecency in the public sphere*

The sequence of events which was to destroy relations between Cardiff WLA and the party began with the general election of 1906; the association therefore had an early lesson in the betrayal by their party experienced by Liberal suffragists nationally over the next few years. Cardiff's Liberal candidate in the 1906 general election was Ivor Guest, a Unionist who now supported the Liberals on free trade. Guest was a known opponent of women's suffrage; his family had developed an anti-suffrage tradition, his mother Lady Wimborne, a founder of the Ladies' Grand Council of the Primrose League, having been one of the signatories of the notorious 1889 Appeal Against Female Suffrage.[19] Guest needed the WLA to work for his election, so the association was able to extract a pledge from him that he would not oppose women's suffrage, and 200 women worked to get him elected. While technically honouring his pledge by abstaining from voting on women's suffrage in the Commons, Guest intervened in the second reading debate on the women's franchise bill of February 1908 to warn of 'the serious menace which would be the result if women had the vote'.[20] Thereafter, as anti-suffragism entered its organized and active phase, Guest took a prominent role, as a speaker and as secretary, then treasurer, to the Women's National Anti-Suffrage League, formed in the summer of 1908.[21] The demoralization of at a least a section of the Cardiff association must have been significant, the extent to which their loyalty had been abused being all too clear; these members now began to turn to alternative methods of pursuing their suffrage aims. The formation of the C&DWSS was announced in July; while the president of the new society was a Tory, Liberal domination of the new society was evident among the names of the executive committee, including that of WLA president Edith Lester Jones.[22]

Many of the political events in Cardiff and south Wales more generally in this period can be understood in terms of the 'politics of disruption'.[23] The WSPU had, since 1905, developed the tactic of interruption of political meetings addressed by ministers, including continuous interruption, which meant that speeches might go completely unheard, or meetings abandoned.[24] This gave rise to a number of responses, at the level of government and local party. The rank and file of young men in the party – their numbers swollen by other opponents of women's suffrage and by freelance hooligans –

turned the tables (as they saw it) on the suffragists by breaking up their meetings, preventing speeches being heard, in some cases creating near-riot conditions. As a prominent member of the Liberal cabinet against which the WSPU was waging war, Lloyd George was the frequent target of disruption, inside and outside Wales. Following his experience when speaking in support of women's suffrage at the Albert Hall meeting of 5 December 1908, Lloyd George announced 'reluctantly' that he would address no more meetings at which women were present, and a private bill criminalizing conduct which prevented the business of a public meeting and sanctioning the use of private stewards to keep order was quickly passed into law. Liberal party organizations and national leadership attempted to prevent women attending political meetings at which ministers were speaking, or forbade them from asking questions. The ticketing of meetings was tightened up, creating, as the C&DWSS put it, 'humiliating' conditions on women's entry. There was no attempt in any of this to distinguish between militant and constitutionalist suffragists, or between Liberal and non-party women. Indeed, the militant speakers who toured south Wales at this time, holding meetings on street corners and at factory or dock gates, got off more lightly from the impromptu crowds which gathered – mainly of young boys and working men – than did suffragists at the indoor meetings subject to organized wrecking by Liberal supporters.[25]

In south Wales, the most vivid examples of the 'politics of disruption', containing very real threats of violence and bodily harm, were provided by male Liberals and anti-suffragists. In 1908, meetings in Cardiff, Pontypridd and Caldicot, organized by Liberal women and members of local branches of the WFL, were to be addressed by NUWSS president Millicent Fawcett and WFL president Charlotte Despard, with platforms arranged to represent local male Liberal support. Despard, a long-time socialist, also spoke at Llanelli and Swansea for the ILP. The meetings were broken up, and women were driven from the meeting halls and hunted through the streets with a ferocity which requires explanation. That the demonstrators were government supporters is clear from the interpretation of the crowd's behaviour as 'paying back in their own coin' those who disrupted meetings of Cabinet ministers.[26] However, the organizers and speakers at these events were themselves wholly innocent of the disruptive tactics against government ministers being imitated, as it was claimed, by the crowd.[27] Martin Pugh's explanation for the Liberal party's 'extraordinarily hostile reaction' to the WSPU can be extended to the reaction to suffragists more generally: the party and its supporters were venting their anger and embarrassment at the pressure from Liberal women, their 'own' women, their 'natural' supporters and irreplaceable election workers, who were now deserting in large numbers.[28] Millicent Fawcett, a Liberal Unionist who had moved increasingly towards conservatism (although supporting free trade), may particularly have been perceived as embodying this dangerous apostasy.

The incidents reveal the contest for occupancy of political spaces and representation in the life of the nation and the locality; a contest not, as was customary in local political life, of parties or factions, but of gender.[29] By force of numbers, volume of noise and the threat of violence – sheer, massed maleness – the suffragists were denied a hearing. Just how effectively this was achieved was shown in the Pontypridd meeting at which communication from the platform was reduced to two placards held up to plead 'Give Mrs Fawcett one minute' and to announce the end of the meeting![30] Women's spaces within the halls were invaded and occupied, as were the streets of the towns; violence and threats of violence thus denying to suffragists the freedom of public political space.[31] A distinctly masculinist version of local and national identity was projected against the suffragist platform by the singing of the Welsh national anthem and of 'Sosban fach', and the 'New Zealand war chant', the last two linked with national pride and Welsh masculinity through the rugby field. The implication was that the suffragists lacked legitimacy in the face of national sentiment and that their presence in the city was not to be suffered. In response, the women and their supporters attempted to deploy a different version of Welsh manliness: appealing to chivalry and respect, they called for 'a characteristic Welsh welcome'; the demonstrators were asked to 'be men, have some respect for women; have some respect for courage'. Cllr Edward Thomas shouted from the platform of the Cardiff's Cory Hall that he was 'ashamed as a Welshman' – but he could be heard no further back than the press table, while the anti-suffragists mockingly sang music-hall songs about gender confusion.[32] As in Aberdare's 'hooligan carnival' the following year (see chapter 5), these were partisan crowds; the Cardiff rioters hunted the suffragists through the political geography of the city, from the Cory Hall to the Unionist headquarters and then to the Ruskin Institute, which was defended by 'stalwart socialists' while the women held a small meeting. As in Aberdare the following year, the meeting demonstrated the ability and willingness of women to act together across the divisions of militant and constitutional, party and non-party, while those who broke up the meetings were not interested in such distinctions, seeing all suffragists as a danger to the Liberal party and government, as well as to Welsh integrity.

The conditions under which women were now licensed to enter the Liberal tent were demonstrated in April 1909, when the anti-suffragist Cabinet minister Lewis Harcourt addressed a ticketed meeting of Cardiff Liberals.[33] Despite the fact that a number of women were subscribers to the Liberal Association, women were able to obtain tickets only through male members, who extracted a pledge of good behaviour from them and were then held responsible for their guests. Women were excluded from the body of the hall, confined to the balcony, distant from the stage and – in the event of interjections – inaudible to most below. As Harcourt ranged widely over government policy and issues of the day, he provided ample openings to suffra-gettes to point out the anomalous position of women, and there were three shouted interjections. Only the first heckler was able to make her point; as Harcourt spoke about taxation, she stood up in the balcony and shouted 'The tax is paid by women who want the vote' – an impec-cably Liberal suffragist position. After that, preventing the words coming out of the women's mouths was as urgent as ejecting them; the press described the second incident, as Harcourt spoke about tariffs versus free trade: 'At this point another suffragette made herself heard in the gallery. What she said was inaudible, but she was speedily silenced. A handkerchief was firmly held over her mouth, and she was passed towards the door, amid much good-natured chaff from the audience.'[34] It would be hard to find a more vivid image of the silencing of women. In closing remarks both Harcourt and Guest made refer-ence to the interjections, both referring to 'the decencies of public meetings', contrasting the right sort of women – local and decently silent – to indecorous, vocal, strangers. Again, the implication was that women's protest was an importation, and therefore lacked legitimacy. However, Harcourt's respect for local women who observed the 'decen-cies' did not extend to answering their written questions.[35]

The range of political issues covered by Harcourt allowed him to make frequent reference to 'the people': free trade and the 'cheap loaf', 'the Peers versus the people', the People's Budget; religious equality and Welsh desires for disestablishment; all gave plenty of scope for moving populist rhetoric. The irony was not lost on suffragists of all stripes in the audience. Ethel Lester Jones, daughter of the WLA president, whose father had a place on the platform, sent up a written question, asking 'how Mr. Harcourt thought it possible for the Government to express the will of the people while the women had no votes'.[36] It was, of course, only the vocal interjections of the militants, and their suppression, which were reported by the press. The attempt at written questions was recorded in a letter, written in the heat of her anger immediately after the meeting by Dr Erie Evans, one of the founders of C&DWSS. Evans had obtained a ticket from Mr Lester Jones, having promised that she would be silent throughout, 'a pledge it was easy for me to give in as much as I am strongly opposed to any attempt to interfere with free speech'. Her protestations were a reference to the accusation that suffragettes, by interrupting meetings, were attacking freedom of speech. In other circumstances, suffragists pointed out that free speech had tradition-ally meant the right of public assembly without interference from the authorities, not the silencing of individuals at meetings,[37] but Evans was demonstrating her reasonableness. She went on to develop the broader issue of women's place within the political nation, protesting at the way women's claims were increasingly cast outside the pale of legitimate political discourse. She claimed that after the meeting, Mr Lester Jones had been censured by the Cardiff Liberal Association (CLA) executive, amongst whom the feeling was that it was illegiti-mate for women to submit written questions at a public meeting. Reasonable to a fault, Evans was willing to accept that unenfran-chised women should not take up time at meetings with spoken questions, time which really belonged to voters – or, she might have said, to men, since no test of enfranchisement was applied to male questioners; but she expressed astonishment and dismay at the impli-cations of the new restrictions for women's political participation: 'that it should be regarded as illegitimate for unenfranchised sections of the people to put <u>written</u> questions had never occurred to me . . . It is well for us to clearly understand what are the disabilities imposed on us by our disfranchisement . . .'[38]

## Women or 'the people'?: political crises 1910–1911

The year 1910 was full of intersecting political events with national and local significance for Liberal suffragists. Both general elections of

1910 were called in response to the constitutional crisis, and the government's determination to resolve it by the introduction of the Parliament Bill, which would limit the Lords' power of veto. The January election having produced a House of Commons without a strong majority, a cross-party approach to the question of women's suffrage was attempted, with the formation of a Conciliation Committee of MPs. The committee's first bill had a successful second reading in July 1910, despite cabinet opposition. However, when a general election was called for December it became clear that no further parliamentary time would be available.

The opposition to women's suffrage of the prime minister, Asquith, in the context of the complex politics of the period, was crucial to the fate of the cause. However, it was Lloyd George who moved to the centre of suffragists' attention in 1910; having hitherto presented himself as a supporter of women's enfranchisement, he strenuously opposed the Conciliation Bill as being too narrow and undemocratic. For the militants, he henceforward stood for Liberal perfidy, and as an enemy of women's suffrage. The position was more fraught for Welsh Liberal suffragists: Lloyd George held iconic status as a representative of Welsh aspirations, acquired when, as leader of Cymru Fydd, he had appeared to embody the hopes of national progress. That status reached new heights in this period as he attained greater prominence on the British stage.[39] Opposition to Lloyd George, or criticism of his position, might cast the suffragists outside the pale of the nation, further delegitimizing their claims and drawing real hostility.

The chancellor, in his turn, was wont to wrap himself in national sentiment and populist language, as in a flag, in response to challenges from suffragists. At the end of September, having made a strong attack on the 'undemocratic' character of the bill in the House and outside it, he further annoyed suffragists nationally, but especially in Wales, when he told a delegation of local women at his home in Cricieth, that women's suffrage 'was not the cause which he had nearest his heart'. He was fighting, he said, 'the battle of the poor and oppressed'; the old causes of Welsh Nonconformist liberalism were 'the cause of the people from whom I have sprung', which he placed before all else.[40] When casting the House of Lords as the citadel of reactionary privilege, Lloyd George could speak eloquently and movingly of the evils of poverty.[41] 'The People' might then take on dual meaning: on one hand, all those united against power and privilege, which included Lloyd George and his audience; and, at the same time, 'the poor and oppressed', the agents of whose deliverance the Liberals would be.[42] Here, however, 'the cause of the people' was further recast in terms of the causes of Cymru Fydd, and moreover connected to Lloyd George's own origins, which in Cymru Fydd mythology had made him an emblematic representative of Welshness.[43] 'The people' of Lloyd George's British discourse became the *gwerin* of the Welsh national story, as he addressed his Welsh constituency through his visitors. The four-woman delegation included active local Liberals, who protested at the chancellor's assumption that they were not interested in the same causes as he. But the chancellor had explained to his visitors, as the newspaper headline put it, 'Why Wales is Unsympathetic': distinctive national institutions, Wales itself, he seemed to suggest, were under attack; the suffragette actions were laid at the door of the whole women's movement, and Lloyd George's position became that of the nation.

Lloyd George's populist discourse was both echoed and challenged in the response of Cardiff suffragists. Olive Stevenson-Howell, secretary of the Cardiff WFL, protested at the chancellor's intense identification with causes such as disestablishment, for which, she declared, there was now no demand.[44] She protested at the exclusiveness of that identification, in a government minister with wider responsibilities: were not women 'to be included in the people?' Responding to his rhetoric of 'the poor and oppressed', Stevenson-Howell pointed out that women were 'notoriously the worst paid class of workers and the most oppressed by sweating employers', but also suggested that they would soon find their way to the chancellor's heart if they withheld their taxes. Thus, like Lloyd George, Stevenson-Howell also divided the people, and women, into parts: since the first formulations of their demands for enfranchisement, women had based their claim on their status as taxpayers; but increasingly in the late nineteenth century, they had claimed citizenship for the sake of poor, oppressed and exploited women, both in Britain and in the empire. Cardiff Liberal suffragists continued, in this period, to remind themselves that they wanted the vote 'to guard against tyrannical laws for women, both in England and India, especially in the interests of purity', to combat the 'white slave traffic', as well as to look after the interests of working women in Cardiff.[45] The language of altruistic liberalism had been to a great extent shaped by women and, indeed, it was difficult for women to make claims not based on altruism: hence the necessity of dividing 'women' into groups with differing levels of agency.[46] But Stevenson-Howell's letter also signalled the alienation of suffragists from the long-standing visions of Welsh nationhood. Her anger was vividly conveyed by her biting letter, as had been the anger of Erie Evans the previous year. In happier times, both would have been active Liberals; however, these were not women of the Cymru Fydd generation and, excluded from the Liberal conversation, they now declared that its terms were bogus.

The following day, it was announced that the chancellor had given instructions that women were to be excluded from the annual meetings of the Welsh National Liberal Council (WNLC), to be held at Mountain Ash, near Aberdare. WLAs had been affiliated to the WNLC since its formation in 1898, and while women's representation on the council was weak, those women who kept up the connection included such party stalwarts as Maria Richards of Aberdare, Susannah Gee from Denbigh, Kate Freeman of Swansea and Lady Brynmor Jones, all of whom, in the 1890s, had been instrumental in building women's Liberal organization and in bringing male and female liberalism closer. In the event, the meetings were cancelled when a general election was announced,[47] but the damage done was not cancelled. The council's conventions have been seen as representing 'the idea of the political unity – almost the general will – of a nation';[48] it was a nation from which women could be excluded, it seemed, by edict.

## *Losing Cardiff*

The national crisis and the deteriorating relations between the government and the women's movement came together in Cardiff in the last three months of 1910. The suffragist MP D. A. Thomas was about to retire. With the lesson learned from their support for Ivor Guest in 1906, the prominent part taken by other Welsh Liberal MPs against suffrage bills over the last two or three years and with Lloyd George's hostility providing legitimacy to Welsh anti-suffragists, the Cardiff WLA executive called a national conference of Welsh Liberal women. The conference was an attempt to produce a united voice in support of the Conciliation Bill, but it was also intended to go further, with an application of the 'test question' in Wales: that is, that WLAs should refuse electoral help to candidates whose position on women's suffrage was not satisfactory. The conference was reported at great length by the Cardiff press, under headlines like 'Welshwomen in fighting mood. Boycott of Liberal MPs', and 'Vote Before Party. Liberal Women's Resolve'. The meeting was haunted by the absent Lloyd George, as one speaker after another referred to him, beginning with the president in her opening remarks. The first resolution, asking that the period of truce in Parliament be used to pass the Conciliation Bill into law, reaffirmed in its preamble 'demands for Welsh Disestablishment . . .', a clear reference to Lloyd George's argument with Welsh suffragists, and a sign that as yet Liberal suffragists, unlike the non-party campaigners like Stevenson-Howell, felt the need to placate the old Nonconformist sentiments of Wales. There were only three dissentients to the potentially divisive resolution which proposed that, should the government not grant facilities for the bill, Liberal women should cease work for their party until the vote was won and that, in the coming election, they should work only for Liberals who supported the bill. The resolution was 'a challenge to all Liberal women to do something practical in their own cause' and to 'bring some pressure on [the chancellor] as the Welsh Liberal leader'.[49] However, Lloyd George increased his majority in the December election: reports to the NUWSS in this period suggest that an anti-suffragist stance could only improve his standing in his constituency.[50] Analysis of attendance at the conference suggests that this first attempt in some years to produce a Welsh voice for women's liberalism was not indicative of strength or unity at this time. The main impact of the resolution was to be felt in Cardiff.

When the Cardiff Liberal Association announced that it had invited Sir Clarendon Hyde, an anti-suffragist tycoon, to be their candidate,[51] the executive of the WLA quickly announced that, in line with the conference resolution, the association would not work for Hyde's election. A split in the association immediately emerged, to be cynically exploited by Hyde and his agents. A number of WLA activists held a meeting with Lady Clarendon Hyde, giving rise to a report that 'the women Liberals of Cardiff are enthusiastic in the people's fight against the Peers, and . . . determined to do their part in securing victory'. Hyde issued the report as an election leaflet, with the message 'Men of Cardiff – The Women want you to Vote thus: Hyde X'.[52] Suffragists must have ground their teeth at this exploitation of unenfranchised women by a candidate who would deny them the vote. Numbers of the anti-Hyde camp took themselves off to other constituencies, notably Swansea, to work for suffragist candidates. The constitutional crisis was too serious for them to remain idle during the election – women Liberals had a long history of opposition to the power of the unelected peers – but the bitter experience of Cardiff politics in recent years had made them determined to work only for 'the right candidate'.[53] Cardiff was lost to the Conservative Ninian Crichton Stuart, who had given the right answers on women's suffrage to the C&DWSS. According to his wife – and it must have given satisfaction to report it – 'a great number of women workers of all classes' had helped in his election.

In the post-mortems on 'Who Lost Cardiff?' women who had withdrawn their support from Hyde got their share of the blame, which they were happy to accept, since it demonstrated the importance of the women's associations in election work.[54] Blaming the women went further: despite their protestations that 'there were no truer Liberals', they were also accused of 'treachery', indicative of the extent to which it was assumed that women would and should set aside their own political aims at such a time, while the various categories of male voters who had stayed away from the poll or given their vote elsewhere were regarded as having legitimate political reservations. It was 'treachery' because women's efforts were deemed to belong to the party, or to the causes of liberalism, and never to themselves; the language of altruistic liberalism, of duty and citizenship, which women themselves had done so much to develop, was turned against them. There might be 'no truer Liberals', but they were, over the next few months, to redefine what that meant. They retained, they declared, their belief that 'the full representation of the people' was a 'Liberal principle', but they had their self-respect to consider.[55] Now there was no attempt to conciliate the old Welsh party: WLA president Edith Lester Jones declared that women's suffrage was more important 'even than Home Rule and Disestablishment'. The declaration indicated the distance travelled: home rule and disestablishment, with the enfranchisement of women and support for temperance, had formed fixed points of political identity for Welsh women Liberals in the 1890s. After being censured by the party, Lester Jones, four of her vice-presidents, eight members of the executive committee and many ordinary members resigned from the WLA to form the Cardiff Progressive Liberal Women's Union (CPLWU) in April 1911. There came a time, said Lester Jones, 'when they had to put principle before anything else . . . when they saw some of the best of their women leaving them, it was time for them to consider their position'.[56]

As the formation of the new society shows, some of these women had not cut themselves off from liberalism, but they had fundamentally redefined what their liberalism meant, rejecting the language of Welsh radicalism: in the WLF, the term 'progressive' had long signified those who put their own enfranchisement first, and this is what many women in south Wales now decided to do. With a nominal membership of 845 and new officers, Cardiff WLA retained its affiliation to the WLF for just one more year.[57] After that, the association, or at least its leading figures, appear simply to have been absorbed into the Liberal Association, becoming visible mainly as the Ladies' Social Committee of the association, and as the Cardiff Free Trade Bazaar Committee. When a prospective Liberal candidate began to cultivate the constituency in 1913, he met women of the party only in this guise, and their fund-raising skills rather than their political or electoral organization were the object of his flattery.[58] The Ladies' Social Committee appears to have provided an alternative focus for women who wished to put party before women's suffrage after 1910, providing continuity within the party for women's activities into the First World War, fund-raising for the association, keeping social events going and sewing and fund-raising for the Red Cross.[59] The progressives remained a small and ineffectual group into the post-war years.[60] However, as Cardiff WLA collapsed, the C&DWSS reached a membership of over one thousand, as the WLA had once done.

### Cardiff suffragists and the Election Fighting Fund

Given the history of the disillusionment of Cardiff Liberal suffragists with their party, the position taken by the C&DWSS on the Election Fighting Fund (EFF) needs to be revisited and re-examined as an episode in the history of women's Liberal politics in Cardiff. The response of the NUWSS to the conciliation crisis, and the setting up of the EFF have, thanks to a number of histories produced in the 1980s and 1990s, become central to the understanding of the suffrage struggle in the few years before the outbreak of war in 1914, and especially in its relationship with the Liberal and Labour parties and the ILP. In so far as the suffrage movement was successful, the EFF has been established by these histories as the keystone of effective strategies in those years. While the alliance between the NUWSS and Labour was tactical as far as some of the NUWSS leadership was concerned, it has also been read by historians as a policy motivated not just by disillusionment with the Liberal government by a predominantly Liberal women's movement, but as one driven by socialist or leftward-moving women to bring about a democratic alliance for adult suffrage.[61] Cardiff, which led south Wales's resistance to the new policy, affords an opportunity to consider the impact of the strategy at local level. Such a study reveals the complexities of women's politics in this period; it provides a rather enigmatic postscript to the story of the Cardiff WLA

Wales provided more than one front of early opposition to the new policy, which I have examined in two articles exploring the politics of Welsh suffragists and the relationship between national and local structures in the NUWSS, to support the argument that the opposition from Wales was more complex than simple Liberal loyalism.[62] Those articles were written before further research had revealed the nature of the crisis which had occurred in the Cardiff WLA in 1910–11. It is now possible to see the history of exploitation and betrayal of the constituency's hard-working Liberal suffragists, from the election of Guest in 1906 to the selection of Hyde in December 1910. Also clear is the extent to which leading women, along with some newer activists whose names first appear in accounts of meetings in these years, were already helping to set up an alternative sphere of suffrage activity in 1908.

As Liberal women's organization imploded in 1910–11, so the C&DWSS grew. Its subscription lists in 1912–13 were as impressive as those of the Cardiff WLA at its height, as in that year it became, briefly, the biggest society outside London.[63] The rapidity of its growth, from a late start, is significant, reflecting the crisis of women's liberalism. The society was a federation, in all but name, of eight local societies, in greater Cardiff, Barry and Penarth. It was larger and wealthier than other societies in the South Wales and Monmouthshire Federation of Women's Suffrage Societies (SWMFWSS), formed in December 1910, which were to some extent dependent on it, for financial as well as organizational help; the president and secretary of the Cardiff society filled the same offices in the SWMFWSS.[64]

The Cardiff and District Society exemplified the party political mix of constitutional suffragism,[65] and now clearly provided an alternative sphere of activity for Liberal women, by whom it was numerically dominated, not least in its committees. The vice-presidents and executive committee of the C&DWSS elected in 1913 shared at least half a dozen members with the same body in the CPLWU, and others had been leading members of the old WLA.[66] But the leadership also included a strong presence of Conservative women, including its president, and leading members of the Penarth branch. There were, perhaps, others, like Millicent Mackenzie, a committee member of the CPLWU, who was also a Fabian, and was to be the Labour candidate for the new University seat, the only woman candidate in Wales, in the 1918 parliamentary election. Apart from Mackenzie, it has not been possible to identify other Labour supporters amongst those whose names surface in the records of the suffrage society, perhaps reflecting lack of knowledge about Labour women in Cardiff at this time. The profile of class and social status presented by the C&DWSS – or, again, of its most visible members – was , not surprisingly, very like the old WLA.[67] These were all women who, it must be safe to say, should have harboured no illusions about what the Liberal party might do for them; the experiences of 1910–11 make the C&DWSS role in the NUWSS controversies over election policy, in 1912–14, all the more complex.

In support of her understanding of Welsh suffragism, Sandra Holton cites Kenneth O. Morgan on the survival, despite signs of the rise of Labour, of community as opposed to class politics.[68] Morgan necessarily provides the long view, synthesizing evidence over time and across the coalfield to support his argument for the continuing unity of outlook until after the First World War.[69] In the midst of the bitter industrial tensions of those years, things may have felt rather different: other historians have emphasized the 'fracturing [of] the Edwardian illusion of a Liberal consensus' throughout south Wales, in a period of class conflict from 1910–14, a time 'when little heed was taken of the proponents of class harmony'.[70] It must also be asked whether the political consensus described by Morgan and Holton, based exclusively on the forms taken by male Lib–Lab politics, holds good when the gaze is turned to *women's* politics, and their own accounts of this period.

Catherine Marshall, leading the EFF strategy, herself clearly believed that liberalism was the reason for Cardiff's opposition, and one cannot ignore evidence in the records of Marshall and the NUWSS that support for the Welsh Liberal agenda affected attitudes in the Welsh societies to operation of the new policy.[71] According to

Barbara Foxley, an academic active in the C&DWSS, writing about a Swansea by-election, south Wales suffragists were wedded to the Liberal party programme, would put that first in by-elections and were still inclined to put their faith in men who, despite the contrary evidence of their voting records, claimed to be convinced suffragists.[72] This is the very kind of hopeless faith in the Liberals on which the NUWSS had turned its back with the creation of the EFF, and which Cardiff Liberal suffragists had learned, from bitter experience, to reject. It is clear that the Liberal women who joined the suffrage movement in Cardiff from 1908–14, while some still remained attached to Liberal women's organization, were prepared to abandon the old Welsh Nonconformist Liberal programme and declare the question of women's enfranchisement the foremost question of the day.[73] The Swansea society presented the case against EFF involvement in the by-election rather differently from Foxley, emphasizing above all the delicate balance of the cross-party nature of their society, with all the parties represented in the leadership.[74] Foxley's presentation of the case looks all the more out of step in face of the evidence that by early 1913, despite the continuing opposition of some members of the federation committee, the south Wales societies had, in the face of what they considered as Asquith's betrayal of his pledges, come round to endorsing NUWSS policy.

However, the signals from south Wales continued to be ambiguous for some time. Until Foxley's letter of 1914, the south Wales suffragists appear not to have stated that it was loyalty to the Liberals which made them oppose the election policy, rather than mistrust of the Labour party in south Wales.[75] In their resolutions of June 1912, the Cardiff society had included amongst the grounds of their objections the fear that they could not rely on the support of miners' MPs in the votes on the Franchise Bill, a fear based on the record of the miners' delegates at Labour party conference, and the absence of miners' MPs and failure to secure pairs in the vote the previous March for the Conciliation Bill.[76] The feeling that the support of the Labour MPs was not to be relied on was not confined to south Wales: Isabella Ford had reported to the EFF committee, following discussions with ILP members, that an increase in the number of trade union, and especially miners', MPs following the general election, could mean that the Labour party's resolution to oppose any further franchise reform which did not include women might be rescinded, and support given to a third reading of the Franchise bill without the women's suffrage amendments.[77] But, while Ford appeared to be offering a cool assessment of the political situation on which to base strategy, the tone of some of the communications from Cardiff was more bitter, claiming the superiority of local knowledge of coalfield politics. Writing to NUWSS secretary Kathleen Courtney, Mabel Howell reiterated the Cardiff society's distrust of the miners' influence, its belief that the new policy was an abandonment of the national union's non-party election line and that it would involve the loss of control of funds to Labour organizations. And, importantly, like the Swansea society, she feared the effect on the Cardiff society, and on the suffrage struggle as a whole, of a partisan policy.[78] Similarly, there is evidence that maintaining the cross-party mix was also important to the Penarth society, in which Conservative women seem to have had a presence: in this period riven with class and party hostility, it was perhaps all the more important to suffragists to preserve the non-partisan culture of their societies, which in a relatively short period of activity, compared to other regions of Britain, had produced an impressive level of organization.[79]

After the fiasco of Asquith's Franchise Bill, however, the evidence suggests gradual acceptance of the policy by Cardiff, rather than entrenched opposition based on loyalty to the government. In December 1912, the south Wales committee was still unanimously opposed to the election policy, but indicated that if Labour MPs voted the right way for the women's suffrage amendments to the Franchise Bill it would reconsider.[80] The Cardiff executive's report for 1912–13 indicated that with the collapse of the Franchise Bill, and what it saw as Asquith's failure to redeem his pledges to suffragists, 'the political outlook has completely changed', private members' bills were clearly futile: 'we must brace ourselves for a longer fight . . . we must work now so that when the time comes it shall seem wise to the powers that be to see that the Prime Minister is a Suffragist'.[81] The following year, the Cardiff annual report displayed the general election and by-election policies of the national union underneath its own rules, without comment.[82]

This evidence of the disaffection rather than the loyalty of Liberal women in Wales is supported by the decline, already discussed, of WLAs and individual membership. All of this may reflect the state of the Welsh Liberal party in this period; it must also indicate the strain on the loyalties of Liberal women as the political philosophy and the party on which they had based their ideals and hopes for generations so clearly failed to match their expectations or to acknowledge their demands. The seismic events in Cardiff were just the most dramatic playing-out of that disaffection. It might justifiably be said that by 1914 suffrage organization had effectively replaced Liberal organization for women, in Cardiff and south Wales. The NUWSS in Wales had more societies, and a wider geographical spread of membership in 1912–14, than did the Liberal women's associations. There was a growth in both membership and new constitutional suffrage societies in south Wales in these years, and vocal support for the movement in the coalfield, which the adoption of the EFF policy appears to have encouraged. Together with the membership of other smaller suffrage societies, this suggests a commitment on the part of women in Wales to the suffrage cause now far outstripping their active involvement in the Liberal party.[83]

Is it possible to suggest which women, what kinds of women, might chose which side in the split of 1910–11? Or can the split tell us more about the nature of Cardiff liberalism? The CPLWU and the C&DWSS included representatives of the families who did much to provide Cardiff with a more liberal civic culture, and there were a number of those who put women before party in the 1894 guardians' elections who were also to be found on the suffragist side in 1910–11: Annie Mullin and Kate Jones were examples. On the other hand, the suffragist side also included prominent members of old Cardiff liberalism and Nonconformity: during the post-election bitterness, Fred H. Jotham, owner of a men's outfitter, identified with the old, economizing, conservative liberalism of the city, was a public ally of the suffragists, and his wife became president of the executive of the CPLWU. Women of the Marychurch family, best known for a history of Nonconformist good works, also made the move from WLA to C&DWSS.[84] Mrs (Principal) Edwards, president of the Glamorgan union of the BWTA, endorsed the suffragist policy from the beginning: she believed that there would be no reform until the law of the country was 'womanised'.[85] Cllr Edward Thomas, a venerable temperance campaigner and promoter of Welsh cultural identity, played a role in Cardiff liberalism, as supporter of women's suffrage, akin to that played by Keir Hardie and George Lansbury on the national stage. All this suggests that old liberalism of the city still had something to offer women, and that the clear divide between it and the progressive or New Liberal tendency was less marked, when support for women's suffrage was part of the picture, than has previously been suggested.[86]

It might be argued that there had long been at least two WLAs in Cardiff, one looking towards the party, interested in support and fund-raising, the other having a clear political agenda of its own, in which women's enfranchisement was central and seen as in conformity with the frequently invoked 'Liberal principles'. The disputes of 1894 had already indicated the nature of the division. Both sides will have seen themselves as ardent, loyal and 'true' Liberals. It is not possible simply to characterize and contrast the two groups according to class, status, national identity, 'old' radicalism versus New Liberalism, or other characteristics, at least partly because the extant sources do not permit such an analysis. There was clearly a greater ease amongst the women who formed the Progressive Union with throwing off the old Welsh Liberal programme. While both groups included many temperance supporters, it was the Progressive Union which contained the well-known activists. The progressives appear to have been, on the whole, better educated, with a number of academics, secondary school teachers and heads and graduates. The best-known women from the old WLA, those who had a distinct public profile, were overwhelmingly on the Progressive Union side, while for many of the others, one is attempting to draw some conclusions about them from the little known about their husbands or families. Perhaps that is the real difference: women who were inclined to put their own enfranchisement first in this crisis had embraced the public political sphere, were known political and philanthropic figures in their own right and took leadership positions in other causes such as temperance or the education of girls and women. Those who put party first were those more likely to be doing what Aberdare WLA called 'quiet work for the Liberal party', welcoming the auxiliary role. These differences could in the normal run of things be accommodated within the association; the ward structure of a large association provided space for them, and there was plenty of work of different kinds for all to do. But the conditions of 1910–11 were not in the normal run of things: a real national constitutional crisis, a threat to cherished Liberal aims, occurred at a time when both the suffrage movement and the anti-suffrage movement were most active and militant, and when the suffrage movement was in conflict with the government. Into that mixture was thrown the insulting indifference of Liberal associations to the political desires of the women on whom they relied for electoral work. What had appeared to be a large and strong WLA then split along a natural fault, in a way which appears to have destroyed it as a political force.

171

The problem of the leadership, or lack of leadership, provided by the WLF on the suffrage issue must be taken into account in considering the fate of Cardiff WLA. Wales's test-question resolution of 1910 had been passed against a background of a resolve on the part of the WLF to do nothing to endanger the return of a Liberal government, and the break-away group in Cardiff was uncomfortably aware that the unwillingness of Liberal women to take a stand on women's suffrage was exploited by the party, and taken as evidence that women did not wholeheartedly desire their own enfranchisement.[87] The new CPLWU identified itself with the Forward Suffrage Union founded by Eva McLaren in 1907, which aimed to make WLAs concentrate on women's suffrage while remaining active Liberals; but the lack of success of the movement is indicated by the creation, in 1913, of yet another Liberal suffrage ginger group, the Liberal Women's Suffrage Union. In that year it was reported that the WLF 'has just declared its willingness to continue to work for the Liberal government in spite of the Government's breach of faith with the women over the suffrage question' and that women in the Liberal party 'are generally content to be merely parts of the party machine'.[88] As Cardiff WLA found, there was, indeed, 'very little leadership' nationally,[89] and very little cohesion at the Welsh level. However, it should be emphasized that, while the new CPLWU was tiny compared to the old WLA, the latter ceased to exist entirely shortly after the split, becoming a rump which was absorbed into the CLA, while it must be safe to assume that many erstwhile members turned to the massively expanding C&DWSS. The lesson of Cardiff is not supine adherence to the party, but the polarizing and destructive potential of the party's refusal to take the suffragists seriously.

Despite the bitter words, and their president's ringing rejection of the Welsh Liberal programme, the CPLWU accepted an invitation from Lord St Davids to be represented in the WNLC.[90] It may have felt, as a very small association, that such membership would give it legitimacy. Might it have taken on electoral work again for the right parliamentary candidate? The opportunity was not to arise again in the pre-war years, and by the end of the war the association was too small, with twenty-five members, to have been a factor in what became three new constituencies. The CPLWU was not listed in the WLF returns after 1921; a new Cardiff and District WLA was affiliated in 1926, with Mabel Howell as secretary, and the following year claimed a membership of over four hundred.

## Conclusions

From 1906, Liberal suffragists found an increasing strain in maintaining their party identity; the confidence of most nineteenth-century suffragists that liberalism would – eventually – deliver full citizenship to women was lost.[91] Despite overwhelming electoral support for the party, Wales was not immune to the destructive conflict. In Cardiff WLA, as throughout Britain, 'some of the best of their women' were leaving the WLA and seeking new ways to work for enfranchisement.[92] They were able to find a home in the suffrage societies; as a result of the reconstitution and revived organization of the NUWSS, societies had been formed in Wales, including Cardiff in 1907, a society which was to become large and influential within a few years. It provided a channel for the energies of Liberal women: as membership of the WLA plummeted, the C&DWSS became the largest suffrage society outside London. By the spring of 1908, the city also had branches of the WSPU and of the WFL.[93] The year 1908 has been described as 'this inauspicious year' for Liberal women:[94] it was so in Cardiff. In that year, and into the following year, a number of public political meetings, organized by suffragists and by the Liberal party, provided the opportunity for the growing hostility between the two movements to manifest itself.

Similar, and in the long term more damaging, strains were experienced in 1910–11. In their refusal to repeat their mistake of 1906, instead boycotting the election campaign of another known anti-suffragist candidate, the association – or at least a section of its executive committee and activists – effectively destroyed women's distinct Liberal organization in the city. In the process, they revealed fractures and fault lines at the many levels of liberalism: the potential for division in a large, broad-church WLA; the weakness of their organization on an all-Wales basis, a sad decline from the late 1890s; the feebleness of the WLF position in refusing to withdraw its support from the Asquith government; and the weakness of local (male) Liberal organization which fell back on blaming the women, after failing to chose an acceptable candidate or to work effectively for him, in a period when the coalition of interests and identities which was Cardiff liberalism was falling apart.[95] In all this one can see the seeds of the post-war decline of liberalism, supporting the historiography of a crisis of liberalism in which feminism and the women's movement played their part. 'This was the beginning of the disintegration of the Liberal party.'[96] Given the disillusion of Liberal women, their role in the C&DWSS, in its opposition to the national union pact with Labour from 1912, is less easy to fathom than has been previously suggested, but supports, eventually, a picture of disillusionment and apostasy rather than loyalty.

The complexities and contradictions of the period were very fully played out in Cardiff. However, the story is not just an example of national trends, but also reflects local circumstances and conditions. Liberalism in Cardiff, never safe in electoral terms, has been described as a 'bizarre coalition', complicated by militant Protestantism, Irish and Catholic interests and the rise of Labour, with all the concomitant tendencies to splits. The fact that it was also the largest single-member constituency in the United Kingdom made it very expensive electorally[97] – hence the liking for wealthy candidates, and the need for volunteer organization provided by women. By the turn of the century, women's Liberal organization in Cardiff was also a coalition of different identities and interests, as the social and civic development of Cardiff brought into liberalism – and women's politics more broadly – activists who did not necessarily put first the old agenda of Welsh radicalism. While temperance and education reform remained central to these new women, those goals were linked to a feminist agenda, and not necessarily to one of nation-building. Some of them were able to work, at least on some issues, with socialist and labour-movement women, and militant and constitutionalist suffragists, cooperating in the interests of 'working women', as well as of their own emancipation. And, in the choice between party and women's suffrage, it was still possible for some representatives of the old radicalism to make common cause with the newer elements in Cardiff society, and with those who put 'women' first. This is a complex picture of women's politics and, indeed, of urban politics and social movements in Cardiff more broadly.

In his seminal work on Cardiff, Martin Daunton provided a schematic understanding of Liberal politics in the town, dividing the town between the 'puritans' and the rationalists: 'There were two largely separate groups of men, agencies and attitudes, a difference between encouraging the full use of potentiality, and purifying the working class and urban society.'[98] Gender changes the picture: not only were there not just 'groups of men', but in a range of social organizations and a variety of causes, the picture is of women (and men), attitudes and agencies now making common cause, now separating, in the making of a complex modern society. Effective work in elections, a now established place in poor law work, their contribution to the political and cultural development of the city and the growth of a wider female urban political culture in which they participated had given Liberal women a sense of their own worth and entitlement. Thus, an independent suffragist identity was forged over two decades of political and social activism, enabling them to cut their losses, shrugging off the undervaluation of their aims and ambitions by the party. This was the local context for the formation of broader political identities.

In the late nineteenth century, women had been able to identify with, and expand, the language of altruistic liberalism, producing a highly developed discourse of citizenship as 'womanly duty'.[99] In Wales, the closeness of this to the agenda of Welsh Nonconformity had meant that the progress of women and of the nation was seen as advancing 'hand in hand'. It has been argued that English feminism abandoned the language of populism, replacing it with 'womanhood' in the 1880s and 1890s.[100] The national resurgence of the Cymru Fydd period, during which women placed themselves at 'the spoken centre'[101] of the Welsh national conversation, enabled 'womanhood' and 'the people' to retain their connection rather longer in the Welsh context. That connection weakened under the impact of divisions in Wales. In the crisis of liberalism of the Edwardian years, a popular masculinist nationalism was deployed by the Liberal crowd, while the party's refusal to take women's political ambitions seriously combined with its deployment of the old idiom of Welsh liberalism to enforce party loyalty, and to delegitimize the voice of unenfranchised women. It was at one level a battle for possession of political spaces, the right to a presence, to speak certain words and be heard to speak them. That battle was easily won, in the short term, by aggressive masculinity. At another level, words were themselves the area of contestation; it was about the relationship of women to the Liberal party, and it was also about their relationship to the language of radical liberalism. However, the context should not be forgotten. It was not inevitable that national feeling should be roused against 'incomers' and 'alien' ideas. The robust patriarchalism of Welsh society is not an adequate explanation; nor, alternatively, is the threatened masculinity of the public sphere.[102] All of these may have been conjured up in the 1890s, when national feeling was at its height, but when, in contrast, there was enthusiastic support for women's role in public life and their enfranchisement and a warm welcome for visiting women speakers who came to spread the message. By 1908, transgressive militancy had licensed men to abandon chivalry towards middle-class ladies, but in a very specific context: as the Liberal government moved into its sought-for confrontation with the Lords, the challenge from women who had once been relied on as the party's 'natural' supporters was not to be endured. By spring of 1911, the context had changed; Liberal and Labour suffragists, local women and visitors together occupied the stage of the Cory Hall before a large and appreciative audience, even as, in the House of Commons, Lloyd George voted in favour of the second Conciliation Bill.[103] However, with the constitutional fight behind it, home rule now became the crucial source of pressure on the government, and the years 1912–13 were to be marked by further legislative setbacks for suffragists: the loss of the third Conciliation Bill in March 1912; the introduction of the government's Home Rule Bill without a women's suffrage clause, and the defeat of an attempt to amend it in November; the withdrawal of the 'manhood suffrage' Franchise and Registration Bill, after the attempt to introduce a women's suffrage amendment, in January 1913. The maleness of the British constitution was entrenched and extended.[104] In 1914, the WLF noted that E. T. John's Welsh Home Rule Bill included provision for equal enfranchisement of men and women,[105] so restoring to Welsh liberalism its reputation for enlightenment in the matter. However, as the statistics of decline of women's Liberal organization in south Wales show, the breach between women and the party was not healed.

# Conclusion

This book has demonstrated the intersections of gender, nation and party which created a complex and distinctive political context for women in Wales at the end of the long nineteenth century. It has suggested important continuities, in personnel, aims and ethos, between the women's Liberal movement which burgeoned in the 1890s and earlier campaigns which united votes for women with temperance and the campaign to repeal the Contagious Diseases Acts; and between the earliest Women's Liberal Associations (WLAs) and Welsh national causes of the 1880s. Because of the political and ideological hegemony of a form of Nonconformist liberalism which had successfully represented itself as embodying Welsh nationhood, tensions between party and 'women', and party and feminism, which historians have described in the British context, were further complicated for Welsh Liberal women as those dimensions were cross-cut by nationalism. For some, this would have been a real, felt, political and ideological dilemma; for others, including the first, non-Welsh, leadership of the Welsh Union of Women's Liberal Association (WUWLA), it was a tactical one in the context of feminist aims for the Women's Liberal Federation (WLF). The book has also demonstrated that in parts of Wales women's Liberal organization gave place to women's membership of suffrage societies, as the crisis of faith of Liberal suffragists manifested itself in dramatic fashion, challenging previous understandings of the loyalty to party of women in Wales. Then, the sacred tenets of Welsh liberalism were explicitly rejected by significant groups, in favour of their own emancipation. Such a narrative is essential to the further development of studies of women's political history in nineteenth century Wales, which contrasts with English women's political history, where the long gap which once existed between Mary Wollstonecraft and the Edwardian suffrage movement has been filled by the history of women in early socialism and Chartism, in the anti-slavery and anti-Corn Law movements and in radical dissent, as well as a rich history of the suffrage movement from the 1860s onwards. The narrative provided here, and the example of English women's history, suggest the value of further research in the nineteenth century.

While claiming important elements of continuity, two distinct periods of activity have been highlighted, in the context of which the nature of women's liberalism, feminism and national identity have been examined. These periods were the 1890s, when women's Liberal organization was at its impressive height, and when it intersected both with a feminist agenda in the Women's Liberal Federation (WLF) and with the high point of Welsh national political identity, in Cymru Fydd; and the Edwardian period, when the incumbency of a Liberal government with a radical reforming agenda, within which women's suffrage was not a priority, coincided with, or gave rise to, the most polarizing manifestations of the suffrage movement, with a demonstrably highly destructive impact on women's Liberal organization. Both of these periods illustrate the difficulties – perhaps the impossibility – of the aim set by the WUWLA, of working for women's emancipation, for party and for nation, bearing out the claims of theorists and historians of gender and nation that nationalism and feminism have been mutually inimical. For the Edwardian period the south Wales perspective supports the view that the poisoning of relations between women Liberals and their party contributed to, perhaps was 'a major cause of',[1] the fatal weakness of Liberal organization after the war, thus complicating the well-worn analyses of the challenge of Labour and the impact of war. However, the local studies suggest that, while driving a wedge between women and party, feminism, and the desire to work for women, was a source of unity and cooperation, at least occasionally, between women of different parties, and from different points on the suffrage spectrum. A narrative of rise and decline has been presented, through national and local dimensions. The rise of women's Liberal organization has been seen to have been connected to Welsh conditions, including the 'rebirth of nation' from 1868, when Welsh grievances and aspirations could be given political form, but also to the suffragist push in the WLF which found ready support in Wales. Decline has been linked to British Liberal crises after 1895, to the splits in Welsh liberalism in the same period and to women's disillusionment with the party and the polit-

ical philosophy which they had believed would deliver their emancipation. However, that story of decline, though compellingly linked to
the longer history of the decline of the party, should not be allowed to
obscure the strength and importance of women's Liberal organization in its time, and the extent to which it enriches the political history
of Wales in this period.

The history provided here is not the only one possible. Studies in
other areas and localities, on other organizations and periods and
into the lives and activities of individual women might lead to
dramatic revisions and extensions of the analysis I have presented
here. One of my aims has been to provide a ground for such investiga-
tions. Further research would build on Ryland Wallace's useful
examination (published in 1991) of the earliest period of women's
suffrage and reform organization, and would test my suggestion that
support for women's suffrage in Wales had deeper and more indigenous roots (in so far as 'indigenous' has meaning in a nation of
migrants) than historians have suggested. Research and publication
on the suffrage movement as a whole is very much needed. In the
British context, publications offering new and ever deeper insights
into the women's suffrage movement and its connections to other
forms of politics proliferate, but in Wales the subject awaits system-
atic examination. The period between 1896 and the end of the South
African War has not been examined in detail here. The war has
recently been ascribed an important role in shaping understandings
of citizenship and in creating militant suffrage identities.[2] Women's
reactions to the war have also been included in an examination of the
way in which empire and understandings of empire afforded opportunities to feminists to claim citizenship, with a focus on the writings of
Josephine Butler, who was so influential in evangelical feminist circles
in Wales.[3] A closer examination of opposition to and support for the
war amongst women in Wales might be fruitful, contributing to the
growing literature on Wales and empire; and might well provide a
starting point for a study of women's anti-war activism in Wales in the
twentieth century. The period 1912–14, brought into closer focus,
might tell us to what extent Welsh Liberal suffragists were participants in the 'transnational feminisms' which have been discerned in
these years, and examine their enthusiasm for 'federal suffragism',
through support for the Welsh Home Rule Bill of 1914.[4] Studies
giving more attention to the diversity of women's politics would also
be useful: the Liberal Unionists had a small presence in Wales; the

records of the Welsh National Liberal Association may show which, if any, Welsh associations joined it after the 1893 WLF split, for which there is inconclusive evidence in the sources of the WUWLA and the WLF. Crucially, the identification and examination of more Welsh-language sources might reveal much about the differences which emerged at several points between 'north' and 'south'. My case studies, based on rich sources though they are, both present the view from the industrial and commercial, and rapidly anglicizing, south.

Issues which I have presented as part of the whole might be investigated as major themes in themselves. One such theme is the intersection of religion and women's public sphere. It has been a popular, and historiographically acceptable idea, that Nonconformity imposed an extreme form of 'respectability' on women in Wales, isolating them from a wider public sphere. On the contrary, it is clear that religion was a spur to action, and shaped political aims and ethos, imbuing politics with moral earnestness and reforming energy. It may also, I have suggested, have narrowed women's liberalism in places like Aberdare so that it was unable fully to respond to social realities in the industrial communities. Bringing religion and the public sphere to the centre of focus, as is now increasingly the case in British and US women's histories, would be an important contribution to Welsh women's and gender history. Another major theme might be the women's temperance movement in all its manifestations: Lambert's work on the movement in Wales makes no mention of the involvement of women; his discussion ends in 1895, and suggests that the temperance movement declined in Wales after 1890. As Ceridwen Lloyd-Morgan has pointed out, it is precisely in the early 1890s that the autonomous women's temperance organizations began to establish themselves. Lloyd-Morgan's work on women's organizations concentrates on those which conducted their business in Welsh, and suggests that the British Women's Temperance Association (BWTA) 'remained weak in Wales'.[5] Evidence suggests that this was not the case in south Wales, where many leading Liberal women were also active in the BWTA, as well as in other temperance organizations, suggesting the value of further research on the topic. Liberal women saw local government work as an important vehicle for temperance and other moralizing aims, but local government in Wales in this period is greatly under-researched; the terms on which women might be accepted as suitable candidates, and elected by the voters; how they were able to function when elected; and the reasons why this was still, after 1894 and well into the twentieth century, a very rare occurrence, might tell us a great deal about gender relations in Welsh communities and the nature of local political cultures. The relations between Liberal and Labour women, as for a few years they served side by side, either as elected representatives or as co-optees on local bodies, would cast a fresh light on the history of the familiar narrative, 'from Liberal to Labour', and what that shift meant for women's political practices, as well as the opportunities for public service and political careers.

These possible alternative analyses would contribute to our under-standing of the historical development of women's reforming, radical and suffragist political identities in Wales. More needs to be done on working-class, labour movement and socialist strands.[6] In the analysis of continuities and discontinuities, the period when, in communities like Aberdare, the Labour movement was displacing the Liberals from their dominance of local government and local affairs more generally might shed much light on the making and remaking of women's political identities in Wales. The study of Aberdare suggests that the shift did not open up wider opportunities for women, while in Cardiff, Labour women's organizations contributed to the making of a female political sphere in which women could, at least occasionally, make common cause. More work on this area would be fruitful, contributing to the growing field of Welsh urban histories.

Despite the gaps, the research for this book has opened up a new view on the landscape of Welsh politics in the period 1880–1914, revealing it to be alive with women's political activity, and in many respects actively shaped by women and their organizations. An effec-tive Women's Liberal Association was probably the greatest electoral asset for a parliamentary candidate, in a period – it appeared to be the consensus – when party organization in the constituencies was poor. They were inspired by Nonconformist ideals of moral and civic reform and public duty, devoted to Liberal causes and, up to a point, loyal to the party. But that point was, for a significant proportion, the choice between party and their own emancipation. The book has demonstrated that women's suffrage was always capable of creating tensions between women, while the evidence suggests that the major-ities were on the side of suffrage. Liberal ideological and organizational accommodation of feminism could become rejection when the party felt weak or threatened; in Wales, both acceptance and rejection would be linked to national identity and loyalty to Welsh causes. It is that intersection with nationalism which makes for the distinctiveness of Liberal politics for women in Wales. After the First World War, almost all the elements which have shaped this study had shifted: the suffrage struggle was partly won, the Labour party rapidly replaced the Liberals as the dominant party at every level and, while Labour inherited an interest in home rule or devolution, in the devastation of the depression, centralist solutions appeared more useful;[7] a nationalist party, Plaid Cymru, was established in 1925 which, though small until the 1950s, became a focus for both cultural and political nationalism. What happened to women's Liberal politics in the changed context? In 1928, there were records for an astonishing ninety-four associations in Wales, in WLF and Welsh Constituency Council records. While more than one-fifth recorded no membership figures for that year, there was a combined stated membership of over 6,400. However, eighty of those associations had been newly formed, or revived after a long hiatus, between 1925 and 1928, more than half of those in the last year; others had only a slightly longer history, and several associations formed in the mid-1920s had not made it to 1928.[8] Clearly, the picture in the mid-1920s was dire, a determined effort of organization had been made between the 1924 and 1929 general elections, and the prospect of the equal franchise act may have been a spur to political activity amongst women. But the party did not improve its position in Wales, and lack of WLF affiliation records 1928–36 makes it difficult to understand where women's Liberal organization was going at the end of the 1920s.

Such intractable data on its own reveals little of the characteristics of women's politics, or the reshaping of political identities in these years. However, the changes wrought in individuals and communities by political changes, and by the war and its aftermath, must often have been profound. Brief biographical details for one woman, Sarah Kate Evans, of Gadlys, Aberdare, suggest that women's political ideas might take unexpected directions. From a family of colliers and iron-founders, friendly society and trade union pioneers, Baptist ministers and Liberal activists, Kate Evans is remembered by her family as 'particularly emancipated'. She served as an army telegraphist in France during the war and then became a sub-postmistress in Swansea. She is described as 'suffragette to the core, admirer of Clara Zetkin, Helen Crawfurd, Sylvia Pankhurst, Aleksandra Kollontai, Inesse Armand, Emma Goldman',[9] a pantheon comprising British socialist suffragettes, a German socialist, two bolsheviks and an anarchist, some of them holding 'advanced' ideas on gender, marriage and sexuality. Clearly, in the early twentieth century, and perhaps especially as a result of the experiences of war, some very interesting changes occurred in the political and ideological mentalities of women nurtured in the cradle of Welsh Nonconformist liberalism. Such tantalizing glimpses provide the spur to further research.

# Appendix

## *1894 Elections for Board of Guardians, Cardiff Union: Brief Biographies of Women Candidates*

There were eleven women candidates out of ninety-two candidates in Cardiff wards, and one woman out of an unknown number of candidates in Penarth. Ten of the twelve were successful. Their party status was not always clear, as the notes below indicate, but all 'Independents' in the election were women, and all Independents came top of the poll in their wards. In only one ward where a woman ran did a man head the poll.

### *Biographies*

**Andrews, Mrs Emily Jane:** Independent/Liberal, Nonconformist. Top of the poll for Splott ward with 1,128 votes (17 candidates for 6 places). She was, at various times, Splott ward WLA president and a treasurer and vice-president of Cardiff WLA (Annual Reports). She was 'well known among the poorer classes in Roath and Splott', and had 'for several winters past . . . superintended a soup kitchen at Roath'. According to the press, she took a great interest in the welfare of the poor, worked with the Dorcas Society, 'and thoroughly knows the wants of the poor' (*WM*, 15 December 1894). Husband was councillor for Splott ward, and proprietor of a wagon-building business. She was born in Stroud, Gloucestershire; aged thirty-three in 1891, with two young daughters and two living-in servants (1891 census).

The problematic nature of Andrews's political alignment in the election was symptomatic of the controversial and contested position of women candidates. Andrews was variously described in the press as Independent, or as one of the official party slate of Progressive candidates. The Liberal agent Allgood listed her as Independent. The *WM*, in an editorializing post-election piece regretting some women's candidates abandonment of Independent status, said that Andrews had been 'Independent to the end', but that politics had been introduced into her campaign by the ward party, without her consent. In the 1898 guardians' elections, Andrews was on the official Liberal slate for St Mary's ward.

**Bleby, Emily Rose:** 'spinster'. A successful candidate in Penarth, the only woman candidate for an outlying ward of the Cardiff Union. A member of the first management committee of the Cardiff Charity Organisation Society (COS) (First quarterly and annual reports, CCL) along with her father, Revd R. H. Bleby, but is not listed in later extant reports. No profiles provided in the Cardiff-based press. Bleby wrote her thoughts on the role of women guardians for the Liberal journal *Young Wales*. Not all the contributors appear to have been Liberal, so Bleby's party alignment remains uncertain. The qualification for a woman guardian, she wrote, was 'domesticity enlarged and enlightened' (*YW*, May 1896).

**Davies, Mrs Margaret L.:** St John's ward, 4th in poll with 898 votes (20 candidates, 8 places). Nonconformist, Liberal. While listed in most sources as an official Liberal candidate, she was described as 'not a political candidate' by the *SWDN*, though the daughter of 'advanced Liberals'. Husband Revd Charles Davies of Tabernacle Baptist Church, the Hayes: she had been involved in his ministerial work during twenty-four years of marriage, had 'wide experience among the poorer classes', had lived in Liverpool, where she did philanthropic and nursing work. 'Not a platform speaker', Welsh-speaking. (*SWDN*, 14 December 1894; *WM*, 15 December 1894). One of the official Liberal candidates for St John's ward in the 1898 guardian's elections (Allgood papers, CCL).

**Gridley, Mrs Agnes Jane:** Liberal, Splott. Elected 3rd in the poll with 891 votes (17 candidates, 6 places). Nonconformist, Progressive. Described as 'the wife of a working man'. '[I]n the Splott parish, where there are a large number of very poor people, she has been a kind of good genius', responsible for 'many kind acts, especially among the sick' (*WM*, 15 December 1894). Official Liberal candidate in 1898 guardians' elections (Allgood papers, CCL).

**Jones, Edith Marion (Miss Rees-Jones):** Independent/Liberal, Nonconformist. Top of poll in Roath ward, with 1,108 votes (13 candidates, 6 places). Had had five years' experience on the workhouse visiting committee, was 'well known among the poor of Roath', had worked in the Cardiff Refuge Society and promoted a society for aid to 'friendless' and unemployed girls. According to the press, 'Well knowing, as she does, the needs of the poor, and as women and children form the great majority of the inmates of the workhouse, she thinks women should be on the board' (*WM*, 15 December 1894); 'Miss Rees-Jones had made it very clear that she was a non-political candidate' (*SWDN*, 3 December 1894). Jones's mother had been a member of the original 1890 committee of the Cardiff Women's Liberal Association (WLA). Her father, a former mayor of Cardiff, had presided over a women's suffrage meeting in the Town Hall in March 1881. She was cited as one of the women candidates who had retained Independent status throughout the campaign, and had considerable Conservative support in the campaign, but was also sometimes described as Liberal. In the 1898 guardians' election, she was an official Liberal candidate (Allgood papers, CCL).

**Mullin, Mrs Annie:** Liberal, Roman Catholic. Elected 2nd in Roath ward, with 657 votes (13 candidates, 6 places). Member of Cardiff WLA committee, and Cathays ward secretary 1891–4; Cardiff vice-president 1898–1901. Member of workhouse visiting committee. '[H]aving spent a great deal of time on the continent her views with regard to the treatment of the poor are based on a broad basis.' Had done a great deal of visiting among the poor and had tried to alleviate distress (*WM*, 15 December 1894). Her husband was James Mullin MD, surgeon, JP and president of the Irish National League in Cardiff.

> [S]ome difficulty had been experienced in the case of Mrs Mullin on the ground that she had been brought out as a Roman Catholic. Mrs Mullin indignantly repudiated this assertion, saying that she had been selected by the Liberals, and that her religion had nothing whatsoever to do with it.
>
> (*SWDN*, 4 December 1894)

Mullin was on the Liberal ticket for Roath in the February 1898 election. Her platform was the introduction of 'greater humanity' into the care of the poor, the extension of outdoor relief and greater comfort for the aged poor inside the workhouses, an extension of the boarding-out system for children to remove the taint of the workhouse and the stigma of poverty, and 'increased tenderness for those who have grown old and helpless in the service of the community'. The statement also stressed greater economy and efficiency, but with final emphasis on humanity (election leaflet 1898, Allgood papers, CCL).

In 1894, shortly before the guardians' elections, Mullin was one of the founders of the Cardiff Women's Local Government Association (WLGS). In 1910, she was on the platform for the Cardiff conference of Welsh Liberal women who voted to boycott anti-suffragist Liberal candidates, which led to the split and demise of the Cardiff WLA. In 1913, she was treasurer of the suffragist Cardiff Progressive Liberal Women's Union. A Mrs Mullin appears in the extant subscription lists of the C&DWSS.

**Norman, Mrs Lavinia:** 2nd in poll in Grangetown ward with 457 votes (8 candidates, 4 places). Nonconformist, Liberal. Member of Cardiff WLA committee, Splott ward secretary. One of four official candidates for Grangetown ward, after a male candidate stood down in her favour. The Cardiff Fabians saw her candidature as evidence that the ward had effectively adopted its policies. She had worked with several societies in Canton parish 'which had for their object the betterment of the condition of the poor', and was 'well acquainted with the needs of the class of people who frequent workhouses' (*WM*, 15 December 1894). A founder committee member of the Cardiff WLGS. Born in Swansea, husband was proprietor of a carriage-building business in Market Road, Canton. She had six children and one general living-in servant in 1891, when aged thirty-four (1891 census). Norman was on the official Progressive Liberal ticket for February 1898 guardians' elections, again the only woman candidate for the ward, among a total of sixteen candidates (Allgood papers, CCL).

**Pudge, Mrs Eugenie:** Liberal Progressive, Nonconformist, but formerly a member of St John's Parish Church, as the press thought it worthwhile to mention. An unsuccessful candidate in St Mary's ward, 17th with 372 votes (18 candidates, for 8 places). She had a '[l]ong connection with Liberalism', especially in the south ward, was a member of the executive committee of the Cardiff WLA and secretary of the ward WLA, had 'worked hard and earnestly' for the Liberal candidate in recent municipal elections. Had 'a wide experience among the poor' (*SWDN*, 14 December 1894; *WM*, 15 December 1894).Widowed, lived with her father, James Dyke, hatter, in his Bute Street premises. Former member of St John's church. Born Gloucester; aged thirty-four in 1891 (1891 census).

**Thomas, Miss Mabel Elizabeth:** Independent. Top of the poll in St Mary's ward, with 758 votes (18 candidates, 8 places). Identified as Conservative by both papers, and Church by *WM*, though *SWDN* claimed she described herself as Fabian, which her supporters denied; this appears to be a case of mistaken identity. Had 'many years experience of visiting among working and pauper classes', was a member of the executive of the COS, and working member of several societies for the relief of the poor, better training for poor children etc. Was 'well known among the poor in Swansea' (*WM*, 15 December 1894). The COS supported her as their 'direct representation' on the board of guardians, the effort being 'amply justified by the way in which the interests of poor and of the ratepayers have been served by her kindness and judgement' (COS Ninth Annual Report, CCL). Thomas had introduced herself to the electorate in 'an election address which is characterised by pleasing modesty ... Miss Thomas is nominated by members of divers political parties, and is herself no politician' (*SWDN*, 8 December 1894).

**Thompson, Mrs Harriett Charlotte:** Independent/Liberal, 'Church'. Top of the poll in St John's ward (20 candidates, 8 places). Wife of the vicar of St John's, she had

> for many years done a great deal of work among the poor in parish and also in Cathays. She is foremost in promoting the Whitsun treats for children, manages a Sunday School of 200 girls, has a clothing club at Cathays of over 200 members, and in addition to a vast amount of work on the Dorcas Society, arranges a big dinner at Christmas for the poor people of her parish.
>
> (*WM*, 15 December 1894)

Thompson had been a member of the management committee of the Cardiff COS since its formation in November 1886 (COS papers,

CCL). She appears to have had much Conservative support during the elections. In the February 1898 guardians' elections, however, she was an official Liberal candidate (Allgood papers, CCL)

**Watson, Miss Florence Coldough:** Independent/Conservative, 'Church'. Top of the poll with 860 votes in Canton ward (16 candidates, 6 places). She was a member of a Llandaff family 'well known for interest in the welfare of the poor'. Watson had been a workhouse visitor, was active in the Girls' Friendly Society, and had 'taken a great deal of interest in the Ely [poor law] schools' (*WM*, 15 December 1894). Writing in the Liberal journal, *Young Wales*, Watson emphasized the careful placing of girls in work after their 'training' in the workhouse schools, and their continued supervision, to avoid the danger of 'drift into bad companionship or sin' (*YW*, March 1896).

**Williams, Mrs Mary Jane:** Liberal, Nonconformist (English Congregational), Canton ward. An unsuccessful 12th with 316 votes (16 candidates, 6 places). In a list of candidates which described other women only by their marital status, Mrs Williams was identified as 'bedding manufacturer and married woman' (*WM*, 6 December 1894. See also *SWDN* of same date). Born Dublin 1843, educated in seminary in Drumcondra, active in 'early womanhood' in 'many philanthropic and reformatory measures'. Had worked with well-known women in the philanthropic movement, including Mary Carpenter and Francis Power Cobbe and others in London and Bristol. She was described as active in the religious, social and political life of the parish, and had been for two years honorary secretary of her ward WLA. 'Although an ultra-Liberal, she is a woman of broad and generous views towards those who may differ from her opinions' (*SWDN*, 14 December 1894).

# Notes

## Introduction

[1] The use of 'British', 'national' and other relational terms is fraught with difficulty. The Women's Liberal Federation (WLF) actually represented England and Wales only, which would be cumbersome to spell out each time; while the Welsh Union of Women's Liberal Associations (WUWLA) was considered a 'national' body for Wales, while regarded as a regional union inside the WLF. Generally, I trust to context to make my meaning clear.

[2] Helen Rogers, *Women and the People: Authority, Authorship and the Radical Tradition in Nineteenth Century England* (Aldershot, 2000), p. 7.

[3] Patrick Joyce, 'The constitution and the narrative structure of Victorian politics', in James Vernon (ed.), *Re-reading the Constitution: New Narratives in the Political History of England's Long Nineteenth Century* (Cambridge, 1996), pp. 196–7; also discussed in Rogers, *Women and the People*, pp. 284–5.

[4] Linda Walker, 'Party political women: Liberal women and the Primrose League, 1890–1914', in Jane Rendall (ed.), *Equal or Different: Women's Politics 1800–1914* (Oxford, 1987), p. 167.

[5] Joyce, 'The constitution and the narrative structure'; Rogers, *Women and the People*, p. 285; Laura E. Nym Mayhall, 'The rhetorics of slavery and citizenship: suffragist discourse and canonical texts in Britain, 1880–1914', *Gender & History*, 13, 3 (2001), 481–97.

[6] *Western Mail* (*WM*), 19 July 1915.

[7] Monika Bernold and Johanna Gehmacher, 'A private eye on feminist agency: reflections on self-documentation, biography, and political consciousness', *Women's Studies International Forum*, 22, 2 (March 1999), 237–47. And see: Linda Walker, 'Philipps [née Gerstenberg] Leonora (1852–1915)', in H. C. G. Matthew and Brian Harrison (eds), *Oxford Dictionary of National Biography* (*ODNB*, Oxford, 2004).

[8] Lesley Hall, 'Finding women in the archive', *Women's History Notebooks*, 2, 1 (winter 1995), 3–11; Maria Grever, 'The pantheon of feminist culture:

women's movements and the organization of memory', *Gender and History*, 9, 2 (August 1997), 364–74; Alison Tyler, 'A library of our own: the potential for a women's library in Wales', unpublished Ph.D. thesis, University of Wales Aberystwyth, 2006.

9 Ludmilla Jordanova, *History in Practice* (2nd edn, London, 2006), pp. 96–7.

10 Aled Jones, *Press, Politics and Society: A History of Journalism in Wales* (Cardiff, 1993), pp. 1–6; Kenneth O. Morgan, *Rebirth of a Nation: Wales 1880–1980* (Oxford, 1981), pp. 49–51; Tom O'Malley, Stuart Allan and Andrew Thompson, 'Tokens of antiquity: the newspaper press and the shaping of national identity in Wales, 1870–1900', in Michael Harris and Tom O'Malley (eds), *Studies in Newspaper and Periodical History, 1995 Annual* (Westport, Connecticut, 1997), pp. 127–52.

11 Morgan, *Rebirth of a Nation*, p. 50.

12 See examples in the minute book of the Aberdare WLA, reprinted in Ursula Masson (ed.), *Women's Rights and 'Womanly Duties': The Aberdare Women's Liberal Association 1890–1910* (Cardiff, 2005).

13 Bernold and Gehmacher, 'A private eye on feminist agency', 2–3 (electronic pagination).

14 Masson, *Women's Rights*, p. 89.

15 The now classic critique is Amanda Vickery, 'Golden age to separate spheres: a review of the categories and chronology of women's history', *Historical Journal*, 36, 2 (1993) 383–414; among the revisions of Vickery's position, see Anne Summers, *Female Lives, Moral States: Women, Religion and Public Life in Britain 1800–1930* (Newbury, 2000), pp. 5–30.

16 Julia Bush, 'Ladylike lives? Upper-class women's autobiographies and the politics of late Victorian and Edwardian Britain', *Literature & History*, 10, 2 (autumn 2001), 42–61, 43.

17 Jordanova, *History in Practice*, p. 45.

18 Viscountess Rhondda, *This Was My World* (London, 1933).

19 Bush, 'Ladylike lives?'; Hilda Kean, 'Suffrage autobiography: a study of Mary Richardson – suffragette, socialist and fascist', in Claire Eustance, Joan Ryan and Laura Ugolini (eds), *A Suffrage Reader: Charting Directions in British Suffrage History* (London, 2000); Kean, 'Searching for the past in present defeat: the construction of historical and political identity in British feminism in the 1920s and 1930s', *Women's History Review*, 3, 1 (1994), 57–80; Maroula Joannou, 'She who would be free herself must strike the first blow: suffragette autobiography and suffragette militancy', in Julia Swindells (ed.), *The Uses of Autobiography* (London, 1995).

20 S. Smith, *A Poetics of Women's Autobiography* (Bloomington IN, 1987), p. 19, quoted by Bush, 'Ladylike lives?', p. 48.

21 The impact of post-structuralism on historical studies, and specifically on women's history, was hotly debated in the 1990s. For a summary, and the

term 'feminist women's history', see June Purvis, 'From women worthies to poststructuralism? Debate and controversy in women's history in Britain', in June Purvis (ed.), *Women's History: Britain 1850–1945* (London, 1995).

22  International Federation for Research in Women's History (IFRWH) *Newsletter*, 27 (January 1999); Yvonne Knibiehler, 'Chronology and women's history', in Michelle Perrot (ed.), *Writing Women's History* (English edn, Oxford, 1984), p. 36.

23  Catherine Hall, 'Gender, nationalism and national identities: Bellagio Symposium, July 1992', *Feminist Review*, 44 (summer 1993), 97–103.

24  Angela V. John, 'A draft of fresh air: women's suffrage, the Welsh and London', *Transactions of the Honourable Society of Cymmrodorion* (1994), 82, 90.

25  Masson (ed.), *Women's Rights*, pp. 12, 89, 91.

26  Robert Self, *The Evolution of the British Party System 1885–1940* (London, 2000), ch.3.

27  WLF Annual Reports, 1888–1914; Walker, 'Party political women', p. 169, table 6.1.

28  *South Wales Daily News* (*SWDN*), 19 April 1895.

29  An exception has been Emyr W. Williams, 'Liberalism in Wales and the politics of Welsh Home Rule 1886–1910', *Bulletin of the Board of Celtic Studies*, 37 (1990), 191–207, discussed in chapter 3.

30  Ray Strachey, *The Cause: A Short History of the Women's Movement in Great Britain* (London, 1988, first pub. 1928), pp. 278–83.

31  Constance Rover, *Women's Suffrage and Party Politics in Britain 1866–1914* (London and Toronto, 1967), p. 143.

32  David Morgan, *Suffragists and Liberals: The Politics of Woman Suffrage in England* (Oxford, 1975), pp. 17–18, 52–3, 60, 126, 156.

33  Martin Pugh, *The March of the Women: A Revisionist Analysis of the Campaign for Women's Suffrage, 1866–1914* (Oxford, 2000), ch. 6.

34  Jane Rendall, 'Introduction', in eadem (ed.), *Equal or Different: Women's Politics 1800–1914* (Oxford, 1987), pp. 4–5.

35  Walker, 'Party political women', pp. 165–6.

36  Ibid., pp. 171, 177–8.

37  Olive Banks, *Faces of Feminism: A Study of Feminism as a Social Movement* (Oxford, 1986, first pub. 1981), pp. 7, 13–27.

38  *SWDN*, 18 April 1895.

39  Walker, 'Party political women', p. 187.

40  Claire Hirshfield, 'Fractured faith: Liberal party women and the suffrage issue in Britain, 1892–1914', *Gender & History*, 2, 2 (1990), passim.

41  Ibid., 184–5.

42  Jo Vellacott, *From Liberal to Labour with Women's Suffrage: The Story of Catherine Marshall* (Montreal and Kingston, 1993), pp. 423–4, n. 58.

43  Ibid., pp. 102, 364–6.

[44] Sandra Stanley Holton, *Feminism and Democracy: Women's Suffrage and Reform Politics in Britain 1900–1918* (Cambridge, 1986).

[45] Ursula Masson, '"Political conditions in Wales are quite different": party politics and votes for women in Wales, 1912–1915', *Women's History Review*, 9, 2 (2000), 369–88; eadem, 'Divided loyalties: women's suffrage and party politics in south Wales, 1912–1915', *Llafur: Journal of Welsh Labour History*, 7, 3 and 4 (1998–9), 113–26.

[46] Krista Cowman, '*Mrs Brown is a Man and a Brother*': *Women in Merseyside's Political Organisations, 1890–1920* (Liverpool, 2004); eadem, 'Engendering citizenship: the political involvement of women on Merseyside, 1890–1920', unpublished Ph.D. thesis, University of York, 1994.

[47] Cowman, *Mrs Brown*, pp. 6–11, 45–53, 121–9.

[48] Megan Smitley, '"Woman's mission": the temperance and women's suffrage movement in Scotland, c.1870–1914', unpublished Ph.D. thesis, University of Glasgow, 2000, 'Abstract'; eadem, '"Inebriates", "heathens", templars and suffragists: Scotland and imperial feminism c.1870–1917', *Women's History Review*, 11, 3 (2002), 455–79.

[49] Antoinette Burton, 'Rules of thumb: British history and "imperial culture" in nineteenth- and twentieth-century Britain', *Women's History Review*, 3, 4 (1994), 491, quoted in Smitley, 'Woman's mission', 'Abstract'; Smitley, 'Inebriates', 459.

[50] Smitley, 'Inebriates', 460–2.

[51] Ibid.; Ceridwen Lloyd-Morgan, 'From temperance to suffrage?', in Angela V. John (ed.), *Our Mothers' Land: Chapters in Welsh Women's History, 1830–1939* (Cardiff, 1991).

[52] 'The Women's Liberal Federation of Scotland – Address by the Countess of Aberdeen of Scotland' to the World's Congress of Representative Women, Chicago 1894; Smitley, 'Woman's mission', 11–16; Leah Leneman, 'A truly national movement: the view from outside London', in Maroula Joannou and June Purvis (eds), *The Women's Suffrage Movement: New Feminist Perspectives* (Manchester, 1998), p. 48.

[53] Kay Cook and Neil Evans, '"The petty antics of the bell-ringing, boisterous band"?: the women's suffrage movement in Wales, 1890–1918', in John (ed.), *Our Mothers' Land*, esp. pp. 163–6, 180.

[54] Ibid.

[55] Karen Offen, 'Defining feminism: a comparative historical approach', *Signs: Journal of Women in Culture and Society*, 14, 1 (1988), 119–57, 141.

[56] There is a large body of writing on definitions and types of feminism, including: Banks, *Faces of Feminism*; Offen, 'Defining feminism'; Barbara Caine, *English Feminism 1780–1980* (Oxford 1997), Introduction, pp. 1–10 and especially 8–9; Carol Dyhouse, *Feminism and the Family in England 1880–1930* (Oxford, 1989), Introduction, pp. 3–5; Jane Rendall, *The Origins of Modern Feminism: Women in Britain, France and the United*

*States, 1780–1860* (London, 1985), pp. 1–2; June Hannam and Karen Hunt, *Socialist Women: Britain 1880s-1920s* (London, 2002), pp. 8–9.

57  Rendall, 'Introduction', p. 2.

58  Martin Pugh, 'Liberals and women's suffrage, 1867–1914', in Eugenio F. Biagini (ed.), *Citizenship and Community: Liberals, Radicals and Collective Identities in the British Isles 1865–1931* (Cambridge, 1996), p. 46. See also Aberdare WLA minutes, 4 February 1892.

59  *Aberdare Times* (*AT*), 4 June 1892.

60  A classic expression is Helen Taylor's 1867 article, 'The claim of Englishwomen to the suffrage constitutionally considered', reprinted in Jane Rendall (ed.), *Before the Vote Was Won: Arguments for and Against Women's Suffrage* (New York and London, 1987), pp. 21–37.

61  Carole Pateman, *The Sexual Contract* (Cambridge, 1988); eadem, *The Disorder of Women: Democracy, Feminism and Political Theory* (Cambridge, 1989).

62  Stefan Collini, *Public Moralists: Political Thought and Intellectual Life in Britain, 1850–1930* (Oxford, 1993); Jane Rendall, 'Citizenship, culture and civilisation: the language of British suffragists 1866–1874', in Caroline Daley and Melanie Nolan (eds), *Suffrage and Beyond: International Feminist Perspectives* (New York, 1994); Sandra Stanley Holton, 'British freewomen: national identity, constitutionalism and languages of race in early suffragist histories', in Eileen Janes Yeo (ed.), *Radical Femininity: Women's Self-Representation in the Public Sphere* (Manchester, 1998); Rogers, *Women and the People*; Mayhall, 'Rhetorics', 481–97.

63  Rogers, *Women and the People*, ch. 6; Summers, *Female Lives*, pp. 66–77, ch. 8; Helen Mathers, 'Evangelicalism and feminism: Josephine Butler, 1828–1906', in Sue Morgan (ed.), *Women, Religion and Feminism in Britain, 1750–1900* (Basingstoke, 2002); Suzanne Rickard, 'Victorian women with causes: writing, religion and action', ibid.

64  Rogers, *Women and the People*, pp. 207–12, quoting Josephine Butler, emphasis original.

65  Amanda Vickery, 'Introduction' in eadem (ed.), *Women, Privilege and Power: British Politics, 1750 to the Present* (Stanford, 2001), p. 5; Jane Rendall, 'John Stuart Mill, Liberal politics, and the movements for women's suffrage, 1865–1873', in Vickery (ed.), *Women, Privilege and Power*, p. 195; Rendall, 'Citizenship, culture', p. 129; Mayhall, 'Rhetorics', 481–97; Rogers, *Women and the People*, chs 1, 8.

66  WUWLA Annual Report, 1893; *SWDN*, 24 March 1908.

67  *SWDN*, 1 April 1892.

68  Cook and Evans, 'The petty antics', p. 180.

69  Angela V. John, 'Beyond paternalism: the ironmaster's wife in the industrial community', in John (ed.), *Our Mothers' Land*, pp. 54–64; Ryland Wallace, *Organise! Organise! Organise!: A Study of Reform Agitations in Wales, 1840–1886* (Cardiff, 1991), pp. 163–4, 168.

[70] *Young Wales* (*YW*), January 1895, 23.

[71] Sian Rhiannon Williams, 'The true "Cymraes": images of women in women's nineteenth century Welsh periodicals', in John (ed.), *Our Mothers' Land*; Jane Aaron, 'Finding a voice in two tongues: gender and colonization', in Jane Aaron, Teresa Rees, Sandra Betts and Moira Vincentelli (eds), *Our Sisters' Land: The Changing Identities of Women in Wales* (Cardiff, 1994).

[72] More light is shed on this period in D. R. Hughes, *Cymru Fydd, 1886–1896* (Cardiff, 2006).

[73] Jon Lawrence, *Speaking for the People: Party, Language and Popular Politics in England, 1867–1914* (Cambridge, 1998), p. 198.

[74] Alan Butt Philip, *The Welsh Question: Nationalism in Welsh Politics 1945–70* (Cardiff, 1975), p. 4.

[75] Charlotte Aull Davies, 'Women, nationalism and feminism', in Aaron et al. (eds), *Our Sisters' Land*; eadem., 'Nationalism, feminism and Welsh women: conflicts and accommodations', in Ralph Fevre and Andrew Thompson (eds), *National Identity and Social Theory: Perspectives from Wales* (Cardiff, 1999); Nira Yuval-Davies and Floya Anthias (eds), *Woman–Nation–State* (London, 1989); Sylvia Walby, 'Woman and nation', in Gopal Balakrishnan and Benedict Anderson (eds), *Mapping the Nation* (London, 1996); Ida Blom, Karen Hagemann and Catherine Hall (eds), *Gendered Nations: Nationalism and Gender Order in the Long Nineteenth Century*, (Oxford and New York, 2000).

[76] Ida Blom, 'Gender and nation in international comparison', in Blom et al. (eds), *Gendered Nations*, p. 8.

[77] Kumari Jayawardena, *Feminism and Nationalism in the Third World* (London and New Delhi, 1986), cited in Blom, 'Gender and nation', pp. 3–5 and 11–14.

[78] Laura E. Nym Mayhall, Philippa Levine and Ian Christopher Fletcher, 'Introduction', in Ian Christopher Fletcher, Laura E. Nym Mayhall and Philippa Levine (eds), *Women's Suffrage in the British Empire: Citizenship, Nation, and Race* (London and New York, 2000), pp. xvi–xvii.

[79] Charlotte Williams, Neil Evans and Paul O'Leary (eds), *A Tolerant Nation? Exploring Ethnic Diversity in Wales* (Cardiff, 2003); Jane Aaron and Chris Williams (eds), *Postcolonial Wales* (Cardiff, 2005).

[80] Kirsti Bohata, '"For Wales, see England?": suffrage and the New Woman in Wales', *Women's History Review*, 11, 4 (2002), 643–56; Ursula Masson, '"Hand in hand with the women, forward we will go": Welsh nationalism and feminism in the 1890s', *Women's History Review*, 12, 3 (2003), 357–86. Twentieth-century nationalism has had more attention: see n. 75 above, and Laura McAllister, 'Gender, nation and party: an uneasy alliance for Welsh nationalism', *Women's History Review*, 10, 1 (2001), 51–69.

[81] June Hannam and Katherine Holden, Editorial: 'Heartland and

periphery: local, national and global perspectives on women's history',
*Women's History Review*, 11, 3 (2002), 341–2.

[82] *YW*, January 1895, 17–19; WUWLA Annual Report, 1896.

[83] WUWLA Annual Report, 1895; *YW*, May 1896, 118.

[84] Lawrence, *Speaking for the People*, p. 4.

[85] Ibid., p. 3.

[86] For a discussion of broader and persistent discourses linking 'woman' and 'the local', see Doreen Massey, *Space, Place and Gender* (Cambridge, 1998), pp. 9–11.

[87] *Nineteenth Century*, June 1889, reprinted in Rendall, *Before the Vote*, pp. 409–17; Sir Almroth Wright, *The Unexpurgated Case Against Woman Suffrage* (1913) part II, ch. 1.

[88] Lawrence, *Speaking for the People*, p. 66.

[89] June Hannam, '"I had not been to London": women's suffrage – a view from the regions', in June Purvis and Sandra Stanley Holton (eds), *Votes for Women* (London, 2000), p. 229.

## 1: Women's Liberal Organization in Wales, 1880–1914

[1] Patricia Hollis, 'Women in council: separate spheres, public space', in Jane Rendall (ed.), *Equal or Different: Women's Politics, 1800–1914* (Oxford, 1987), p. 194.

[2] Jane Rendall, 'Introduction', in Rendall (ed.), *Equal or Different*, p. 4.

[3] Ibid.

[4] Women's Liberal Federation (WLF) Annual Report, May 1891; Welsh Union of Women's Liberal Associations (WUWLA) Annual Report, March 1895; *Cambrian News* (*CN*), 1 April 1892. The *CN* reports list the associations and their representatives in a slightly confusing way, and the number of associations was variously reported as thirty and thirty-three.

[5] WLF Annual Reports, 1888–1928; WUWLA Annual Report, 1895; *Young Wales* (*YW*), March 1896, 66; *Welsh Review* (*WR*), 1, 7, 678ff; *South Wales Daily News* (*SWDN*), 18 April 1895.

[6] Kenneth O. Morgan, *Wales in British Politics, 1868–1922* (Cardiff, 1991), p. 17.

[7] Ibid., pp. 84–5. In 1886, the League for the Support of the Tithe Oppressed became the Welsh Land, Commercial and Labour League; NLW XJN 1159 L 24.

[8] Rosemary Jones, 'Women, community and collective action: the "ceffyl pren" tradition', in Angela V. John (ed.), *Our Mothers' Land: Chapters in Welsh Women's History* (Cardiff, 1991), pp. 17–41, esp. 33–4.

[9] See the celebration of Peggy Lewis at Liberal Party events; *SWDN*, 5 February 1890.

[10] Ceridwen Lloyd-Morgan, 'From temperance to suffrage?', in John (ed.), *Our Mothers' Land*, p. 136.

11  WLF Annual Reports, 1892–8; WUWLA Annual Report, 1895. All data on officers of WLAs and membership figures comes from WLF and WUWLA annual reports, unless otherwise indicated.

12  *SWDN*, 10 March 1881.

13  Jane Rendall, 'Who was Lily Maxwell? Women's suffrage and Manchester politics 1866–1867', in June Purvis and Sandra Stanley Holton (eds), *Votes for Women* (London, 2000), p. 62.

14  Ieuan Gwynedd Jones, *Explorations and Explanations: Essays in the Social History of Victorian Wales* (Llandysul, 1981), p. 84.

15  *YW,* April 1896, 92; Morgan, *Wales in British Politics*, p. 72.

16  Alan Butt Philip, *The Welsh Question: Nationalism in Welsh Politics, 1945–1970* (Cardiff, 1975), p. 6; Elizabeth Crawford, *The Women's Suffrage Movement: A Reference Guide, 1866–1928* (London 2001, first published 1999), p. 716.

17  Gwyn A. Williams, *When Was Wales? A History of the Welsh* (London, 1985), 213–16; Jones, *Explorations*, pp. 83–164.

18  Morgan, *Wales in British Politics*, p. 109.

19  WLF Annual Reports, 1890, 1892.

20  WLF Annual Report, 1890.

21  Ibid.

22  Ibid.

23  WLF Annual Report, 1888.

24  See, for example, *South Wales Weekly Argus* (*SWWA*), December 1894, reports on local elections. On the impact of Irish immigrant communities on Welsh politics, Paul O'Leary, *Immigration and Integration: The Irish in Wales 1798–1922* (Cardiff, 2000), ch. IX passim.

25  W. R. Lambert, *Drink and Sobriety in Victorian Wales c.1820–c.1895* (Cardiff, 1983), pp. 206–8.

26  WLF Annual Report, 1889.

27  The first WUWLA Annual Report gives 1888 for the foundation of Cardiff WLA, but in reports thereafter, 1890. *SWDN* reported on the formation of the association, 28 February, 21 March 1890.

28  WLF *Monthly News,* January, February 1912.

29  WUWLA and WLF Annual Reports, 1892–6.

30  Ryland Wallace, *Organise! Organise! Organise!: A Study of Reform Agitations in Wales, 1840–1886* (Cardiff, 1991), p. 168.

31  Morgan, *Wales in British Politics*, pp. 65, 72–3; Beti Jones, *Etholiadau'r Ganrif/Welsh Elections 1885–1997* (Talybont, 1999), pp. 29, 33.

32  WUWLA Annual Report, 1893.

33  John Wynford Philipps represented Mid-Lanark 1888–94. He gave up his parliamentary career for some time, but played an increasingly active part in Cymru Fydd, before standing for election in Pembrokeshire.

34  *SWDN*, 7 January 1898.

[35] On the role of paid secretary-organizers in suffrage organizations, see Crawford, *Women's Suffrage Movement*, pp. 474–9. Krista Cowman discusses WSPU organizers and their local impact, but appears to suggest that WSPU organizers in the Edwardian period were 'the first women to make politics a career'; Krista Cowman, *'Mrs. Brown is a Man and a Brother': Women in Merseyside's Political Organisations, 1880–1920* (Liverpool, 2004), ch. 5.

[36] Martindale, sister of the local MP, Albert Spicer (1892–1900), was also a leading figure in the BWTA, and while in Newport addressed the annual meeting of the Newport branch, exhorting women to use their local government votes to support the temperance candidates; *SWWA*, 3 November 1884. Spicer was also a temperance and women's suffrage supporter.

[37] The second 'Rule' reads: 'To secure equal justice and political rights for all, rich and poor, men and women, and especially to press forward the claims of women to the Parliamentary franchise' ('New Rules and Objects of Newport Women's Liberal Association', *South Wales Weekly Argus*, 8 December 1894).

[38] *SWWA*, 3 November, 8 December 1894; *SWDN*, 6 December 1894.

[39] *SWWA*, 8, 15 December 1894.

[40] John Grigg, *Lloyd George: The Young Lloyd George* (London 1997, first pub. 1973), p. 174.

[41] WLF Annual Reports, 1889–1914.

[42] Ibid., 1891–2.

[43] WUWLA Annual Report, 1893.

[44] WLF Annual Reports, 1891–2.

[45] *SWDN*, 4 March 1891; unidentified cutting in minute book of Aberdare Women's Liberal Association, dated by hand, 10 November 1891, 'Formation of a Branch at Aberdare'.

[46] Nora Philipps, *The Aim and Object of the Welsh Union* (1893), pp. 11–12.

[47] Cardiff Liberal Association (CLA) Annual Report, 1889; WLF Annual Reports, 1889, 1893; WUWLA Rules, and model rules for associations, in Philipps, *Aim and Object*; New Rules of the Newport WLA, *SWWA*, 8 December 1894; Aberystwyth WLA Annual Report, 1902.

[48] Aberystwyth WLA Annual Report, 1897, 1902.

[49] Eileen Janes Yeo, 'Radical femininity: women's self-representation in labour movements in the 19th and 20th centuries', in *North East Labour History*, 29 (1995), 7–8; eadem, 'Introduction: some paradoxes of empowerment', in eadem (ed.), *Radical Femininity: Women's Self-Representation in the Public Sphere* (Manchester, 1998), pp. 1–24.

[50] WUWLA Annual Reports, 1893–6.

[51] The WLF was one of about eight women's party, suffrage and temperance organizations involved in coordinating the petition, which gathered over a quarter of a million signatures by the end of March 1894, to be presented

to Parliament at the same time as Viscount Wolmer's attempt to amend a Registration Bill; Crawford, *The Women's Suffrage Movement*, pp. 648–9.

52  WUWLA Annual Report, 1893.

53  Ibid., 1894.

54  Ibid.

55  For a discussion of the meanings of 'public' and 'private' in relation to philanthropy, religion and women's work, see Anne Summers, *Female Lives, Moral States: Women, Religion and Public Life in Britain 1800–1930* (Newbury, 2000), ch. 1, esp. pp. 13–18.

56  WUWLA Annual Reports, 1893–6.

57  Crawford, *The Women's Suffrage Movement*, pp. 716–20.

58  WUWLA Annual Report, 1895.

59  Ibid.,1893–6.

60  Martin Pugh, *The March of the Women: A Revisionist Analysis of the Campaign for Women's Suffrage, 1866–1914* (Oxford, 2000), ch. 6, esp. pp. 140ff.

61  WLF and WUWLA Annual Reports, 1895. WUWLA Annual Reports provide membership figures for associations, something which the WLF did not provide until after the turn of the century. WLF reports provide records over a longer period.

62  Neil Evans and Kate Sullivan, 'Yn llawn o dân Cymreig (full of Welsh fire): the language of politics in Wales', in Geraint H. Jenkins (ed.), *The Welsh Language in its Social Domains, 1801–1911* (Cardiff, 2000), p. 561.

63  W. T. R. Pryce, 'Language zones, demographic changes, and the Welsh culture area, 1800–1911', in Jenkins (ed.), *The Welsh Language*, pp. 64–5. The WLAs were Bala, Conway, Dolgellau, Holyhead and Wrexham in the north, and Cadoxton, Maesteg and South Monmouthshire in the south.

64  Cardiff WLA Annual Report, 1902.

65  Aberdare WLA minutes, 17 November 1893; WLF Annual Report, 1898.

66  Aberdare WLA minutes, 26 February 1892, 18 March 1892.

67  Ibid., 7 February 1896, 28 January 1898.

68  WLF Annual Report, 1904.

69  Ibid., 1901.

70  Morgan, *Wales in British Politics*, pp. 149–56.

71  Cardiff WLA Annual Report, 1902.

72  WLF Annual Reports, 1901, 1902.

73  Morgan, *Wales in British Politics*, pp. 178–80; Kenneth O. Morgan, *Modern Wales: Politics, Places and People* (Cardiff, 1995), pp. 46–58, 260–1; Kenneth O. Fox, 'Labour and Merthyr's khaki election of 1900', *Welsh History Review* (*WHR*), 2, 3 (1965), 351–66; Wil Jon Edwards, *From the Valley I Came* (London, 1956), pp. 79–80.

74  Claire Hirshfield, 'Fractured faith: Liberal party women and the suffrage issue in Britain, 1892–1914', *Gender & History*, 2, 2 (1990), 179. The impact of the war for women's claims for citizenship has been explored by

Laura E. Nym Mayhall, 'The South African War and the origins of suffrage militancy in Britain, 1899–1902', in Ian Christopher Fletcher, Laura E. Nym Mayhall and Philippa Levine (eds), *Women's Suffrage in the British Empire: Citizenship, Nation and Race* (London and New York, 2000), pp. 3–18.

[75] Aberdare WLA minutes, 26 January 1900; *SWDN*, 6 September 1900.

[76] Morgan, *Wales in British Politics*, p. 168; *YW*, June 1903, 123, also quoted in Morgan, *Wales in British Politics*, p. 166 .

[77] WLF Annual Reports, 1890s.

[78] Ibid., 1896–8.

[79] Kay Cook and Neil Evans ' "The petty antics of the bell-ringing, boisterous band"? The women's suffrage movement in Wales, 1890–1918', in John (ed.), *Our Mothers' Land*, p. 165.

[80] WLF Annual Reports, 1897–1904.

[81] Cardiff WLA Annual Report, 1902.

[82] Cardiff Liberal Association (CLA) subscription lists and Annual Reports, 1892–1911; NLW Mss. XJN 1163, 1164.

[83] Cardiff WLA Annual Reports, 1894, 1897, 1898, 1901, 1902; WLF Annual Reports, 1892–1914.

[84] WLF Annual Reports, 1888–1914. The Gower constituency was won by the ILP in 1906 and remained a Labour seat. It had never had a separate WLA.

[85] *WLF News*, 1912, nos 2–6 and 12.

## 2: The WUWLA and the impact of women's suffrage

[1] Jon Lawrence, *Speaking for the People: Party, Language and Popular Politics in England, 1867–1914* (Cambridge 1998), pp. 3–4.

[2] Ceridwen Lloyd-Morgan, 'From temperance to suffrage?', in Angela V. John (ed.), *Our Mothers' Land: Chapters in Welsh Women's History, 1830–1939* (Cardiff, 1991); Kay Cook and Neil Evans, '"The petty antics of the bell-ringing, boisterous band"? The women's suffrage movement in Wales, 1890–1918', in ibid.

[3] Lawrence, *Speaking for the People*, pp. 19, 210–17.

[4] *Cambrian News (CN)*, 1 April 1892; 'The Women's Liberal Federation of Scotland – Address by the Countess of Aberdeen to the World's Congress of Representative Women, Chicago, 1894', Harvard University Library Page Delivery Service.

[5] Lloyd-Morgan, 'From temperance to suffrage?', pp. 135–8.

[6] W. Gareth Evans, *Education and Female Emancipation: The Welsh Experience* (Cardiff, 1990).

[7] Linda Walker, 'Party political women: a comparative study of Liberal women and the Primrose League, 1890–1914', in Jane Rendall (ed.), *Equal*

or *Different: Women's Politics, 1800–1914* (Oxford, 1987), pp. 186–8. Those who believed that associations should concentrate on their work for the Liberal party were also known as 'neutrals'; Claire Hirshfield, ' Fractured faith: Liberal party women and the suffrage issue in Britain, 1892–1914', *Gender & History*, 2, 2 (1990), 177.

8   Margaret Barrow, 'Teetotal feminists: temperance leadership and the campaign for women's suffrage', in Claire Eustance, Joan Ryan and Laura Ugolini (eds), *A Suffrage Reader: Charting Directions in British Suffrage History* (London and New York, 2000), pp. 80–1.

9   Ursula Masson, '"Hand in hand with the women, forward we will go": Welsh nationalism and feminism in the 1890s', *Women's History Review*, vol. 12, no. 3 (2003), 357–85, 365–7.

10   *CN,* 25 March 1892.

11   Ibid., 22 January, 25 March, 1 April 1892; Aberdare WLA Minute book, newspaper cutting.

12   For a summary of the career of Eva McLaren (née Muller, 1853–1921), and the extent of these family and political networks, see Elizabeth Crawford, *The Women's Suffrage Movement: A Reference Guide* (London and New York, 2001), pp. 397–9; for more on her work in the LNA, in the temperance movement and in local government, see P. Hollis, *Ladies Elect: Women in English Local Government, 1865–1914* (Oxford, 1987), pp. 49–50, 57, 61.

13   Nora Philipps was usually known as Mrs Wynford Philipps and later Lady St Davids. For an account of her life, see Linda Walker, 'Philipps [née Gerstenberg] Leonora '(1852–1915), *Oxford Dictionary of National Biography (ODNB)* (Oxford, 2004), an account which indicates the breadth of Philipps's involvement in many aspects of the women's movement of the late nineteenth century. See also, Walker, 'Party political women', pp. 186–9.

14   Obituary, *South Wales Daily News (SWDN)*, 31 March 1915.

15   *Letters of Well Known Women to Nora Philipps,* NLW Ms. 21971B; Crawford, *The Women's Suffrage Movement*, pp. 170–1, 715; Walker, *ODNB*; eadem, 'Party political women', pp. 187–8; cutting, *The Star*, 22 April 1891, D. A. Thomas papers, NLW.

16   *The Welsh Review (WR)*, 1, 4, February 1892, 355.

17   Obituary, *SWDN*, 5 April 1915; *WR*, 1, 5, 467; ibid., 1, 7, 672–80; WUWLA Annual Report, 1893.

18   Ursula Masson, 'Gender and national memory in *Young Wales*, 1895–1903', unpublished paper to the annual conference of the North American Association for Welsh Culture and History (NAASWCH), Syracuse, New York, 2002.

19   *Young Wales (YW)*, January 1895, 18.

20   *CN*, 1 April 1892; Masson, 'Hand in hand', 367–9.

21   *CN*, 1 April 1892.

22  Masson, 'Hand in hand', 368.
23  *CN*, 1 April 1892.
24  WLF Annual Report, 1892.
25  *CN*, 8 and 22 January 1892; newspaper cuttings, Aberdare WLA minute book, 1891–2.
26  See also Masson (ed.), *Women's Rights and Womanly Duties: The Aberdare Women's Liberal Association, 1891–1910* (Cardiff, 2005), Introduction.
27  WLF Annual Report, 1892; WUWLA Annual Report, 1893.
28  Kenneth O. Morgan, *Wales in British Politics, 1868–1922* (Cardiff, 1980), p. 78.
29  *SWDN*, 3 October 1894.
30  Aberdare WLA minutes, 8, 25 February 1895.
31  WUWLA Annual Report, 1896.
32  Ibid., 1895; programme for Fifth Annual Meetings, Newtown, March 1896.
33  WLF Annual Report, 1892.
34  Ibid., 1894.
35  Lloyd-Morgan, 'From temperance to suffrage?', pp. 145–6.
36  WLF Annual Report, 1901.
37  Ibid., 1893, 1901; Aberdare WLA minutes, October 1900–February 1903; see also part II, ch. 5, and Masson, *Women's Rights*, p. 59. After the inaugural meetings at Aberystwyth in 1892, there are references to, and in some cases records, for annual councils of the WUWLA 1893–7, at Swansea, Rhyl, Cardiff, Newtown and Pembroke Dock.
38  Gwyneth Vaughan Papers (Gwynedd RO, Caernarfon) and Cochfarf Papers (CCL) show that Vaughan and the temperance activist Cranogwen (Sarah Jane Rees) were both the subject of appeals to friends and sympathizers for their support in later life.
39  WUWLA Annual Reports, 1893–6.
40  See above, pp. 35–6.
41  WUWLA Annual Reports, 1894, 1895.
42  For example, the public meeting following the annual council at Swansea, 15 March 1893; WUWLA Annual Report, 1893.
43  WUWLA Annual Report, 1893.
44  Mrs Wynford Philipps, 'The Aim and Object of the Welsh Union' (1893), 5.
45  Walker, *ODNB*.
46  Philipps, 'An Appeal to Welsh Women' and 'Apel at Ferched Cymru' (London 1893). The style was copied in 'Apel at Ferched Rhyddfrydol Cymru', published in 1909 by Cynghrair Rhyddfrydol y Merched (Liberal Women's League), in the sole reference to such a 'League' I have encountered.
47  WUWLA Annual Report, 1896; Ada Thomas was misprinted as Ann Thomas.

[48] Ibid.

[49] See, for example, essays in Sue Morgan (ed.), *Women, Religion and Feminism in Britain, 1750–1900* (Basingstoke and New York, 2002); Megan Smitley, '"Woman's mission": the temperance and women's suffrage movements in Scotland c.1870–1914', unpublished Ph.D. thesis, University of Glasgow, 2002.

[50] Press representations, of Philipps and others, and of public meetings and events, are discussed in the context of the local studies in part II.

[51] WUWLA Annual Report, 1893.

[52] Helen Rogers, *Women and the People: Authority, Authorship and the Radical Tradition in Nineteenth-Century England* (Aldershot, 2000). Rogers also quotes Butler, in a 'Letter to the Women of Oxford' in 1874, in which the vote was represented as a covenant with God, 'the God of purity', to whom voters would have to answer for their use of the trust.

[53] Mrs Dilys Glynne Jones, *The Duty of Welshwomen in Relation to the Welsh Intermediate Education Act* (London, 1894); Eva McLaren, *The Duties and Opportunities of Women with Reference to the Parish and District Councils* (London 1894); Mrs D. M. Richards, 'Dyledswydd Merched a Gwragedd i geisio seddau ar y Cyngorau Plwyfol &c' (Aberdare, undated).

[54] WUWLA Annual Report, 1895.

[55] Ibid., 1896.

[56] *Nineteenth Century*, June 1889. George Osborne Morgan MP (Denbigh 1868–97) was vocal in Parliament in opposing women's enfranchisement from the 1870s, apparently because of the close links between suffragists and those who campaigned for repeal of the Contagious Diseases Acts; Ryland Wallace, *Organise! Organise! A Study of Reform Agitations in Wales, 1840–1866* (Cardiff, 1991), pp. 61–2.

[57] *SWDN*, 18–20 March 1896; *Pall Mall Gazette*, 19 March 1896.

[58] *SWDN*, 24 March 1896.

[59] Programme for 1896 Annual Meetings; *SWDN*, 2 March 1896, 18–27 March 1896.

[60] *YW*, January 1895, 18.

[61] 'The Women's Liberal Federation of Scotland – Address by the Countess of Aberdeen of Scotland, to the World's Congress of Representative Women, Chicago 1894'.

[62] WLF Annual Report, 1894.

[63] *YW*, March 1896, 67.


### 3: The WUWLA and the National Movement in Wales

[1] Kenneth O. Morgan, *Wales in British Politics 1868–1922* (Cardiff, 1991, first pub. 1963), especially chs III and IV; idem., *Rebirth of a Nation:*

*Wales 1880–1980* (Oxford and Cardiff, 1982, first pub. 1981), especially chs 1–4; idem., 'Tom Ellis *versus* Lloyd George: the fractured consciousness of fin-de-siècle Wales', in Geraint H. Jenkins and J. Beverley Smith (eds), *Politics and Society in Wales 1840–1922* (Cardiff, 1988); Emyr Wynn Williams, 'The politics of Welsh home rule, 1886–1929:a sociological analysis', unpublished Ph.D. thesis, University of Wales, Aberystwyth, 1986; idem., 'Liberalism and the politics of Welsh home rule 1886–1910', *Bulletin of the Board of Celtic Studies*, 37 (1990), 191–207; Chris Williams, 'Democracy and nationalism in Wales: the Lib–Lab enigma', in Robert Stradling, Scott Newton and David Bates (eds), *Conflict and Coexistence: Nationalism and Democracy in Modern Europe: Essays in Honour of Harry Hearder* (Cardiff, 1997); David Adamson, 'The intellectual and the national movement in Wales', in Ralph Fevre and Andrew Thompson (eds), *Nation, Identity and Social Theory: Perspectives from Wales* (Cardiff, 1999); Tom O'Malley, Stuart Allan and Andrew Thompson, 'Tokens of antiquity: the newspaper press and the shaping of national identity in Wales 1870–1900', in Michael Harris and Tom O'Malley (eds), *Studies in Newspaper and Periodical History: 1995 Annual* (Westport, Connecticut, 1997).

2  Sian Rhiannon Williams, 'The true "Cymraes": images of women in women's nineteenth-century Welsh periodicals', in Angela V. John (ed.), *Our Mothers' Land: Chapters in Welsh Women's History, 1830–1939* (Cardiff, 1991); Jane Aaron, 'Finding a voice in two tongues: gender and colonization', in Jane Aaron, Teresa Rees, Sandra Betts and Moira Vincentelli (eds), *Our Sisters' Land: The Changing Identities of Women in Wales* (Cardiff, 1994); Rosemary Jones, '"Separate spheres"? Women, language and respectability in Victorian Wales', in Geraint H. Jenkins (ed.), *The Welsh Language in its Social Domains, 1801–1911* (Cardiff, 2000); Mari A. Williams, 'Women and the Welsh language in the industrial valleys of south Wales, 1914–1945', in Geraint H. Jenkins and Mari A. Williams (eds), *'Let's Do Our Best for the Ancient Tongue': The Welsh Language in the Twentieth Century* (Cardiff, 2000). For a recent discussion based on literary sources, Kirsti Bohata, *Postcolonialism Revisited: Writing Wales in English* (Cardiff, 2004), especially ch. 3, which considers some of the sources and events discussed here.

3  Alan Butt Philip, *The Welsh Question: Nationalism in Welsh Politics 1945–1970* (Cardiff, 1975), p. 3.

4  See n. 1, above.

5  Emyr Williams, 'Liberalism'; Chris Williams, *Democratic Rhondda: Politics and Society 1885–1951* (Cardiff, 1996), pp. 44–5; idem., 'Democracy and nationalism', p. 117ff.

6  Emyr Williams, 'Liberalism'.

7  Nira Yuval-Davies and Floya Anthias (eds), *Woman–Nation–State* (London, 1989); Sylvia Walby, 'Woman and nation', in Gopal

Balakrishnan and Benedict Anderson (eds), *Mapping the Nation* (London, 1996); Ann Curthoys, 'Feminism, citizenship and national identity', *Feminist Review,* 44 (summer 1993), 19–38; Ida Blom, Karen Hagemann and Catherine Hall (eds), *Gendered Nations: Nationalisms and Gender Order in the Long Nineteenth Century* (Oxford and New York, 2000). On Wales: Charlotte Aull Davies, 'Women, nationalism and feminism', in Aaron et al., *Our Sisters' Land*; eadem., 'Nationalism, feminism and Welsh women: conflicts and accommodations', in Fevre and Thompson (eds), *National Identity*; Laura McAllister, 'Gender, nation and party: an uneasy alliance for Welsh nationalism', *Women's History Review*, 10, 1 (2001), 51–69.

[8] For discussions covering the period of this study, see Anna Clark, 'Gender, class and the nation: franchise reform in England, 1832–1928', in James Vernon (ed.), *Re-reading the Constitution: New Narratives in the Political History of England's Long Nineteenth Century* (Cambridge, 1996); Jon Lawrence, *Speaking for the People: Party, Language and Popular Politics in England, 1867–1914* (Cambridge, 1998); Jane Rendall, 'Citizenship, culture and civilisation: the languages of British suffragists', in Caroline Daley and Melanie Nolan (eds), *Suffrage and Beyond: International Feminist Perspectives* (New York, 1994); eadem, 'The citizenship of women and the Reform Act of 1867', in Catherine Hall, Keith McLelland and Jane Rendall (eds), *Defining the Victorian Nation: Class, Race, Gender and the Reform Act of 1867* (Cambridge, 2000); eadem, 'John Stuart Mill, Liberal politics, and the movements for women's suffrage, 1865–1873', in Amanda Vickery (ed.), *Women, Privilege and Power: British Politics, 1750 to the Present* (Stanford, 2001); Helen Rogers, *Women and the People: Authority, Authorship and the Radical Tradition in Nineteenth Century England* (Aldershot, 2000); Laura E. Nym Mayhall, 'The rhetorics of slavery and citizenship: suffragist discourse and the canonical texts in Britain, 1880–1914', *Gender & History*, 13, 3 ( 2001), 481–97.

[9] I have based my summary on Walby, 'Woman and nation', pp. 236–7.

[10] Davies 'Nationalism, feminism', pp. 90–1.

[11] Curthoys, 'Feminism, citizenship and national identity', 25–6.

[12] Ruth Roach Pierson, 'Nations: gendered, racialized, crossed with empire', in Blom et al. (eds), *Gendered Nations*, pp. 53–4.

[13] Margaret Ward, 'The Ladies' Land League and the Irish Land War 1881/2: defining the relationship between women and nation', in Blom et al. (eds), *Gendered Nations*, pp. 229–32.

[14] WUWLA Annual Report, 1893.

[15] See a special 'Celebration Issue', 'The Progress of Wales During the Queen's Reign', *YW*, July 1897.

[16] Eugenio F. Biagini, 'Introduction: citizenship, liberty and community', in idem (ed.), *Citizenship and Community: Liberals, Radicals and Collective*

*Identities in the British Isles, 1865–1931* (Cambridge, 1996), p. 13; Jane Rendall, 'Citizenship, culture', pp. 136–8; eadem, 'The citizenship of women', pp. 164–5; Mayhall, 'Rhetorics', passim.

17 Mayhall, 'Rhetorics', 484–5.

18 For Welsh women, Nora Philipps found historical models in the Ancient British and Celtic histories influentially provided by C. C. Stopes in *British Freewomen* (1894), but not much else in the way of 'example' between Boadicea and the mid-nineteenth century; *YW*, March 1896, 64–6. For a discussion of suffragist histories of the second half of the nineteenth century, see Sandra Stanley Holton, 'British freewomen: national identity, constitutionalism and languages of race in early suffragist histories', in Eileen Janes Yeo (ed.), *Radical Femininity: Women's Self-Representation in the Public Sphere* (Manchester, 1998), pp. 149–171.

19 For the question, and some of the answers, see especially the first year of the journal's publication.

20 Giuseppe Mazzini, *The Duties of Man and Other Essays* (London and New York, 1966), pp. 61–4, 122.

21 Rendall, 'The citizenship of women', pp. 164–5.

22 *YW*, February 1895, 37.

23 *YW*, June 1897, 134–6; December 1897, 273–7.

24 *Aberdare Times* (*AT*), 14 November 1868, quoted in Morgan, *Wales in British Politics*, p. v.

25 For the significance of the construct, see especially the work of Prys Morgan, 'The *gwerin* of Wales – myth and reality', in Ian Hume and W. R. T. Pryce (eds), *The Welsh and Their Country: Selected Readings in the Social Sciences* (Llandysul, 1986); Gwyn A. Williams, *When Was Wales? A History of the Welsh* (London, 1985), pp. 206, 237–9.

26 *South Wales Daily News* (*SWDN*), 9 October 1888.

27 Emyr Williams, 'Liberalism', 197.

28 Morgan, *Wales in British Politics*, p. 160; idem., *Rebirth of a Nation*, p. 114.

29 Emyr Williams, 'Liberalism', 197–204.

30 Ibid.

31 Ibid., 199; Morgan, *Wales in British Politics*, pp. 136ff.

32 *To Young Wales*, manifesto of Liverpool and Manchester Cymru Fydd Societies, uncertain date, but after May 1894; NLW Mss. XJN 273. Also quoted by Emyr Williams, 'Liberalism', 199.

33 D. A. Thomas papers.

34 Ibid.; *SWDN*, 4 January 1895.

35 *SWDN*, 16, 23, 24 August 1894, 5 January 1895.

36 *SWDN*, 17 September 1894.

37 Morgan, *Wales in British Politics*, p. 164.

38 WUWLA Annual Reports, 1895, 1896.

39 Ibid.

40 WUWLA Annual Report, 1895.

41 Ibid.

42 *SWDN*, 19 April 95; Morgan, *Wales in British Politics*, pp. 160ff; Emyr Williams, 'Liberalism', 201–2.

43 See also the discussion in David Adamson, *Class, Ideology and the Nation: A Theory of Welsh Nationalism* (Cardiff, 1991), chs 4 and 5.

44 *SWDN*, 18, 19 April 1895.

45 On 'the 'platitudes [of] romanticise[d] and exaggerate[d] notions of Welsh freedom and justice', see Angela V. John, 'A draft of fresh air: women's suffrage, the Welsh and London', *Transactions of the Honourable Society of Cymmrodorion* (*THSC*), 1994, 82, 90; Kirsti Bohata, '"For Wales, see England"?: Suffrage and the New Woman in Wales', *Women's History Review*, 11, 4 (2002), 649–50; Bohata also cites Jane Aaron's discussion in *Pur Fel y Dur: Y Gymraes yn Llên Menywod y Bedwared Ganrif ar Bymtheg* (Cardiff, 1998).

46 Blom, 'Gender and nation', pp. 6, 8.

47 Aberdare WLA minute book, newspaper cutting, 11 February 1892.

48 Blom, 'Gender and nation', p. 6.

49 *SWDN*, 18 April 1895; WUWLA Annual Report, 1896; programme for Annual Meeting, Newtown, March 1896. At its foundation in January 1893, the ILP stated itself to be 'in favour of every proposal for extending electoral right'; Keith Laybourn, *The Labour Party, 1881–1951: A Reader in History* (Gloucester, 1988), p. 31.

50 *SWDN*, 18 April 1895.

51 *SWDN*, 19, 20 April 1895.

52 *SWDN*, 6 November 1895, 17 January 1896; Morgan, *Wales in British Politics*, pp. 163–5; idem., *Rebirth of a Nation*, pp. 117–19; Williams, *When Was Wales?*, pp. 230–1; Emyr Williams, 'Liberalism', 204, 231, 303; Chris Williams, 'Democracy and nationalism', p. 124; *YW*, February 1896, 30–3.

53 Emyr Williams, 'Liberalism', 200–1; Dewi Rowland Hughes, 'Y coch a'r gwyrdd: Cymru Fydd a'r mudiad llafur Cymreig (1886–96)', in *Llafur: Journal of Welsh Labour History*, 6, 4 (1995), 60–79.

54 *SWDN*, 18, 24 March 1896.

55 A. Confino, 'The nation as a local metaphor: heimat, national memory and the German empire, 1871–1918', *History and Memory*, 5, 52; Ann McClintock, '"No longer in a future heaven": nationalism, gender and race', in G. Eley and R. G. Suny (eds), *Becoming National: A Reader* (New York, 1996), p. 260; both quoted in Silke Wenk, 'Gendered representations of the nation's past and future', in Blom et al. (eds), *Gendered Nations*, pp. 66, 67.

56 See n. 2 above.

57 See also Kirsti Bohata's work on the cultural nationalist journal, *Cymru Fydd*, in which a futuristic tale depicts Wales in the year 2000, when the president is Lady Gwen Tudor, 'typical of what was best in the past, and what would be in the future'; Bohata, 'For Wales, see England', 648; eadem, *Postcolonialism Revisited*, pp. 62–72.

58 K. Lentzner, 'Man or woman: which is woman to be?' *YW*, October 1897, 232–3.

59 An example of the 'progressive' version of nationalist history, I suggest, is Anna Jones, 'Women and religious freedom', *YW*, March 1895, 55–6; for the more reactionary construction of nation and women's role, see 'Patriotism and the women of Cymru' by 'Un o'r ddau Wynne' (Mallt Williams), *YW*, May 1898, 115; and Mallt Williams's profile of the novelist Gwyneth Vaughan, *YW*, August 1901, as well as Lentzner, 'Man or woman?'. A conference paper on this subject has prompted some responses with alternative interpretations: see Bohata, *Postcolonialism Revisited*, pp. 71–2.

60 Williams, *When Was Wales?*, p. 192; Stuart Woolf (ed.), *Nationalism in Europe, 1815 to the Present: A Reader* (London, 1996), pp. 2, 9.

61 A recent and comprehensive treatment is Neil Evans, 'Finding a new story: the search for a usable past in Wales 1869–1930', *Transactions of the Honourable Society of Cymmrodorion*, 10 (2004), 144–62. See also Adamson, *Class, Ideology and Nation*.

62 Morgan, *Rebirth of a Nation*, pp. 49–51; Aled Jones, *Press, Politics and Society: A History of Journalism in Wales* (Cardiff, 1993); Adamson, 'The intellectual and the national movement'; O'Malley et al., 'Tokens of antiquity'.

63 *YW*, January 1895, 19, 23; Februry 1895, 20.

64 *YW*, 1895–1903.

65 O'Malley et al.,' Tokens of antiquity', p. 148.

66 *YW*, March 1895, 69; also 'Thoughts from Mazzini', *YW*, August 1895, June 1897.

67 For example, *YW*, February 1895, 8–9; June 1898, 129.

68 *YW*, August 1896, 188.

69 *YW*, April 1896, 89–94; August 1896, 196–9.

70 Blom, 'Gender and nation', pp. 8–9; Wenk, 'Gendered representations', pp. 63, 67–8; Pierson, 'Nations: gendered', p. 44, makes the point that, according to feminist scholars of nationalism, 'most noteworthy. . . is the inverse relationship between the prominence of female figures in the allegorizations of nation and the degree of access granted women to the political apparatus of the state'.

71 *YW*, December 1897, 273–7.

72 *YW*, June 1897, 134–6.

73 Ibid., 134, emphasis original.

74  Ibid.

75  Davies, 'Women, nationalism and feminism', pp. 252–5.

76  'Patriotism and the women of Cymru' by 'Un o'r ddau Wynne' (Mallt Williams), *YW*, May 1898, 115; and Mallt Williams's profile of the novelist Gwyneth Vaughan, *YW*, August 1901; Lentzner, 'Man or woman?'.

77  McClintock, 'No longer in a future heaven', quoted by Wenk, 'Gendered representations', p. 69.

78  Emyr Williams, 'Liberalism', 204; *SWDN*, 4–5 February 1898.

79  Aberdare WLA minute book, cutting, February 11 1898.

80  Morgan, *Wales in British Politics*, p. 168.

81  Ibid., p. 171.

82  WLNC Revised Scheme of Organisation, undated but c.1907; NLW Political Ephemera collections, boxes XJN 1156–1160.

83  Programmes for WNLC Great National Convention, 1 October 1908, and Disestablishment Convention, 20 May 1909.

84  Neil Evans, '"A nation in a nutshell": the Swansea disestablishment demonstration of 1912 and the political culture of Edwardian Wales', pp. 218–19, in R. R. Davies and Geraint H. Jenkins (eds), *From Medieval to Modern Wales: Historical Essays in Honour of Kenneth O. Morgan and Ralph A. Griffiths* (Cardiff, 2004), pp. 214–29.

85  Kay Cook and Neil Evans, '"The petty antics of the bell-ringing boisterous band"? The women's suffrage movement in Wales, 1890–1918', in John (ed.), *Our Mothers' Land*, p. 165.

86  *YW*, January 1895, 18, also quoted in Bohata, 'For Wales see England', 652.

87  Bohata, 'For Wales, see England', 651.

88  *YW*, August 1901.

## 4: *Aberdare Women's Liberal Association, 1891–1914*

1  Ursula Masson (ed.), *Women's Rights and 'Womanly Duties': The Aberdare Women's Liberal Association, 1891–1910* (Cardiff, 2005), p. 5.

2  WUWLA Annual Reports; Aberdare WLA minutes, undated final entry; *Aberdare Leader* (*AL*), 16 March 1907; WLF Annual Reports, 1903–22.

3  Masson (ed.), *Women's Rights*, appendix 1, pp. 232–6.

4  Aled Jones, *Press, Politics and Society: A History of Journalism in Wales* (Cardiff, 1993), pp. 1–6; Kenneth O. Morgan, *Rebirth of a Nation: Wales 1880–1980* (Oxford and Cardiff, 1982), pp. 49–51; Tom O'Malley, Stuart Allan and Andrew Thompson, 'Tokens of antiquity: the newspaper press and the shaping of national identity in Wales, 1870–1900', in Michael Harris and Tom O'Malley (eds), *Studies in Newspaper and Periodical*

*History, 1995 Annual* (Westport, Connecticut, 1997), pp. 127–52. On the Cardiff press and its political positions: Neil Evans, 'The Welsh Victorian city: the middle class and national consciousness in Cardiff, 1850–1914', *Welsh History Review*, 12, 3 (1985), passim.

5 *AL*, 6 February 1892; *Merthyr Express* (*ME*), 14 November 1891, 5 December 1891; *SWDN*, 9, 12 November 1891, 4 February 1892. The Lady Lewis Habitation of the Primrose League existed in 1891, got its first woman officer, the treasurer, in 1893, and in 1895 had a full complement of women officers from the Ruling Councillor down; *Aberdare Illustrated Almanack*, 1891–5.

6 *SWDN*, 4 February 1892.

7 Aberdare WLA minutes, 20 January 1893, 7 February 1896, 7 September 1900; cutting, January 1893.

8 Martin Barclay, 'Aberdare 1880–1914: class and community' (MA thesis, University of Wales, Cardiff, 1985), 9–10.

9 Ibid.,11; John Williams (ed.), *Digest of Welsh Historical Statistics* (Cardiff, 1985), vol. I, p. 63.

10 Minutes of the Aberdare Nonconformist Election Committee, 1868.

11 Barclay, 'Aberdare', 6, 33, 56.

12 Ibid., iii.

13 Chris Williams, *Democratic Rhondda: Politics and Society, 1885–1951* (Cardiff, 1996), pp. 29–30, 45–6; Jon Parry, 'Labour leaders and local politics, 1888–1902: the example of Aberdare', *Welsh History Review (WHR)*, 14, 3 (1989), 409.

14 Eddie May, 'The mosaic of Labour politics, 1900–1918', in Duncan Tanner, Chris Williams and Deian Hopkin (eds), *The Labour Party in Wales, 1900–2000* (Cardiff, 2000), p. 68; Beti Jones, *Welsh Elections, 1885–1997 Etholiadau'r Ganrif* (Talybont, 1999), pp. 45–58.

15 Minutes of the Aberdare Nonconformist Election Committee, 1867–8; Helen Blackburn, *Women's Suffrage: A Record of the Women's Suffrage Movement in the British Isles* (London, 1902), p. 258.

16 Ryland Wallace, *Organise! Organise! Organise! A Study of Reform Agitations in Wales, 1840–1886* (Cardiff, 1991), pp. 164–5, 182, 218; Blackburn, *Women's Suffrage*, pp. 261–4.

17 Aberdare WLA minutes, 26 November 1891.

18 Aberdare WLA minutes, 8 March 1899.

19 J. Ifano Jones, 'One of the daughters of Wales', *Cymru,* November 1899, reprinted in translation from the original Welsh, in an unidentified cutting, Biographical Collection, Aberdare Reference Library.

20 Ibid.

21 For a discussion of the way liberal feminists used the rhetoric of 'woman's mission' to 'relocate' the 'sense of sexual difference ... in a new and public setting' after 1867, see Jane Rendall, 'The citizenship of women and the Reform Act of 1867', in Catherine Hall, Keith McClelland and Jane

Rendall (eds), *Defining the Victorian Nation: Class, Race, Gender and the Reform Act of 1867* (Cambridge, 2000), pp. 163–4.

22  Ieuan Gwynedd Jones, 'Dr Thomas Price and the election of 1868 in Merthyr Tydfil, a study in Nonconformist politics', *WHR*, 2, 1 and 2 (1964), 147–72, 251–70; Kenneth O. Fox, 'Labour and Merthyr's khaki election of 1900', *WHR*, 2, 3 (1965), 351–66; Jon Parry, 'Labour leaders and local politics, 1888–1902: the example of Aberdare', *WHR*, 14, 3 (1989), 399–416; Barclay, 'Aberdare'.

23  Kenneth O. Morgan, *Wales in British Politics 1868–1922* (Cardiff, 1980), p. 243.

24  *Aberdare Times (AT)*, 14, 20 November 1891, 2 April 1892; *South Wales Daily News (SWDN)*, 11–12 November 1891, 29 January 1892, 4, 6 February 1892.

25  Lucy Bland, *Banishing the Beast: English Feminism and Sexual Morality, 1885–1914* (London, 1995), pp. 114–15; Elizabeth Crawford, *The Women's Suffrage Movement: A Reference Guide, 1866–1928* (London and New York 2001), p. 105.

26  On women's pressure-group politics and their 'interlocking membership', see Patricia Hollis, *Ladies Elect: Women in English Local Government, 1865–1914* (Oxford, 1987), pp. 47–59.

27  'Rules of the Aberdare Women's Liberal Association', Aberdare WLA minute book, 26 November 1891.

28  *SWDN*, 12 November 1891; *Merthyr Express (ME)*, 14 November 1891.

29  Cutting in Aberdare WLA minute book (hereafter 'cutting[s]'), 4 February 1892.

30  Eileen Janes Yeo, 'Radical femininity: women's self-representation in labour movements in the 19th and 20th centuries', in *North East Labour History*, 29 (1995), 7–8; eadem, 'Introduction: some paradoxes of empowerment', in eadem (ed.), *Radical Femininity: Women's Self-Representation in the Public Sphere* (Manchester 1998), pp. 1–24.

31  *Nineteenth Century*, June 1889.

32  Aberdare WLA minutes, 14, 29 April 1892, 6 June 1892, and cutting reporting 'Tea Meeting' of 30 May 1892.

33  Aberdare WLA minutes, 8, 29 April 1892, 25 June 1892, 21 October 1893, 13, 30 March 1894, 6 June 1894, 21 February 1895, 5 July 1895, 27 January 1897.

34  Cutting, March 1894, report of meeting of 6 November 1894.

35  Aberdare WLA minutes, 10 June 1892, 6 June 1894.

36  Ibid., 23 February 1900. Gwyneth Vaughan, novelist and leading Welsh Liberal and suffragist, was a member of the executive of the UPS; Crawford, *Women's Suffrage Movement*, pp. 693–4.

37  Claire Hirshfield, 'Fractured faith: Liberal Party women and the suffrage issue in Britain, 1892–1914', *Gender & History*, 2, 2 (1990), 179.

38  Aberdare WLA minutes, 23 February 1900, 12 January 1901, 27 January 1903, 13 March 1903.

39  Fox, 'Merthyr's khaki election', 361.

40  Martin Pugh, *The Making of Modern British Politics, 1857–1939* (Oxford, 1995), p. 41.

41  A few of the places where these reforms appear yoked together: Aberdare WLA minutes, 11 November 1892; cutting, report of meeting of 13 December 1892; cutting, report of annual meeting February 1894; minutes, 10 February 1900. On the House of Lords, which was seen as a permanent obstacle to reform, especially to Irish Home Rule and the enfranchisement of women, see cutting, report of public meeting of 13 December 1892, speech by D. A. Thomas; cutting, report of meeting of March 1894, when a paper on the history of the House of Lords was read by Maria Richards, and the meeting passed a resolution calling for reform.

42  Margaret Barrow, 'Teetotal feminists: temperance leadership and the campaign for women's suffrage', in Claire Eustance, Joan Ryan and Laura Ugolini (eds), *A Suffrage Reader: Charting Directions in British Suffrage History* (London, 2000), p. 69; W. R. Lambert, *Drink and Sobriety in Victorian Wales, c.1820–c.1895* (Cardiff, 1983).

43  Cutting, report of meeting of March 1893; *Cambrian News* (*CN*), 1 April 1892.

44  D. A. Thomas papers, letter from Aberdare BWTA to D. A. Thomas, signed by Mary S. Lloyd, undated, but probably December 1893; WWP Biographical Index (BI*)*, XVI p. 4, XXIV p. 55. Newport and Cardiff BWTA branches also shared membership with the WLAs in those towns.

45  Cuttings, report of meeting of 17 March 1893, speech by Mrs Massingberd; report of annual meeting of 19 February 1894, speech by Miss Conybeare; report of speech by Nora Philipps, 17 October 1894; *CN*, 1 April 1892.

46  Aberdare WLA minutes, 15 December 1893, 27 April 1894; D. A. Thomas papers, letters from Aberdare WLA, 15 December 1893, from Aberdare branch BWTA (undated), and from Dowlais Primitive Methodists, undated. The WLA resolution of 27 April 1894 and that from the BWTA shared the same wording, supplied by Josephine Butler.

47  Aberdare WLA minutes, 28 October 1892, 6 January 1893, 2 March 1894, 1 May 1896, 28 May 1897, 10 February 1899, 5 May 1900, 10 February 1900; cuttings, reports of 17 March 1893, 6 December 1893, March 1894.

48  Aberdare WLA minutes, 15, 25 February 1895, 8 March 1895, 3 January 1896; cuttings, 27 January 1896, 23 April 1900.

49  Cutting, meeting of 11 November 1895; Aberdare WLA minutes, 8 May 1896, 12 May 1902.

50  Morgan, *Wales in British Politics*, pp. 178–80; idem., 'Wales and the Boer War' in idem. (ed.) *Modern Wales: Politics, Places and People,* (Cardiff,

1995), pp. 46–58, 260–1; Fox, 'Merthyr's khaki election', 351–66; Wil Jon Edwards, *From the Valley I Came* (London, 1956), pp. 79–80.

51  Aberdare WLA minutes, 29 December 1899, 26 January 1900; cutting re. 8 February 1900. For a discussion of disruption of public meetings in this period, and the assumption of a certain degree of political legitimacy for that, in contrast to private meetings, see Jon Lawrence, *Speaking for the People: Party, Language and Popular Politics in England, 1867–1914* (Cambridge, 1998), pp. 185–6. The topic is further discussed in following chapters.

52  *SWDN*, 24 August 1894.

53  *SWDN*, 23 October 1894. The phrase 'forward movement' appears to have been capable of use in social, religious or political contexts to denote what would now be described as a 'proactive' approach. Maria Richards may have been talking about the decision of the WLF actively to pursue women's suffrage, or of women's Liberal and Welsh national political activities more generally.

54  Cutting, meeting of 11 February 1898.

55  Cutting, meeting of 29 October 1895.

56  *SWDN*, 7 December 1894.

57  Hollis, *Ladies Elect*, pp. 59–61. The relative importance of local boards and bodies may not have been the same everywhere: Carolyn Steedman, *Childhood, Culture and Class in Britain: Margaret McMillan, 1860–1931* (New Brunswick 1990), p. 38; Parry, 'Labour leaders', 404–5.

58  Aberdare WLA minutes, 2 November 1894; *SWDN*, 15 December 1894.

59  Cuttings, meetings of 17 October 1894, 6 November 1894.

60  Cutting, annual meeting, 21 February 1895.

61  *Young Wales* (*YW*), May 1896, 115–18.

62  Hollis, *Ladies Elect*, p. 227.

63  Aberdare WLA minutes, 26 November 1891.

64  Christine Collette, *For Labour and For Women: The Women's Labour League, 1906–1918* (Manchester, 1989), p. 83.

65  Parry, 'Labour leaders', 404–5; Barclay, 'Aberdare', 124, 136.

66  Aberdare WLA minutes, 29 April 1892. For further material on Sybil Thomas, see Ursula Masson (ed.), *Women's Rights and 'Womanly Duties': Aberdare Women's Liberal Association, 1891–1910* (Cardiff, 2005), pp. 47–51.

67  Ibid., Appendix I, pp. 232–6.

68  Barclay, 'Aberdare', iii, 5–6, 15–20; minutes of the Aberdare Nonconformist Election Committee, 1867–8.

69  *AL*, 16 February 1907.

70  Cutting, March 1894, 'Public meeting at Aberaman'; *Western Mail* (*WM*), 19 October 1909; *SWDN*, 19 October 1909, 6 February 1911; 1891 Census of Population, RG 12/4442–8.

71  Masson (ed.), *Women's Rights*, pp. 51–5.

72 Catherine Davies, wife of a land-owning JP, mother of five children, and with three living-in servants.

73 Aberdare WLA minutes, 4 March 1892; WWP BI XIX, 204–5. No inkling of the bitter events enters the minute book.

74 Cuttings, 'Monster Tea', 30 May 1892, annual meeting, 27 November 1899; 1891 Census, Aberdare, RG 12/4442–8.

75 Cuttings, 8 March 1900, 5 May 1900.

76 Carol Dyhouse, *Feminism and the Family in England, 1880–1930* (Oxford, 1989), ch. 2, especially pp. 81ff.

77 Angela V. John, *By the Sweat of Their Brow: Women Workers at Victorian Coalmines* (London, 1984), pp. 145, 162.

78 Deborah James, '"Teaching girls": intermediate schools and career opportunities for girls in the East Glamorgan valleys of Wales, 1896–1914', *History of Education*, 30, 6 (2001), 513–26.

79 Eddie May, 'The mosaic of labour politics, 1900–1918', in Tanner et al. (eds), *The Labour Party*, p. 63.

80 Barclay, 'Aberdare', 74–6, 134.

81 Profile of Mrs Richards, *ME*, 20 October 1923, WWP BI, XXIV, 55; Barclay, 'Aberdare', 93–4.

82 Aberdare WLA minutes, 22 October 1895, 16, 23 July 1900; cutting, 29 October 1895; Kay Cook and Neil Evans, '"The petty antics of the bell-ringing, boisterous band"? The women's suffrage movement in Wales, 1890–1918', in Angela V. John (ed.), *Our Mothers' Land: Chapters in Welsh Women's History, 1830–1939* (Cardiff, 1991), p. 165.

83 Aberdare WLA minutes, 13 October 1899, 10 February 1900, 23 July 1900, 21 September 1900.

84 Fox, 'Merthyr's khaki election', 361.

85 Aberdare Valley ILP records, GRO D/DXhj 2.

86 *AL*, 20 March 1920; John Williams, 'The economic and social context', in Tanner et al. (eds), *The Labour Party*, p. 32.

87 *SWDN*, 4 April 1911.

88 *AL*, 28 February 1920, 8 April 1920.

89 Aberdare WLA minutes and cutting of 4 February 1892.

90 *AL*, 9 March 1907.

91 Garland was a member of the executive of the WLF, former member of the Union of Practical Suffragists, and later that year helped form the Forward Suffrage Union. The other speaker at this Aberdare event was Kate Freeman, formerly Jenkins, of the WUWLA and Swansea WLA.

92 *AL*, 16 March 1907.

93 Hirshfield, 'Fractured faith', 179; Martin Pugh, *The March of the Women: A Revisionist Analysis of the Campaign for Women's Suffrage, 1866–1914* (Oxford, 2000), pp. 141–3.

94 *WM*, 19 November 1909.

95 *SWDN*, 1, 3 October 1910.

[96] *SWDN*, 7 October 1910. As political events unfolded, the convention was postponed.

[97] WLF Annual Reports, 1911–22. During the war, Maria Richards was president and Ann Gwenllian George secretary.

[98] *SWDN*, 2 January 1911, 1 April 1911; branches at Hirwaun, Neath, Penarth, Barry and Cardiff.

[99] *SWDN*, 30 November 1910.

[100] WLF *Summary*, July 1910. The charter dealt with coverture, right of maintenance, earnings, wife as partner, divorce, assaults on wives, children, marriage service, inheritance and testamentary power, education of girls, immorality, measures for improving the condition of married women of the working class, factory acts and economics.

[101] Her father, Revd J. J. George, had been a member of the Nonconformist Election Committee of 1867.

[102] Claire Eustance, '"Daring to be free": the evolution of women's political identities in the Women's Freedom League, 1907–1930', unpublished Ph.D. thesis, (York University, 1993), 104–6; *Suffrage Annual*, 112. The five branches were Aberdare, Barry, Cardiff, Montgomery and Swansea.

[103] *AL*, 10 February 1906.

[104] Ursula Masson, 'Davies, Florence Rose (1882–1958): Independent Labour party activist, Labour alderman', in Keith Gildart, David Howell and Neville Kirk (eds), *Dictionary of Labour Biography*, Vol. XI (Basingstoke, 2003), pp. 39–47.

[105] For a summary of these debates, see June Hannam, '"I had not been to London": women's suffrage – a view from the regions', in June Purvis and Sandra Holton (eds), *Votes for Women* (London, 2000), pp. 236ff.

### 5: *Cardiff Women's Liberal Association, 1890–1900*

[1] Ryland Wallace, *Organise! Organise! Organise! A Study of Reform Agitations in Wales, 1840–1886* (Cardiff, 1991), ch. XI.

[2] Martin Daunton, *Coal Metropolis: Cardiff 1870–1914* (Leicester, 1977), ch. 11.

[3] Ibid., pp. 6–7.

[4] Daunton, *Coal Metropolis.*, pp. 11–13; John Williams, 'The economic and social context', in Duncan Tanner, Chris Williams and Deian Hopkins (eds), *The Labour Party in Wales, 1900–2000* (Cardiff, 2000), pp. 28–9.

[5] Beti Jones, *Etholiadau'r Ganrif/Welsh Elections, 1885–1997* (Talybont, 1999), pp. 28–40; Daunton, *Coal Metropolis*, pp. 170–1.

[6] Daunton, *Cool Metropolis*, pp. 172–3, 202; Kenneth O. Morgan, 'The New Liberalism and the challenge of Labour: the Welsh experience 1885–1929', in idem, *Modern Wales: Politics, Places and People* (Cardiff, 1995), pp. 65ff.

7   Daunton, *Coal Metropolis*, part three passim; Neil Evans, 'Cardiff's Labour tradition', *Llafur: Journal of Welsh Labour History*, 4, 2 (1985), 77–90; Deian Hopkin, 'Labour's roots in Wales, 1880–1900', in Tanner et al., *The Labour Party*, pp. 50–1; Neil Evans and Dot Jones, '"To help forward the great work of humanity": women in the Labour party in Wales', ibid., pp. 215–40.

8   Evans, 'The Welsh Victorian city: the middle class and national consciousness in Cardiff, 1850–1914', *Welsh History Review*, 12, 3 (1985), 371–3.

9   Hopkin, 'Labour's early roots', 50–51; Kenneth O. Morgan, *Rebirth of a Nation: Wales 1880–1980* (Oxford, 1981), p. 52.

10  Welsh Union of Women's Liberal Associations (WUWLA) Annual Reports, 1893–6; Cardiff WLA Annual Reports, 1894–1902; Women's Liberal Federation (WLF) Annual Reports, 1904–15.

11  Morgan, *Rebirth of a Nation*, p. 72.

12  Evans, 'The Welsh Victorian city', 387; Mari Williams, 'Women and the Welsh language in the industrial valleys of south Wales, 1914–1945', in Geraint H. Jenkins and Mari A. Williams (eds), *'Let's Do Our Best for the Ancient Tongue': The Welsh Language in the Twentieth Century* (Cardiff, 2000), pp. 137–80.

13  Ryland Wallace, *Organise!*, p. 163; *SWDN*, 10 March 1881.

14  Helen Blackburn, *Women's Suffrage: A Record of the Women's Suffrage Movement in the British Isles* (London, 1902), pp. 152–4.

15  Wallace, *Organise!*, pp. 166, 168; *SWDN*, 10 March 1881.

16  Wallace, *Organise!*, pp. 160ff; Crawford, *The Women's Suffrage Movement: A Reference Guide, 1866–1928* (London, 2001, first pub. 1999), p. 83; *SWDN*, 21 March 1908, 24 March 1908; C&DWSS Annual Report, 1912.

17  Cardiff Liberal Association (CLA) Annual Reports, 1889, 1903; Martin Daunton, 'Aspects of the economic and social structure of Cardiff, 1870–1914', unpublished Ph.D. thesis, University of Kent, 1974, 394, 420; *South Wales Daily News (SWDN)*, 22, 27 December 1894, 6, 8 November 1895, 7 January 1896.

18  *SWDN*, 28 February 1890, 21 March 1890.

19  Wallace, *Organise!*, pp. 168–70, 176–83; W. R. Lambert, *Drink and Sobriety in Victorian Wales, c.1820–c.1895* (Cardiff, 1983), p. 89.

20  Daunton, *Coal Metropolis*, pp. 221, 225; Neil Evans, 'Urbanisation, élite attitudes and philanthropy: Cardiff 1850–1914', *International Review of Social History*, XVII (1982), 302.

21  Neil Evans, 'Urbanisation', 294; idem., 'The Welsh Victorian city: the middle class and civic and national consciousness in Cardiff, 1850–1914', *Welsh History Review (WHR)*, 12, 3 (1985), 352–7; Daunton, *Coal Metropolis*, ch. 9.

22  Daunton, *Coal Metropolis*, pp. 151–9.

23  *SWDN*, 25 March 1891, 4, 6 February 1892; Welsh Union of Women's Liberal Association (WUWLA) Annual Report, 1893. Leake went on to

help reorganize the other large urban associations in Swansea and Newport.

[24] WLF Annual Reports, 1892–5.

[25] The accounts for 1897 give the secretary's salary as £65, in 1901 it was £55, perhaps reflecting loss of subscriptions and lower activity; Cardiff WLA Annual Reports, 1894, 1897, 1901.

[26] WUWLA Annual Report, 1895.

[27] Cardiff WLA Annual Reports, 1897–1902.

[28] Ibid., 1897, subscription lists; 1901 Census of Population, Cardiff, RG 13/4970–88.

[29] Ibid.

[30] However, research by Helen Thomas reveals the formation of branches of the Women's Co-operative Guild in south Wales in the 1890s, including in Cardiff. See Helen Thomas, '"A democracy of working women": the women's co-operative guild in south Wales, 1891–1939', MA dissertation, University of Glamorgan, 2006.

[31] Paul O'Leary, *Immigration and Integration: The Irish in Wales, 1798–1922* (Cardiff, 2000), ch. IX, passim and pp. 269–79.

[32] Daunton, *Coal Metropolis*, p. 176.

[33] *SWDN*, 4 December 1894.

[34] O'Leary, *Immigration and Integration*, pp. 275–7; Cardiff WLA subscription lists 1897.

[35] O'Leary suggests that 'in the 1890s it would have been much more likely that the Irish would enter politics through their own religious/ethnic associations rather than join a Liberal association' (correspondence, June 2004). He points to the gap in research on Irish women's political activity in mainland Britain in this period, and has written of the failure of Home Rule politics to organize women, in contrast to the Irish Self-Determination League (ISDL) formed in 1919, after which there is some evidence for the active involvement of women in south Wales; O'Leary, *Immigration and Integration*, pp. 285ff. A Ladies' Branch of the Irish National League existed in Liverpool in 1891, but has apparently left no records; Krista Cowman, *'Mrs Brown is a Man and a Brother': Women in Merseyside's Political Organisations, 1890–1920* (Liverpool 2004), p. 17.

[36] Ursula Masson, 'The Swansea suffragettes' in Luana Dee and Katell Keinig (eds), *Women in Wales: A Documentary of Our Recent History*, vol. I (Cardiff, 1987); Hilda Kean, *Deeds Not Words: The Lives of Suffragette Teachers* (London, 1990); W. Gareth Evans, *Education and Female Emancipation: The Welsh Experience, 1847–1914*, (Cardiff, 1990).

[37] Catherine Carr (ed.), *The Spinning Wheel: City of Cardiff High School for Girls, 1895–1955* (Cardiff, 1955).

[38] Cutting, 17 July 1924, newspaper not identified, in Cardiff Women's Citizens Association papers, GRO D/Dx 158/2/1.

[39] *SWDN*, 1 October 1910; Deirdre Beddoe, 'Collin, Mary (1860–1955) headmistress', *Oxford Dictionary of National Biography* (Oxford, 2004), *www.oxforddnb.com/view/article/51850.*

[40] Evans, 'Urbanisation'; idem., 'The Welsh Victorian city'; Deian Hopkin, 'Labour's roots in Wales', pp. 50–1.

[41] Millicent Mackenzie, professor of education at the university from 1904–15, was Wales's only woman parliamentary candidate in 1918, standing for Labour in the new University of Wales seat. Mackenzie was also active in the Cardiff Progressive Liberal Women's Union and in the C&DWSS, as was her successor in the Education Department, Barbara Foxley, a Liberal elected to the city council in the 1920s. The first, unpaid, 'Lady Principal' of Aberdare Hall, the women's hall of residence in Cardiff, the Hon. Isabel Bruce, was the daughter of Lord and Lady Aberdare, leading Liberals, educational and temperance reformers. Her successor, Miss Hurlbatt, was also an active Liberal in Cardiff and later a member of the suffrage society.

[42] W. Gareth Evans, *Education and Female Emancipation*, pp. 228ff. On 'feminist advocacy of residential provision' for women students, and this role in Cardiff for Kate Jones and Lady Aberdare, see Carol Dyhouse, *No Distinction of Sex? Women in British Universities, 1870–1939* (London, 1995), pp. 94–5.

[43] Daunton, *Coal Metropolis*, p. 225; Evans, 'Urbanisation', 315–18.

[44] Daunton, *Coal Metropolis*, p. 225.

[45] Quarterly and Annual Reports of the Cardiff Charity Organisation Society (COS) 1887–1898; Evans, 'Urbanisation', 316; Daunton, *Coal Metropolis*, p. 225.

[46] Evans, 'Urbanisation', 320.

[47] Ibid., 315–21; materials relating to all these and other organizations can be found in the Cochfarf Collection, especially boxes 3, 5, 6, 7, 9.

[48] Jane Rendall, 'Introduction', in eadem (ed.), *Equal or Different: Women's Politics, 1800–1914* (Oxford, 1987), p. 23.

[49] Cardiff Poor Law Union Year Books 1894–1930. Before the 1894 reforms, the board had fifty-two ex officio and sixty-five elected members.

[50] *SWDN*, 4, 15, 17 October 1894.

[51] Catherine Hall and Leonore Davidoff, *Family Fortunes: Men and Women of the English Middle Class* (London, 1987), p.10.

[52] The significance of 'local social structures and patterns of growth' in the evolution of philanthropic activity is discussed by Evans, 'Urbanisation', 291–5.

[53] WLF *Summary*, no. 15, September 1894, 4; *SWDN*, 8 October 1894.

[54] Patricia Hollis, 'Women in council: separate spheres, public space', in Rendall (ed.), *Equal or Different*, p. 195.

[55] Ibid.

[56] *SWDN*, October–December 1894; *WM*, October–December 1894.

[57] *SWDN*, 19, 22 December 1894; WUWLA Annual Report, 1895.

[58] *SWDN*, 17, 20 October 1894; WLF *Summary*, no. 18, December 1894, 7.

[59] See Appendix, pp. 184–9.

[60] Evans, 'Urbanisation', 298.

[61] *SWDN*, 14 December 1894.

[62] *WM*, 15 December 1894.

[63] Cardiff COS Ninth Annual Report.

[64] Hollis, 'Women in council', pp. 194, 197, 202.

[65] Cardiff COS First Quarterly Report, April 1887.

[66] *SWDN*, 4 October 1894; *WM*, 28 November 1894.

[67] *SWDN*, 13 December 1894.

[68] *SWDN*, 5 October 1894.

[69] *SWDN*, 17 October 1894, 3, 10 December 1894; Cochfarf Collection, Box 8, poster in support of women candidates and of candidature of Miss Mabel Thomas.

[70] *WM*, 28 November 1894, 13 December 1894.

[71] WLF *Summary*, no. 14, August 1894, 2.

[72] *SWDN*, 4 October 1894 . McLaren had been a founder of the Society for Promoting the Return of Women as Poor Law Guardians in 1881, and the Society for Promoting the Return of Women as County Councillors in 1888, which in 1893 changed its name to the WLGS; Elizabeth Crawford, *The Women's Suffrage Movement: A Reference Guide 1866–1928* (London and New York, 2001), p. 642.

[73] This paragraph is based on reports in the *SWDN*, October–December 1894.

[74] See joint Liberal and Conservative meeting, *SWDN*, 3 December 1894.

[75] *WM*, 18 December 1894.

[76] *WM*, 17–19 December 1894; Election Scrapbook of Henry G. C. Allwood, Cardiff Local Studies collection.

[77] *SWDN*, 18 December 1894.

[78] *SWDN*, 22, 27, 31 December 1894.

[79] Cardiff Poor Law Union Year Books 1894–1930; *SWDN*, 26 December 1894.

[80] *SWDN*, 7 November 1895, 1 September 1896, 4 January 1896, 7 January 1896.

[81] *SWDN*, 6 November 1895.

[82] See, for example, the special issue of *Urban History*, 32, 1, May 2005.

[83] WLF *Summary,* no. 20, March 1895, 11.

## 6: *Cardiff Women's Liberal Association, 1900–1914*

[1] Claire Hirshfield, 'Fractured faith: Liberal party women and the suffrage issue in Britain, 1892–1914', *Gender & History*, 2, 2 (1990), 180–93, 191.

2   Jo Vellacott, *From Liberal to Labour With Women's Suffrage: The Story of Catherine Marshall* (Montreal and Kingston, 1993), p. 365; Hirshfield, 'Fractured faith', 183.

3   Sandra Stanley Holton, *Feminism and Democracy: Women's Suffrage and Reform Politics in Britain, 1900–1918* (Cambridge, 1986), pp. 86, 101, 109; Vellacott, *From Liberal to Labour*, pp. 166, 168–9; Ursula Masson, 'Divided loyalties: women's suffrage and party politics in south Wales, 1912–1915', *Llafur: Journal of Welsh Labour History*, 7, 3 and 4 (1998).

4   Jane Rendall, 'Citizenship, culture and civilisation: the language of British suffragists 1866–1874', in Caroline Daley and Melanie Nolan (eds), *Suffrage and Beyond: International Feminist Perspectives* (New York, 1994); Sandra Stanley Holton, 'British freewomen: national identity, constitutionalism and languages of race in early suffragist histories', in Eileen Janes Yeo (ed.), *Radical Femininity: Women's Self-Representation in the Public Sphere* (Manchester, 1998); Helen Rogers, *Women and the People: Authority, Authorship and the Radical Tradition in Nineteenth Century England* (Aldershot, 2000); Jon Lawrence, 'Contesting the male polity: the suffragettes and the politics of disruption in Edwardian Britain', in Amanda Vickery (ed.), *Women, Privilege, and Power: British Politics 1750 to the Present* (Stanford, 2001); Laura E. Nym Mayhall, 'The rhetorics of slavery and citizenship: suffragist discourse and canonical texts in Britain, 1880–1914', *Gender & History*, 13, 3 (2001), 481–97.

5   *SWDN*, 3 April 1909.

6   Lawrence, 'Contesting the male polity', passim.

7   Speaking at Bridgend; *Glamorgan Gazette*, 10 November 1911.

8   Ursula Masson, '"Hand in hand with the women, forward we will go": Welsh nationalism and feminism in the 1890s', *Women's History Review*, 12, 3 (2003), 357–86.

9   Angela V. John, '"Run like blazes": the suffragettes and Welshness', *Llafur*, 6, 3 (1994) 28–43; eadem, '"A draft of fresh air": women's suffrage, the Welsh and London', *Transactions of the Honourable Society of Cymmrodorion* (1994–5), 81–93; eadem, '*Chwarae Teg': Welsh Men's Support for Women's Suffrage* (Aberystwyth, 1998). See also, Kay Cook and Neil Evans, '"The petty antics of the bell-ringing, boisterous band"?: The women's suffrage movement in Wales, 1890–1918', in Angela V. John (ed.), *Our Mothers' Land: Chapters in Welsh Women's History, 1830–1939* (Cardiff, 1991), pp. 180–1; Ceridwen Lloyd-Morgan, 'From Temperance to Suffrage?', in ibid., p. 154.

10  John, 'Run like blazes', 32; Cook and Evans, 'The petty antics', pp. 180–1.

11  John, '*Chwarae Teg'*, pp. 5–6.

12  Cardiff WLA Annual Report, 1902.

13  Ibid.

14  Ibid.

15 WLF Annual Reports, 1904–1914; the WLF reports began to include membership figures for associations from 1904.

16 *SWDN*, 1, 20, 27 October 1910, 10, 11, 21 February 1911, 4 April 1911; *Western Mail (WM)*, 1 October 1910; Minutes, Cardiff City Council, 1910–11.

17 Martin Daunton, 'Aspects of the social and economic structure of Cardiff, 1870–1914', unpublished Ph.D. thesis, University of Kent, 1974, 30–3.

18 Vellacott, *From Liberal to Labour*, pp. 365–6.

19 In the extended Guest family, however, there were also a number of active suffragists; I am grateful to Angela John for this information.

20 *Hansard*, House of Commons Debates (HoC Deb.), 28 February 1908, c.279, division list 28. For Guest's previous record in the House on women's suffrage, see, for example, HoC Deb., 16 March 1904, division list 58.

21 WLF *Summary*, December 1905, February 1906; *SWDN*, 3 March 1908, 5 June 1908, 18, 19 March 1909; Brian Harrison, *Separate Spheres: The Opposition to Women's Suffrage in Britain* (London, 1978), pp. 122, 127. While Cardiff had an active branch of the anti-suffrage organization in 1910–11, there were few branches in Wales until 1913, when there was a sudden increase to seventeen branches.

22 *SWDN*, 15 June, 4 July 1908.

23 Jon Lawrence, *Speaking for the People: Party, Language and Popular Politics in England, 1867–1914* (Cambridge, 1998), ch. 7, esp. pp. 190–1; idem, 'Contesting the male polity', pp. 201–26.

24 Pugh, *March of the Women: A Revisionist Analysis of the Campaign for Women's Suffrage, 1866–1914* (Oxford, 2000), pp. 188–91.

25 *SWDN*, May–June 1908.

26 *SWDN*, 12 May 1908.

27 The WFL policy was not to interrupt speakers but 'to ask questions at the time allowed'; *The Times*, 23 January 1908.

28 Pugh, *March of the Women*, pp. 136–7.

29 Lawrence, 'Contesting the male polity', pp. 201–26.

30 *SWDN*, 14 May 1908.

31 *SWDN*, 12 May 1908; Lawrence, *Representing the People*, pp. 190–1; idem, 'Contesting the male polity', pp. 201–4.

32 *SWDN*, 12–14, 25 May 1908.

33 Cochfarf collection, Box 7, letter from Erie Evans, 2 May 1909; *SWDN*, 3 April 1909.

34 Ibid.

35 Ibid.

36 By 1912, the whole Lester Jones family was enrolled in C&DWSS.

37 *The Times*, 8 October 1908, Emmeline Pethick-Lawrence, in an exchange of letters with Lloyd George, following incidents at a meeting in Swansea.

[38] Erie Evans, 2 May 1909, emphasis original.

[39] Neil Evans, '"A nation in a nutshell": the Swansea disestablishment demonstration of 1912 and the political culture of Edwardian Wales', in R. R. Davies and Geraint H. Jenkins (eds), *From Medieval to Modern Wales: Historical Essays in Honour of Kenneth O. Morgan and Ralph A. Griffiths* (Cardiff, 2004), pp. 218–19.

[40] *SWDN*, 29 September 1910.

[41] *The Times*, 2 October 1908.

[42] On the division of 'the People' into 'different parts with varying capacities' in radical discourse, see Rogers, *Women and the People*, p. 7.

[43] Ursula Masson, 'Gender and national memory in *Young Wales*, 1895–1903', unpublished paper presented to the North American Association for the Study of Welsh Culture and History, Le Moyne College, New York, June 2002.

[44] The disestablishment issue '[i]ncreasingly . . . was beginning to lose its primacy in Welsh life', and particularly in south Wales; Lloyd George had himself lost interest in the question, though he was obliged to continue to support it; Kenneth O. Morgan, *Wales in British Politics, 1866–1922* (Cardiff, 1980), pp. 240, 273–4; Evans, 'Nation in a nutshell', p. 216.

[45] *SWDN*, 24 March 1908, 1 October 1910.

[46] Rendall, 'Citizenship', pp. 127–50, esp. 134–7.

[47] *SWDN*, September–October 1910.

[48] Evans, 'Nation in a nutshell', pp. 216–17.

[49] *SWDN*, *WM*, 4 November 1910.

[50] Catherine Marshall Papers (CM), Cumbria Record Office, D/MAR/3/21, letter, 20 June 1913, from W. H. Wortham.

[51] *SWDN*, 14–16 November 1910. Hyde had been MP for Wednesbury, 1900–10.

[52] *SWDN*, 25–26 November 1910; election leaflet, NLW Welsh Political Ephemera Box XJN 1165.

[53] *WM*, *SWDN*, November–December 1910.

[54] For the attitude of Cardiff labour movement to Hyde's candidacy and the electoral impact, see Daunton, 'Aspects', 466–8.

[55] *SWDN*, 10 March 1911.

[56] *WM*, *SWDN*, December 1910–March 1911.

[57] *SWDN*, 28, 29 March 1911; WLF Annual Report, 1911.

[58] *SWDN*, 11, 14, 15 March 1912.

[59] CLA Annual Reports, 1908–17; *SWDN*, 26 November 1910, 11 January 1911, 9 March 1911.

[60] *SWDN*, 11–15 March 1912.

[61] June Hannam, *Isabella Ford* (Oxford, 1989); Holton, *Feminism and Democracy*; Leslie Parker Hume, *The National Union of Women's Suffrage Societies, 1897–1914* (New York, 1982); Pugh, *March of the Women*, p. 4; Vellacott, *From Liberal to Labour*, ch. 8.

[62] Masson, 'Divided loyalties'; eadem, '"Political conditions in Wales are quite different": party politics and votes for women, 1912–1915', *Women's History Review*, 12, 3 (2003), 357–86. Some of what follows draws on those articles, but there has also been some revision.

[63] C&DWSS Annual Report, 1912–13.

[64] See letterheads on correspondence between Catherine Marshall, the Cardiff society and the SWFWSS, at CM D/MAR/3/17.

[65] Masson, 'Divided loyalties'.

[66] Ibid., 2–3; *SWDN*, 10 March 1913; C&DWSS Annual Reports.

[67] For a more detailed examination of class and party in the C&DWSS, see Masson, 'Divided loyalties', 118.

[68] Holton, *Feminism and Democracy*, p. 101.

[69] Morgan, *Wales in British Politics*, pp. 251–5.

[70] Chris Williams, *Democratic Rhondda: Politics and Society, 1885–1951* (Cardiff, 1996), p. 84; Morgan, *Wales in British Politics*, pp. 247ff ; Neil Evans, '"A tidal wave of impatience": the Cardiff General Strike of 1911', in Geraint H. Jenkins and J. Beverley Smith (eds), *Politics and Society in Wales, 1840–1922: Essays in Honour of Ieuan Gwynedd Jones* (Cardiff, 1988), p. 135.

[71] Catherine Marshall (CM) to Janet Price, 1 August 1912, D/MAR/3/54; Winifred Coombe-Tennant (WC-T) to CM, 22 December 1914, D/MAR/3/39; CM to WC-T, 29 December 1914, ibid; Nancy Griffiths Jones, 31 December 1914, D/MAR/3/39; Barbara Foxley, 3 January 1915, D/MAR/3/43; NUWSS Exec. Committee Minutes, 1 May 1913, NUWSS/A1/14 (Women's Library).

[72] Barbara Foxley to CM, 3 January 1915, CM D/MAR/3/43.

[73] *SWDN*, 11 March 1911, 8 April 1911.

[74] Nancy Griffiths Jones (secretary, NUWSS Swansea branch) to CM, 31 December 1914, D/MAR/3/39.

[75] EFF Minutes, 19 December 1912.

[76] Resolutions of C&DWSS, enclosed with letter to Kathleen Courtney from Mabel E. Howell, C&DWSS secretary, 27 June 1912, D/MAR/3/17.

[77] EFF Committee Minutes, 19 December 1912.

[78] Correspondence between Mabel Howell and Kathleen Courtney, secretary to the national union, June and July 1912, D/MAR/3/17; Resolutions of the C&DWSS members, 18 June 1912.

[79] Masson, 'Divided loyalties', 118; eadem, 'Political conditions', 376, 384.

[80] EFF Committee Minutes, 12 December 1912.

[81] C&DWSS Annual Report, 1912–13.

[82] Ibid., 1913–14.

[83] Ibid., 1912–13; WLF Annual Reports; reports in *The Rhondda Socialist*, May 1912–April 1913.

[84] Martin Daunton, *Coal Metropolis: Cardiff, 1870–1914* (Leicester, 1977),

p. 175; *SWDN*, 26 November 1910, 16 March 1911, 8 April 1911, 10 March 1913.

85 *SWDN*, 4 November 1910.
86 Daunton, *Coal Metropolis*, p. 225.
87 Hirshfield, 'Fractured faith', 183; *SWDN*, 10 March 1911.
88 Vellacott, *From Liberal to Labour*, pp. 228–9.
89 Ibid., pp. 365–6.
90 Cochfarf Papers, Box 7, flyer, Cardiff WLA Social Meeting, 10 November 1911; WLF Annual Report, 1911; *SWDN*, 28, 29 March 1911, 24 April 1911.
91 Pugh, *March of the Women*, ch. 6; Hirshfield, 'Fractured faith', 180–9.
92 *SWDN*, 8 April 1911.
93 Cochfarf Papers, Box 7, letter of 16 May 1908.
94 Hirshfield, 'Fractured faith', 181.
95 Morgan, *Wales in British Politics*, p. 168; Daunton, *Coal Metropolis*, ch. 10.
96 Claire Eustance, '"Daring to be free": the evolution of women's political identities in the Women's Freedom League, 1907–1930', unpublished Ph.D. thesis (University of York, 1993), 7–8, and Introduction, passim; Paul Stigant, 'Foreword: whose history?', in Angela V. John and Claire Eustance (eds), *The Men's Share? Masculinities, Male Support and Women's Suffrage, 1890–1920* (London, 1997), pp. xv–xvi; Pugh, *March of the Women*, pp. 142–3.
97 Morgan, *Rebirth of a Nation: Wales, 1880–1980* (Oxford and Cardiff 1982), p. 168.
98 Daunton, *Coal Metropolis*, p. 225.
99 Rendall, 'Citizenship', pp. 127–50; Mayhall, 'Rhetorics', on what this language owed to the influence on feminists of Mazzini.
100 Rogers, *Women and the People*, pp. 283–301.
101 See ch. 3, above; Patrick Joyce, 'The constitution and the narrative structure of Victorian politics', in James Vernon (ed.), *Re-Reading the Constitution: New Narratives in the Political History of England's Long Nineteenth Century* (Cambridge, 1996), pp. 196–7.
102 Morgan, *Rebirth*, p. 137; John, *'Chwarae Teg'*, p. 10.
103 *SWDN*, 6 May 1911.
104 Constance Rover, *Women's Suffrage and Party Politics in Britain, 1866–1914* (London and Toronto, 1967), app. II, pp. 222–3; Ian Christopher Fletcher, '"Women of the Nations, Unite!": transnational feminism in the United Kingdom, 1912–1914', in Ian Christopher Fletcher, Laura E. Nym Mayhall and Philippa Levine (eds), *Women's Suffrage in the British Empire: Citizenship, Nation, and Race* (London and New York, 2000), p. 105.
105 WLF Annual Report, 1914.

## Conclusion

1 Martin Pugh, *The March of the Women: A Revisionist Analysis of the Campaign for Women's Suffrage, 1866–1914* (Oxford, 2000), p. 141.
2 Laura E. Nym Mayhall, *The Militant Suffrage Movement: Citizenship and Resistance in Britain, 1860–1930* (Oxford, 2003), ch. 2.
3 Antoinette Burton, '"States of injury": Josephine Butler on slavery, citizenship and the Boer War', in Ian Christopher Fletcher, Laura E. Nym Mayhall and Philippa Levine (eds), *Women's Suffrage in the British Empire: Citizenship, Nation, and Race* (London and New York, 2000), pp. 18–32.
4 Ian Christopher Fletcher, '"Women of the Nations, Unite!": transnational feminisms in the United Kingdom, 1912–1914', in Ian Christopher Fletcher, Laura E. Nym Mayhall and Phillippa Levine (eds), *Women's Suffrage in the British Empire: Citizenship, Nation, and Race* (London and New York, 2000), pp. 103–20.
5 W. R. Lambert, *Drink and Sobriety in Victorian Wales, c.1820–1895* (Cardiff, 1983), p. 247; Ceridwen Lloyd-Morgan, 'From temperance to suffrage?', in Angela V. John (ed.), *Our Mothers' Land: Chapters in Welsh Women's History, 1830–1939* (Cardiff, 1991), pp. 136–7.
6 The fullest treatment of women's labour movement history in the period of this book is Neil Evans and Dot Jones, '"To help forward the great work of humanity": women in the Labour party in Wales', in Duncan Tanner, Chris Williams and Deian Hopkin (eds), *The Labour Party in Wales, 1900–2000* (Cardiff, 2000), pp. 215–20.
7 R. Merfyn Jones and Joan Rhys Jones, 'Labour and the nation', in Tanner et al. (eds), *The Labour Party*, pp. 242–6.
8 WLF Annual Reports, 1920–8.
9 Correspondence from Dr H. G. A. Hughes, nephew of Kate Evans, 19 April 2005; quoted by permission.

# Bibliography

## *Manuscript and archival collections*

**Aberdare Reference Library, W.W. Price collections**
Aberdare WLA Minute Book, 1891–1907
Aberdare Nonconformist Election Committee, minutes 1867–8
Aberdare ILP records
Biographical collection (cuttings)
Censuses of Population 1891, RG 12/4442–4448; 1901, RG 13/5034–5039 (microfilm)
W. W. Price *Biographical Index*

**Bristol University Library special collections**
Records of the Women's Liberal Federation, 1886–1928

**Cardiff Central Library, local studies collections (CCL)**
Allwood, Henry G. C., Election Scrapbook
Cardiff Charity Organisation Society (COS) Reports, 1887–98
Cardiff City Council minutes, 1910–12
Cardiff Liberal Association reports, papers and election ephemera
Cardiff Poor Law Union Year Books, 1894–1930
Cardiff Women's Liberal Association, Annual Reports, 1894–1902 (incomplete series)
Censuses of Population 1891, RG 12/4384–4408; 1901, RG 13/4970–4988 (microfilm)
Cochfarf papers
National Liberal Federation, records of annual meetings, Cardiff, 1895
Welsh Union of Women's Liberal Associations: Programme for Fourth Annual Meetings, Cardiff, March 1895; Annual Report, 1895

**Cumbria Record Office, Carlisle**
Catherine Marshall papers (CM)

**Glamorgan Record Office (GRO)**
Aberdare Valley ILP records
Ald. Rose Davies papers
Cardiff and District Women's Suffrage Society papers
Cardiff Women's Citizens Association papers
Merthyr Tydfil Union minute books, 1893–5, 1899–1900, 1910–13
Penarth Women's Suffrage Society minutes

**Gwynedd Record Office (Caernarfon)**
Gwyneth Vaughan papers

**National Library of Wales, Department of Manuscripts and Political Archive**
Cardiff and District Women's Suffrage Society Annual Reports
D. A. Thomas papers
D. M. Richards papers
'Letters of Well Known Women to Nora Philipps' (bound manuscript volume)
Political ephemera (boxes XJN), including:
   Aberystwyth WLA Annual Reports
   Cardiff Liberal Association, Annual Reports, subscription lists, notices etc. c.1889–1918
   WUWLA Annual Reports, conference programmes and published papers

**Women's Library, London Metropolitan University (formerly Fawcett Collection)**
Election Fighting Fund Committee minutes, 1912
National Union of Women's Suffrage Societies, Executive Committee minutes 1912–13

*Newspapers and journals*

*Aberdare Leader* (*AL*)
*Aberdare Times* (*AT*)
*Cambrian News* (*CN*)
*Colliery Workers Magazine*
*Glamorgan Gazette*
*The Labour Woman*
*Merthyr Express* (*ME*)
*Pall Mall Gazette*
*Rhondda Socialist*
*South Wales Argus* (*SWA*)
*South Wales Daily News* (*SWDN*)
*South Wales Daily Post* (*SWDP*)
*South Wales Labour Times and Tocsin*
*South Wales Radical* (*SWR*)
*South Wales Radical & Nonconformist*
*South Wales Weekly Argus* (*SWWA*)
*Swansea and District Workers Journal*
*The Times*

The Tocsin

Welsh Review (WR)

Western Mail (WM)

Women's Liberal Federation News

Women's Liberal Federation
  Summary

Young Wales (YW)


## Published works

### Works of reference

Aberdare Illustrated Almanack (series, Aberdare, 1891–5).

Bellamy, Joyce M. and John Saville (eds), Dictionary of Labour Biography (DLB), vol. I (London, 1972).

Cardiff Census Statistics, Census of 1891 (London, 1893).

Cook, Chris and Brendan Keith, British Historical Facts, 1830–1900 (London, 1975).

Crawford, Elizabeth, The Women's Suffrage Movement: A Reference Guide, 1866–1928 (London, 2001, first pub. 1999).

Gildart, Keith, David Howell and Neville Kirk, Dictionary of Labour Biography, vol. XI (Basingstoke, 2003).

Hannam, June, Mitzi Auchterlonie and Katherine Holden, International Encyclopedia of Women's Suffrage (Santa Barbara, 2000).

Hansard, House of Commons Debates (HoC).

Jones, Beti, Etholiadau'r Ganrif/Welsh Elections, 1885–1997 (Talybont, 1999).

Matthew, H. C. G. and Brian Harrison (eds), Oxford Dictionary of National Biography: From the Earliest Times to the Year 2000 (Oxford, 2004), and online version at www.oxforddnb.com/.

Suffrage Annual and Women's Who's Who (London, 1913).

Williams, John (ed.), Digest of Welsh Historical Statistics, vols I and II (Cardiff, 1985).

Western Mail Cardiff Directory (Cardiff, 1910).

Wright's Cardiff Directory (Cardiff, 1891).


### Works published before 1914

Aberdeen, Countess of, 'The Women's Liberal Federation of Scotland – Address by the Countess of Aberdeen of Scotland to the World's Congress of Representative Women' (Chicago, 1894) (Harvard University Library Page Delivery Service).

Blackburn, Helen, Women's Suffrage: A Record of the Women's Suffrage Movement in the British Isles (London, 1902).

Cardiff District Congregational Board, History of Congregationalism in Cardiff (Cardiff, 1920).

Cynghrair Rhyddfrydol y Merched, Apel at Ferched Rhyddfrydol Cymru (1909).

Garland, C. M., 'Women's interests in Wales. I. Higher education', Young Wales, IX, 101 (May 1903), 102–4.

Gibson, John, *The Emancipation of Women* (Aberystwyth 1891, 1894; reissued with introduction by W. Gareth Evans, Llandysul, 1992).

Gladdish, Miss C. M., 'The interests of women in Wales: a foreword', *Young Wales*, IX, 99 (March 1903), 63–4.

Johnstone, William, *Notable Men of Cardiff* (Cardiff, 1903).

Jones, Anna, 'Women and religious freedom', *Young Wales*, I, 3 (March 1895), 55–6.

Jones, Dilys Glynne, *The Duty of Welshwomen in Relation to the Welsh Intermediate Education Act* (London, 1894).

Kennard, E. F., *Men I Have Known* (Cardiff, 1918).

Lentzner, K., 'Man or woman: which is woman to be?', *Young Wales*, III, 34 (October 1897), 232–3.

McLaren, Eva, *The Duties and Opportunities of Women with reference to the Parish and District Councils* (London, 1894).

Mazzini, Giuseppe, *The Duties of Man and Other Writings* (London and New York, 1966).

Orme, Eliza, 'A commonplace correction', *Welsh Review*, 1, 5 (1892), 467–70.

Philipps, Nora (Mrs Wynford Philipps), 'The problem of the nineteenth century', *Welsh Review*, 1, 4 (1892), 348–58.

——, 'A Reply', *Welsh Review*, 1, 7 (1892), 670–80.

——, *The Aim and Object of the Welsh Union* (1893).

——, *An Appeal to Welsh Women* (London, 1893).

——, *Apel at Ferched Cymru* (London, 1893).

——, 'Notes on the work of Welsh Liberal women', *Young Wales*, I, 1 (January 1895), 17–19.

——, 'Notes on the work of Welsh Liberal Women', *Young Wales*, I, 2 (February 1895), 37–41.

——, and Elsbeth Philipps (eds), 'Progress of women in Wales', *Young Wales*, II, 15 to III, 26 (March 1896–February 1897).

Richards, Mrs D. M. (Maria), *Dyledswydd Merched a Gwragedd i Geisio Seddau ar y Cyngorau Plwyfol &c* (Aberdare, undated, *c*.1894).

Saunders, S. M., 'The Women of Wales' Circle', *Young Wales*, III, 28 (April 1897), 90–1; III, 34 (October 1897), 230–1.

Taylor, Helen, 'The claim of Englishwomen to the suffrage constitutionally considered', *Westminster Review*, January 1867, reprinted in Jane Lewis (ed.), *Before the Vote was Won: Arguments For and Against Women's Suffrage, 1864–1896* (New York and London, 1987).

*To Young Wales*, manifesto of Liverpool and Manchester Cymru Fydd Societies (undated, *c*.1894–5).

Un o'r ddau Wynne (Mallt Williams), 'Patriotism and the women of Cymru', *Young Wales*, IV, 41 (May 1898), 115.

Ward, Mrs Humphry et al., 'An appeal against female suffrage', *The Nineteenth Century*, June 1889, reprinted in Jane Lewis (ed.), *Before the Vote was Won: Arguments For and Against Women's Suffrage, 1864–1896* (New York and London, 1987).

Williams, Alis M. (Mallt Williams), 'The Women of Wales' Circle', *Young Wales*, VII, 78 (June 1901), 137–8; VII, 80 (August 1901), 188–9.

Wright, Sir Almroth, *The Unexpurgated Case Against Woman Suffrage* (1913, available online at Project Gutenberg, *www.gutenberg.org/catalog*).

## Works published after 1914

Aaron, Jane, 'Finding a voice in two tongues: gender and colonization', in Jane Aaron, Teresa Rees, Sandra Betts and Moira Vincentelli (eds), *Our Sisters' Land: The Changing Identities of Women in Wales* (Cardiff, 1994), pp. 183–98.

——, Teresa Rees, Sandra Betts and Moira Vincentelli (eds), *Our Sisters' Land: The Changing Identities of Women in Wales* (Cardiff, 1994).

—— and Chris Williams (eds), *Postcolonial Wales* (Cardiff, 2005).

Adamson, David L., *Class, Ideology and the Nation: A Theory of Welsh Nationalism* (Cardiff, 1991).

——, 'The intellectual and the national movement in Wales', in Ralph Fevre and Andrew Thompson (eds), *Nation, Identity and Social Theory: Perspectives from Wales* (Cardiff, 1999).

Balakrishnan, Gopal and Benedict Anderson (eds), *Mapping the Nation* (London, 1996).

Banks, Olive, *Faces of Feminism: A Study of Feminism as a Social Movement* (Oxford, 1986, first pub. 1981).

Barrow, Margaret, 'Teetotal feminists: temperance leadership and the campaign for women's suffrage', in Claire Eustance, Joan Ryan and Laura Ugolini (eds), *A Suffrage Reader: Charting Directions in British Suffrage History* (London, 2000).

Beddoe, Deirdre, *Out of the Shadows: A History of Women in Twentieth Century Wales* (Cardiff, 2000).

——, 'Collin, Mary (1860–1955) headmistress', *Oxford Dictionary of National Biography* (Oxford, 2004; *www.oxforddnb.com/view/article/51850*).

Bernold, Monika and Johanna Gehmacher, 'A private eye on feminist agency: reflections on documentation, biography and political consciousness', *Women's Studies International Forum*, 22, 2 (March 1999), 237–47.

Biagini, Eugenio F., *Liberty, Retrenchment and Reform: Popular Liberalism in the Age of Gladstone, 1860–1880* (Cambridge, 1992).

——, 'Introduction: citizenship, liberty and community' in Eugenio F. Biagini (ed.), *Citizenship and Community: Liberals, Radicals and Collective Identities in the British Isles, 1865–1931* (Cambridge, 1996).

—— (ed.), *Citizenship and Community: Liberals, Radicals and Collective Identities in the British Isles, 1865–1931* (Cambridge, 1996).

Billington, Rosamund, 'Women, politics and local liberalism: from "Female Suffrage" to "Votes for Women"', *Journal of Regional and Local Studies*, 5, 1 (1985), 1–14.

Bland, Lucy, *Banishing the Beast: English Feminism and Sexual Morality, 1885–1914* (London, 1995).

Blom, Ida, 'Gender and nation in international comparison', in Ida Blom, Karen Hagemann and Catherine Hall (eds), *Gendered Nations: Nationalism and Gender Order in the Long Nineteenth Century* (Oxford and New York, 2000).

Blom, Ida, Karen Hagemann and Catherine Hall (eds), *Gendered Nations: Nationalism and Gender Order in the Long Nineteenth Century* (Oxford and New York, 2000).

Bohata, Kirsti, '"For Wales, see England?" suffrage and the New Woman in Wales', *Women's History Review*, 11, 4 (2002), 643–56.

——, *Postcolonialism Revisited: Writing Wales in English* (Cardiff, 2004).

Bryson, Valerie, *Feminist Political Theory: An Introduction* (Basingstoke, 1992).

Burton, Antoinette ,'"States of injury": Josephine Butler on slavery, citizenship and the Boer War', in Ian Christopher Fletcher, Laura E. Nym Mayhall and Philippa Levine (eds), *Women's Suffrage in the British Empire: Citizenship, Nation and Race* (London and New York, 2000), pp. 18–32.

Bush, Julia, 'Ladylike lives? Upper-class women's autobiographies and the politics of late Victorian and Edwardian Britain', *Literature & History*, 10, 2 (autumn 2001), 42–61.

Caine, Barbara, *English Feminism, 1780–1980* (Oxford, 1997).

Campbell, Beatrix, *The Iron Ladies: Why do Women Vote Tory?* (London, 1987).

Carr, Catherine (ed.), *The Spinning Wheel: City of Cardiff High School for Girls, 1895–1955* (Cardiff, 1955).

Clark, Anna, 'Gender, class and the nation: franchise reform in England, 1832–1928', in James Vernon (ed.), *Re-reading the Constitution: New Narratives in the Political History of England's Long Nineteenth Century* (Cambridge, 1996).

Collette, Christine, *For Labour and For Women: The Women's Labour League, 1906–1918* (Manchester, 1989).

Collini, Stefan, *Public Moralists: Political Thought and Intellectual Life in Britain, 1850–1930* (Oxford, 1993).

Cook, Kay and Neil Evans, '"The petty antics of the bell-ringing, boisterous band"? The women's suffrage movement in Wales, 1890–1918', in Angela V. John (ed.), *Our Mothers' Land: Chapters in Welsh Women's History, 1830–1939* (Cardiff, 1991).

Cowman, Krista, *'Mrs Brown is a Man and a Brother': Women in Merseyside's Political Organisations, 1890–1920* (Liverpool, 2004).

Cragoe, Matthew, '"Jenny rules the roost": women and electoral politics, 1832–1868', in Kathryn Gleadle and Sarah Richardson (eds), *Women in British Politics, 1760–1860: The Power of the Petticoat* (Basingstoke, 2000).

Croll, Andy, *Civilizing the Urban: Popular Culture and Public Space in Merthyr, c.1870–1914* (Cardiff, 2000).

Curthoys, Ann, 'Feminism, citizenship and national identity', *Feminist Review*, 44 (1993), 19–38.

Daley, Caroline and Melanie Nolan (eds), *Suffrage and Beyond: International Feminist Perspectives* (New York, 1994).

Daunton, Martin, *Coal Metropolis: Cardiff, 1870–1914* (Leicester, 1977).

Davies, Charlotte Aull, 'Women, nationalism and feminism', in Jane Aaron, Teresa Rees, Sandra Betts and Moira Vincentelli (eds), *Our Sisters' Land: The Changing Identities of Women in Wales* (Cardiff, 1994).

——, 'Nationalism, feminism and Welsh women: conflicts and accommodations', in Ralph Fevre and Andrew Thompson (eds), *National Identity and Social Theory: Perspectives from Wales* (Cardiff, 1999).

Davies, R. R. and Geraint H. Jenkins (eds), *From Medieval to Modern Wales: Historical Essays in Honour of Kenneth O. Morgan and Ralph A. Griffiths* (Cardiff, 2004).

Dyhouse, Carol, *Feminism and the Family in England, 1880–1930* ( Oxford, 1989).

——, *No Distinction of Sex? Women in British Universities, 1870–1939* (London, 1995).

Edwards, Wil Jon, *From the Valley I Came* (London, 1956).

Eustance, Claire, Joan Ryan and Laura Ugolini (eds), *A Suffrage Reader: Charting Directions in British Suffrage History* (London, 2000).

Evans, Neil, 'Urbanisation, élite attitudes and philanthropy: Cardiff 1850–1914', *International Review of Social History*, XVII (1982), 290–323.

——, 'Cardiff's Labour tradition', *Llafur: Journal of Welsh Labour History*, 4, 2 (1985), 77–90.

——, 'The Welsh Victorian city: the middle class and national consciousness in Cardiff, 1850–1914', *Welsh History Review*, 12, 3 (1985), 350–87.

——, '"A tidal wave of impatience': the Cardiff General Strike of 1911', in Geraint H. Jenkins and J. Beverley Smith (eds), *Politics and Society in Wales, 1840–1922: Essays in Honour of Ieuan Gwynedd Jones* (Cardiff, 1988).

——, 'Region, nation, globe: roles, representations and urban space in Cardiff, 1839–1928', in Andreas Fahrmeir and Elfie Rembold (eds), *Representation of British Cities: Transformation of Urban Space, 1700–2000* (Berlin, 2003).

——, 'Finding a new story: the search for a usable past in Wales, 1869–1930', *Transactions of the Honourable Society of Cymmrodorion*, 10 (2004), 144–62.

——, '"A nation in a nutshell": the Swansea disestablishment demonstration of 1912 and the political culture of Edwardian Wales', in R. R. Davies and Geraint H. Jenkins (eds), *From Medieval to Modern Wales: Historical*

*Essays in Honour of Kenneth O. Morgan and Ralph A. Griffiths* (Cardiff, 2004).

—— and Dot Jones, '"To help forward the great work of humanity": women in the Labour party in Wales', in Duncan Tanner, Chris Williams and Deian Hopkin (eds), *The Labour Party in Wales, 1900–2000* (Cardiff, 2000).

—— and Kate Sullivan, 'Yn llawn o dân Cymreig (full of Welsh fire): the language of politics in Wales', in Geraint H. Jenkins (ed.), *The Welsh Language in its Social Domains, 1801–1911* (Cardiff, 2000).

Evans, W. Gareth, *Education and Female Emancipation: The Welsh Experience, 1847–1914* (Cardiff, 1990).

Fevre, Ralph and Andrew Thompson (eds), *Nation, Identity and Social Theory: Perspectives from Wales* (Cardiff, 1999).

Fletcher, Ian Christopher, '" Women of the Nations, Unite!": transnational feminism in the United Kingdom, 1912–1914', in Ian Christopher Fletcher, Laura E. Nym Mayhall and Philippa Levine (eds), *Women's Suffrage in the British Empire: Citizenship, Nation, and Race* (London and New York, 2000), pp. 103–20.

——, Laura E. Nym Mayhall and Philippa Levine (eds), *Women's Suffrage in the British Empire: Citizenship, Nation and Race* (London and New York, 2000).

Fox, Kenneth O., 'Labour and Merthyr's khaki election of 1900', *Welsh History Review*, 2, 3 (1965), 351–66.

Gallagher, Ann-Marie, Cathy Lubelska and Louise Ryan (eds), *Re-presenting the Past: Women and History* (London, 2001).

Gilbert, David, *Class, Community and Collective Action: Social Change in Two British Coalfields, 1850–1926* (Oxford, 1992).

Gleadle, Kathryn, *The Early Feminists: Radical Unitarians and the Emergence of the Women's Rights Movement, 1831–51* (Basingstoke, 1995).

—— and Sarah Richardson (eds), *Women in British Politics, 1760–1860: The Power of the Petticoat* (Basingstoke, 2000).

Grant, Raymond, *The Parliamentary History of Glamorgan, 1542–1976* (Swansea, 1978).

Graves, Pamela M., *Labour Women: Women in British Working-Class Politics, 1918–1939* (Cambridge, 1994).

Grever, Maria, 'The pantheon of feminist culture: women's movements and the organization of memory', *Gender & History*, 9, 2 (August 1997), 364–74.

Grigg, John, *Lloyd George: The Young Lloyd George* (London 1997, first pub. 1973).

Hall, Catherine, 'Gender, nationalism and national identities: Bellagio Symposium, July 1992', *Feminist Review*, 44 (summer 1993), 97–103.

—— and Leonore Davidoff, *Family Fortunes: Men and Women of the English Middle Class* (London, 1987).

——, Keith McClelland and Jane Rendall (eds), *Defining the Victorian Nation: Class, Race, Gender and the Reform Act of 1867* (Cambridge, 2000).

Hall, Lesley, 'Finding women in the archive', *Women's History Notebooks*, 2, 1 (winter 1995), 3–11.

Hannam, June, *Isabella Ford* (Oxford, 1989).

——, '"I had not been to London": women's suffrage – a view from the regions', in June Purvis and Sandra Stanley Holton (eds), *Votes for Women* (London, 2000).

—— and Katherine Holden, 'Heartland and periphery: local, national and global perspectives on women's history', *Women's History Review*, 11, 3 (2002), 341–9.

——, and Karen Hunt, *Socialist Women: Britain, 1880s to 1920s* (London, 2002).

Harrison, Brian, *Separate Spheres: The Opposition to Women's Suffrage in Britain* (London, 1978).

Hirshfield, Claire, 'Fractured faith: Liberal party women and the suffrage issue in Britain, 1892–1914', *Gender & History*, 2, 2 (1990), 173–97.

Hoffman, P. C., *They Also Serve: The Story of the Shop Worker* (London, 1949).

Hollis, Patricia, *Ladies Elect: Women in English Local Government, 1865–1914* (Oxford, 1987).

——, 'Women in council: separate spheres, public space', in Jane Rendall (ed.), *Equal or Different: Women's Politics, 1800–1914* (Oxford, 1987).

Holton, Sandra Stanley, *Feminism and Democracy: Women's Suffrage and Reform Politics in Britain, 1900–1918* (Cambridge, 1986).

——, *Suffrage Days: Stories from the Women's Suffrage Movement* (London and New York, 1996).

——, 'British freewomen: national identity, constitutionalism and languages of race in early suffragist histories', in Eileen Janes Yeo (ed.), *Radical Femininity: Women's Self-Representation in the Public Sphere* (Manchester, 1998).

Hopkin, Deian, 'Labour's roots in Wales, 1880–1900', in Duncan Tanner, Chris Williams and Deian Hopkin (eds), *The Labour Party in Wales, 1900–2000* (Cardiff, 2000).

Hughes, Dewi Rowland, 'Y coch a'r gwyrdd: Cymru Fydd a'r mudiad llafur Cymreig (1886–96)', *Llafur: Journal of Welsh Labour History*, 6, 4 (1995), 60–79.

Hume, Leslie Parker, *The National Union of Women's Suffrage Societies, 1897–1914* (New York, 1982).

Humphreys, Iwan, 'Cardiff politics, 1850–74', in Stewart Williams (ed.), *Glamorgan Historian*, 8 (1971).

International Federation for Research in Women's History, *Newsletter*, 27 (January 1999).

James, Deborah, '"Teaching girls": intermediate schools and career opportunities for girls in the East Glamorgan valleys of Wales, 1896–1914', *History of Education*, 30, 6 (2001), 513–26.

Jenkins, Geraint H. (ed.), *The Welsh Language in its Social Domains, 1801–1911* (Cardiff, 2000).

—— and J. Beverley Smith (eds), *Politics and Society in Wales, 1840–1922: Essays in Honour of Ieuan Gwynedd Jones* (Cardiff, 1988).

—— and Mari. A. Williams (eds), *'Let's Do Our Best for the Ancient Tongue': The Welsh Language in the Twentieth Century* (Cardiff, 2000).

Joannou, Maroula, 'She who would be free herself must strike the first blow: suffragette autobiography and suffragette militancy', in Julia Swindells, *The Uses of Autobiography* (London, 1995).

—— and June Purvis (eds), *The Women's Suffrage Movement: New Feminist Perspectives* (Manchester, 1998).

John, Angela V., *By the Sweat of Their Brow: Women Workers at Victorian Coalmines* (London, 1984).

——, 'Beyond paternalism: the ironmaster's wife in the industrial community', in Angela V. John (ed.), *Our Mothers' Land: Chapters in Welsh Women's History, 1830–1939* (Cardiff, 1991).

——, '"Run like blazes": the suffragettes and Welshness', *Llafur: Journal of Welsh Labour History*, 6, 3 (1994), 29–43.

——, 'A draft of fresh air: women's suffrage, the Welsh and London', *Transactions of the Honourable Society of Cymmrodorion* (1994–5), 81–93.

——, *'Chwarae Teg': Welsh Men's Support for Women's Suffrage* (Aberystwyth, 1998).

—— (ed.), *Our Mothers' Land: Chapters in Welsh Women's History, 1830–1939* (Cardiff, 1991).

—— and Claire Eustance, 'Shared histories – differing identities: introducing masculinities, male support and women's suffrage', in Angela V. John and Claire Eustance (eds), *The Men's Share? Masculinities, Male Support and Women's Suffrage, 1890–1920* (London, 1997).

—— and Claire Eustance (eds), *The Men's Share? Masculinities, Male Support and Women's Suffrage, 1890–1920* (London, 1997).

Jones, Aled, *Press, Politics and Society: A History of Journalism in Wales* (Cardiff, 1993).

Jones, Ieuan Gwynedd, 'Dr Thomas Price and the election of 1868 in Merthyr Tydfil, a study in Nonconformist politics: I', *Welsh History Review*, 2, 1 (1964),147–72.

——, 'Dr Thomas Price and the election of 1868 in Merthyr Tydfil, a study in Nonconformist politics: II', *Welsh History Review*, 2, 2 (1964), 251–70.

——, *Explorations and Explanations: Essays in the Social History of Victorian Wales* (Llandysul, 1981).

Jones, Rosemary, 'Women, community and collective action: the "ceffyl pren" tradition', in Angela V. John (ed.), *Our Mothers' Land: Chapters in Welsh Women's History, 1830–1939* (Cardiff, 1991).

——, '"Separate spheres"? Women, language and respectability in Victorian Wales', in Geraint H. Jenkins (ed.), *The Welsh Language in its Social Domains, 1801–1911* (Cardiff, 2000).

Jones, R. Merfyn and Joan Rhys Jones, 'Labour and the nation', in Duncan Tanner, Chris Williams and Deian Hopkin (eds), *The Labour Party in Wales, 1900–2000* (Cardiff, 2000).

Jordanova, Ludmilla, *History in Practice* (London 2006, 2nd edn).

Joyce, Patrick, 'The constitution and the narrative structure of Victorian politics', in James Vernon (ed.), *Re-reading the Constitution: New Narratives in the Political History of England's Long Nineteenth Century* (Cambridge, 1996).

Kean, Hilda, *Deeds Not Words: The Lives of Suffragette Teachers* (London, 1990).

——, 'Searching for the past in present defeat: the construction of historical and political identity in British feminism in the 1920s and 1930s', *Women's History Review*, 3, 1 (1994), 57–80.

——, 'Suffrage autobiography: a study of Mary Richardson – suffragette, socialist and fascist', in Claire Eustance, Joan Ryan and Laura Ugolini (eds), *A Suffrage Reader: Charting Directions in British Suffrage History* (London, 2000).

Knibiehler, Yvonne, 'Chronology and women's history', in Michelle Perrot (ed.), *Writing Women's History* (English edn, Oxford, 1984).

Lambert, W. R., *Drink and Sobriety in Victorian Wales, c.1820–c.1895* (Cardiff, 1983).

Lawrence, Jon, *Speaking for the People: Party, Language and Popular Politics in England, 1867–1914* (Cambridge, 1998).

——, 'Contesting the male polity: the suffragettes and the politics of disruption in Edwardian Britain', in Amanda Vickery (ed.), *Women, Privilege, and Power: British Politics, 1750 to the Present* (Stanford, 2001).

Laybourn, Keith, *The Labour Party, 1881–1951: A Reader in History* (Gloucester, 1988).

Leneman, Leah, 'A truly national movement: the view from outside London', in Maroula Joannou and June Purvis (eds), *The Women's Suffrage Movement: New Feminist Perspectives* (Manchester, 1998).

Lewis, Jane (ed.), *Before the Vote Was Won: Arguments for and against Women's Suffrage, 1864–1896* (New York and London, 1987).

Lloyd-Morgan, Ceridwen, 'From temperance to suffrage?', in Angela V. John (ed.), *Our Mothers' Land: Chapters in Welsh Women's History, 1830–1939* (Cardiff, 1991).

McAllister, Laura, 'Gender, nation and party: an uneasy alliance for Welsh nationalism', *Women's History Review*, 10, 1 (2001), 51–69.

McKibbin, Ross, *The Evolution of the Labour Party, 1910–1924* (Oxford, 1974).

Massey, Doreen, *Space, Place and Gender* (Cambridge, 1998).

Masson, Ursula, 'The Swansea suffragettes', in Luana Dee and Katell Keinig (eds), *Women in Wales: A Documentary of Our Recent History*, I (Cardiff, 1987).

——, 'Divided loyalties: women's suffrage and party politics in south Wales, 1912–1915', *Llafur: Journal of Welsh Labour History*, 7, 3 and 4 (1998), 113–26.

——, '"Political conditions in Wales are quite different": party politics and votes for women, 1912–1915', *Women's History Review*, 9, 2 (2000), 369–88.

——, '"Hand in hand with the women, forward we will go": Welsh nationalism and feminism in the 1890s', *Women's History Review*, 12, 3 (2003), 357–86.

——, 'Davies, Florence Rose (1882–1958): Independent Labour Party activist, Labour alderman', in Keith Gildart, David Howell and Neville Kirk (eds), *Dictionary of Labour Biography*, vol. XI (Basingstoke, 2003).

——, 'Women *versus* "the People": language, nation and citizenship, 1906–11', in T. Robin Chapman (ed.), *The Idiom of Dissent: Protest and Propaganda in Wales* (Llandysul, 2006).

—— (ed.), *Women's Rights and Womanly Duties: The Aberdare Women's Liberal Association, 1891–1910* (Cardiff, 2005).

Mathers, Helen, 'Evangelicalism and feminism: Josephine Butler, 1828–1906', in Anne Summers (ed.), *Female Lives, Moral States: Women, Religion and Public Life in Britain, 1800–1930* (Newbury, 2000).

May, Eddie, 'The mosaic of labour politics, 1900–1918', in Duncan Tanner, Chris Williams and Deian Hopkin (eds), *The Labour Party in Wales, 1900–2000* (Cardiff, 2000).

Mayhall, Laura E. Nym, 'The South African War and the origins of suffrage militancy in Britain, 1899–1902', in Ian Christopher Fletcher, Laura E. Nym Mayhall and Philippa Levine (eds), *Women's Suffrage in the British Empire: Citizenship, Nation and Race* (London and New York, 2000).

——, 'The rhetorics of slavery and citizenship: suffragist discourse and the canonical texts in Britain, 1880–1914', *Gender & History*, 13, 3 (November 2001), 481–97.

——, *The Militant Suffrage Movement: Citizenship and Resistance in Britain, 1860–1930* (Oxford, 2003).

Middleton, Lucy (ed.), *Women in the Labour Movement: The British Experience* (London, 1977).

Midgley, Clare, 'Feminist historians and challenges to imperial history', in Ann-Marie Gallagher, Cathy Lubelska and Louise Ryan (eds), *Representing the Past: Women and History* (London, 2001).

Morgan, David, *Suffragists and Liberals: The Politics of Woman Suffrage in Britain* (Oxford, 1975).

Morgan, Kenneth O., 'The new liberalism and the challenge of Labour: the Welsh experience, 1885–1929', *Welsh History Review*, 6, 3 (1973), 288–312.

——, *Wales in British Politics, 1868–1922* (Cardiff, 1980).

——, *Rebirth of a Nation: Wales, 1880–1980* (Oxford, 1981).

——, 'Tom Ellis *versus* Lloyd George: the fractured consciousness of fin-de-siècle Wales', in Geraint H. Jenkins and J. Beverley Smith (eds), *Politics and Society in Wales, 1840–1922* (Cardiff, 1988).

——, *Modern Wales: Politics, Places and People* (Cardiff, 1995).

——, 'Wales and the Boer War', in Kenneth O. Morgan, *Modern Wales: Politics, Places and People* (Cardiff, 1995).

Morgan, Prys, 'The *gwerin* of Wales – myth and reality', in Ian Hume and W. T. R. Pryce (eds), *The Welsh and Their Country: Selected Readings in the Social Sciences* (Llandysul, 1986).

Morgan, Sue (ed.), *Women, Religion and Feminism in Britain, 1750–1900* (Basingstoke and New York, 2002).

O'Brien, Anthony Môr, 'The Merthyr Borough election, November 1915', *Welsh History Review*, 12, 4 (1985), 538–66.

Offen, Karen, 'Defining feminism: a comparative historical approach', *Signs: Journal of Women in Culture and Society*, 14, 1 (1988), 119–57.

O'Leary, Paul, *Immigration and Integration: The Irish in Wales, 1798–1922* (Cardiff, 2000).

O'Malley, Tom, Stuart Allan and Andrew Thompson, 'Tokens of antiquity: the newspaper press and the shaping of national identity in Wales, 1870–1900', in Michael Harris and Tom O'Malley (eds), *Studies in Newspaper and Periodical History, 1995 Annual* (Westport, Connecticut, 1997), pp. 127–52.

Oram, Alison, *Women Teachers and Feminist Politics, 1900–1939* (Manchester, 1996).

——, 'Women teachers and the suffrage campaign: arguments for professional equality', in June Purvis and Sandra Stanley Holton (eds), *Votes for Women* (London, 2000).

Parry, Jon, 'Labour leaders and local politics, 1888–1902: the example of Aberdare', *Welsh History Review*, 14, 3 (1989), 399–416.

Pateman, Carole, *The Sexual Contract* (Cambridge, 1988).

——, *The Disorder of Women: Democracy, Feminism and Political Theory* (Cambridge, 1989).

Perrot, Michelle (ed.), *Writing Women's History* (English edn, Oxford, 1984).

Philip, Alan Butt, *The Welsh Question: Nationalism in Welsh Politics, 1945–1970* (Cardiff, 1975).

Pierson, Ruth Roach, 'Nations: gendered, racialized, crossed with empire', in Ida Blom, Karen Hagemann and Catherine Hall (eds), *Gendered Nations: Nationalism and Gender Order in the Long Nineteenth Century* (Oxford and New York, 2000).

Pryce, W. T. R., 'Language zones, demographic changes, and the Welsh culture area, 1800–1911', in Geraint H. Jenkins (ed.), *The Welsh Language in its Social Domains, 1801–1911* (Cardiff, 2000).

Pugh, Martin, *Women and the Women's Movement in Britain, 1914–1959* (London, 1992).

——, *The Making of Modern British Politics, 1857–1939* (Oxford, 1995).

——, 'Liberals and women's suffrage, 1867–1914' in Eugenio F. Biagini (ed.), *Citizenship and Community: Liberals, Radicals and Collective Identities in the British Isles, 1865–1931* (Cambridge, 1996).

——, *The March of the Women: A Revisionist Analysis of the Campaign for Women's Suffrage, 1866–1914* (Oxford, 2000).

Purvis, June (ed.), *Women's History: Britain, 1850–1945* (London, 1995).

—— and Sandra Stanley Holton (eds), *Votes for Women* (London, 2000).

Rendall, Jane, *The Origins of Modern Feminism: Women in Britain, France and the United States, 1780–1860* (London, 1985).

——, 'Citizenship, culture and civilisation: the languages of British suffragists, 1866–1874', in Caroline Daley and Melanie Nolan (eds), *Suffrage and Beyond: International Feminist Perspectives* (New York, 1994), pp. 127–50.

——, 'Who was Lily Maxwell? Women's suffrage and Manchester politics, 1866–1867', in June Purvis and Sandra Stanley Holton (eds), *Votes for Women* (London, 2000).

——, 'The citizenship of women and the Reform Act of 1867', in Catherine Hall, Keith McClelland and Jane Rendall (eds), *Defining the Victorian Nation: Class, Race, Gender and the Reform Act of 1867* (Cambridge, 2000).

——, 'John Stuart Mill, Liberal politics, and the movements for women's suffrage, 1865–1873', in Amanda Vickery (ed.), *Women, Privilege and Power: British Politics, 1750 to the Present* (Stanford, 2001).

—— (ed.), *Equal or Different: Women's Politics, 1800–1914* (Oxford, 1987).

Rhondda, Viscountess, *This Was My World,* (London, 1933).

Rickard, Suzanne, 'Victorian women with causes: writing, religion and action', in Anne Summers (ed.), *Female Lives, Moral States: Women, Religion and Public Life in Britain, 1800–1930* (Newbury, 2000).

Roberts, Gwyneth Tyson, *The Language of the Blue Books: The Perfect Instrument of Empire* (Cardiff, 1998).

Rogers, Helen, *Women and the People: Authority, Authorship and the Radical Tradition in Nineteenth-Century England* (Aldershot, 2000).

Roper, Michael and John Tosh (eds), *Manful Assertions: Masculinities in Britain since 1800* (London, 1991).

Rover, Constance, *Women's Suffrage and Party Politics in Britain, 1866–1914* (London and Toronto, 1967).

Self, Robert, *The Evolution of the British Party System, 1885–1940* (London, 2000).

Smitley, Megan, ' "Inebriates", "heathens", templars and suffragists: Scotland and imperial feminism c.1870–1917', *Women's History Review*, 11, 3 (2002), 455–79.

Steedman, Carolyn, *Childhood, Culture and Class in Britain: Margaret McMillan, 1860–1931* (New Brunswick, 1990).

Stigant, Paul, 'Foreword: whose history?', in Angela V. John and Claire Eustance (eds), *The Men's Share? Masculinities, Male Support and Women's Suffrage 1890–1920* (London, 1997).

Strachey, Ray, *The Cause: A Short History of the Women's Movement in Great Britain* (London, 1988, first pub. 1928).

Summers, Anne, *Female Lives, Moral States: Women, Religion and Public Life in Britain, 1800–1930* (Newbury, 2000).

Tanner, Duncan, Chris Williams and Deian Hopkin (eds), *The Labour Party in Wales, 1900–2000* (Cardiff, 2000).

Tosh, John, 'The making of masculinities: the middle class in late nineteenth-century England', in Angela V. John and Claire Eustance (eds), *The Men's Share? Masculinities, Male Support and Women's Suffrage, 1890–1920* (London, 1997).

——, *A Man's Place: Masculinity and the Middle-Class Home in Victorian England* (London, 1999).

Vellacott, Jo, *From Liberal to Labour with Women's Suffrage: The Story of Catherine Marshall* (London, Montreal and Kingston, 1993).

Vernon, James (ed.), *Re-Reading the Constitution: New Narratives in the Political History of England's Long Nineteenth Century* (Cambridge, 1996).

Vickery, Amanda, 'Golden age to separate spheres: a review of the categories and chronology of women's history', *Historical Journal*, 36, 2 (1993) 383–414.

—— (ed.), *Women, Privilege, and Power: British Politics, 1750 to the Present* (Stanford, 2001).

Walby, Sylvia 'Woman and nation', in Gopal Balakrishnan and Benedict Anderson (eds), *Mapping the Nation* (London, 1996).

Walker, Linda, 'Party political women: a comparative study of Liberal women and the Primrose League, 1890–1914', in Jane Rendall (ed.), *Equal or Different: Women's Politics, 1800–1914* (Oxford, 1987).

——, 'Philipps [née Gerstenberg] Leonora (1852–1915)', in H. C. G. Matthew and Brian Harrison (eds), *Oxford Dictionary of National Biography, From the Earliest Times to the Year 2000* (Oxford, 2004).

Wallace, Ryland, *Organise! Organise! Organise! A Study of Reform Agitations in Wales, 1840–1886* (Cardiff, 1991).

Ward, Margaret, 'The Ladies' Land League and the Irish Land War 1881/1882: defining the relationship between women and nation', in Ida Blom, Karen Hagemann and Catherine Hall (eds), *Gendered Nations: Nationalism and Gender Order in the Long Nineteenth Century* (Oxford and New York, 2000).

Wenk, Silke 'Gendered representations of the nation's past and future', in Ida Blom, Karen Hagemann and Catherine Hall (eds), *Gendered Nations: Nationalism and Gender Order in the Long Nineteenth Century* (Oxford and New York, 2000).

Williams, Charlotte, Neil Evans and Paul O'Leary (eds), *A Tolerant Nation? Exploring Ethnic Diversity in Wales* (Cardiff, 2003).

Williams, Chris, *Democratic Rhondda: Politics and Society, 1885–1951* (Cardiff, 1996).

——, 'Democracy and nationalism in Wales: the Lib–Lab enigma', in Robert Stradling, Scott Newton and David Bates (eds), *Conflict and Coexistence: Nationalism and Democracy in Modern Europe: Essays in Honour of Harry Hearder* (Cardiff, 1997).

——, *Capitalism, Community and Conflict: The South Wales Coalfield, 1898–1947* (Cardiff, 1998).

Williams, Emyr W., 'Liberalism in Wales and the politics of Welsh home rule, 1886–1910', *Bulletin of the Board of Celtic Studies*, 37 (1990), 191–207.

Williams, Gwyn A., *When Was Wales? A History of the Welsh* (London, 1985).

Williams, John 'The economic and social context', in Duncan Tanner, Chris Williams and Deian Hopkin (eds), *The Labour Party in Wales, 1900–2000* (Cardiff, 2000).

Williams, Mari A., 'Women and the Welsh language in the industrial valleys of south Wales, 1914–1945', in Geraint H. Jenkins and Mari A. Williams (eds), *'Let's Do Our Best for the Ancient Tongue': The Welsh Language in the Twentieth Century* (Cardiff, 2000).

Williams, Sian Rhiannon, 'The True "Cymraes": images of women in women's nineteenth-century Welsh periodicals', in Angela V. John (ed.), *Our Mothers' Land: Chapters in Welsh Women's History, 1830–1939* (Cardiff, 1991).

Woolf, Stuart (ed.), *Nationalism in Europe, 1815 to the Present: A Reader* (London, 1996).

Yeo, Eileen Janes, 'Radical femininity: women's self-representation in labour movements in the 19th and 20th centuries', in *North East Labour History*, 29 (1995), 6–18.

—— (ed.), *Radical Femininity: Women's Self-Representation in the Public Sphere* (Manchester, 1998).

Yuval-Davies, Nira and Floya Anthias (eds), *Woman–Nation–State* (London, 1989).

## *Theses and dissertations*

Barclay, Martin, 'Aberdare 1880–1914: class and community', MA thesis, University of Wales, Cardiff, 1985.

Cowman, Krista: 'Engendering citizenship: the political involvement of women on Merseyside, 1890–1920', Ph.D. thesis, University of York, 1994.

Daunton, Martin, 'Aspects of the social and economic structure of Cardiff, 1870–1914', Ph.D. thesis, University of Kent, 1974.

Eustance, Claire L., '"Daring to be free": the evolution of women's political activities in the Women's Freedom League, 1907–1930', Ph.D. thesis, University of York, 1993.

Smitley, Megan, '"Woman's mission": the temperance and women's suffrage movements in Scotland c.1870–1914', Ph.D. thesis, University of Glasgow, 2002.

Thomas, Helen, '"A democracy of working women": the women's Co-operative Guild in south Wales, 1891–1939', MA dissertation, University of Glamorgan, 2006.

Tyler, Alison, 'A library of our own: the potential for a women's library in Wales', Ph.D. thesis, University of Wales, Aberystwyth, 2006.

Williams, Emyr Wynn, 'The politics of Welsh home rule, 1886–1929: a sociological analysis', Ph.D. thesis, University of Wales, 1986.

# Index